Testimonia

Mark has a gift for sharing tax and legal information. Not only does he clearly explain strategies for lowering taxes and protecting assets, but also, he makes it fun along the way. I strongly recommend *The Business Owner's Guide to Financial Freedom* to all business owners.

—DANIEL TURKEWITZ, JL & A GROUP, INC.

This book is for entrepreneurs who want to be successful. I attended Mark's workshop in Philadelphia with my son, and Mark's legal and tax expertise gave me the knowledge to help me launch my real estate business with confidence!

—FARAH PIERRE, DEVELOPSELF

Since I met Mark and started implementing his strategies, my gross income has grown over 1,000 percent. Mark's strategies have worked flawlessly, and his advice saved my wife and me tens of thousands of dollars and *huge* amounts of stress. Mark is the real deal . . . Get reading!

—GREG GALLAGHER, REAL ESTATE INVESTOR, ADVISOR, BROKER, AND COACH

I love reading Mark Kohler's books! Mark gives you a real-life perspective on tax and legal strategies that you can implement without having to spend a lot of money. I'm able to use his strategies to stay on track with my business and save thousands of dollars in taxes.

—JEIMY RAMIREZ, FIGUEROA PROFESSIONAL SERVICES

Mark Kohler has a gift for making normally dry information interesting and entertaining so it is better absorbed and retained. I have four or five of his books and cannot recommend him highly enough. [...] n. His

—JOE D [...]IATES

Mark Kohler is AMAZING! He makes the boring business of taxes and legal strategies fun to learn. I am very grateful to have someone with such vast knowledge lead me through the complicated world of contracts and law and government forms. He is the most important person to have on my team to create financial freedom.

—SHELLEY SIMS, THRIVE, INC.

My life and business will forever be changed for the better because of Mark Kohler. His books contain pure gold when it comes to understanding the way business, taxes, and asset protection works. I highly recommend *The Business Owner's Guide to Financial Freedom*.

—KYLE PARKS, OWNER, SOUND HARBOR ENTERPRISES, LLC

Do you have a coordinated tax, legal, and financial plan? If not, you should read Mark's book *The Business Owner's Guide to Financial Freedom*. Your professional and personal life is about to get a whole lot better.

—CHRISTIAN HESTER, M.D., LITTLE ROCK EYE CLINIC

Ever since *What Your CPA Isn't Telling You*, I have been following Mark's work. I have saved my clients thousands of dollars by implementing his recommended strategies. Any business owner is missing out on opportunities to save if they are not learning from Mark's newsletters, podcasts, and books.

—ANGIE TONEY, CPA, ANGEL FINANCIAL SERVICES LLC

THE BUSINESS OWNER'S GUIDE TO
FINANCIAL FREEDOM

WHAT WALL STREET ISN'T TELLING YOU

MARK J. KOHLER

CPA, ATTORNEY • WITH RANDALL A. LUEBKE, RFC

Entrepreneur
PRESS®

Entrepreneur Press, Publisher
Cover Design: Andrew Welyczko
Production and Composition: Eliot House Productions

This publication is designed to provide accurate and authoritative information
in regard to the subject matter covered. It is sold with the understanding that
the publisher is not engaged in rendering legal, accounting or other professional
services. If legal advice or other expert assistance is required, the services of a
competent professional person should be sought.

Library of Congress Cataloging-in-Publication Data
 Names: Kohler, Mark J., author. | Luebke, Randy, author.
 Title: The business owner's guide to financial freedom: what Wall Street isn't
  telling you / by Mark J. Kohler and Randy Luebke.
 Description: Irvine, California: Entrepreneur Media, Inc., [2017]
 Identifiers: LCCN 2017027583| ISBN 978-1-59918-616-0 (alk. paper) |
  ISBN 1-59918-616-0 (alk. paper)
 Subjects: LCSH: Businesspeople—Finance, Personal. | Business enterprises—
  Finance.
 Classification: LCC HG179 .K62349 2017 | DDC 332.024—dc23
 LC record available at https://lccn.loc.gov/2017027583

Printed in the United States of America

22 21 20   10 9 8 7 6 5 4 3

This book is dedicated to our amazing spouses, Jennifer and Sandi. They have supported both of us time and time again, including during this huge undertaking to write about such an important topic.

CONTENTS

CHAPTER 8

CHAPTER 9

PART III

DEPLOYING YOUR ASSETS STRATEGICALLY

CHAPTER 10

CHAPTER 11

CHAPTER 12

PART V
PROTECTING YOUR HARD-EARNED ASSETS

ACKNOWLEDGMENTS

I can't thank my amazing wife, Jennifer, enough for her support during the many hours I spent working on this project. She was gracious and understanding as she told me to "go to the den" to finish the book when I was taking valuable time away from the family and missing important family functions. She always understood the importance of this work, and I couldn't ask for a more loving and supportive wife.

Randy consistently reported the same support from his wonderful wife, Sandi. She consistently was patient, supportive, and understanding of the time and energy it takes to put together a book of this magnitude.

Both Jennifer and Sandi's contributions and insights as we would bounce ideas off of them were invaluable in making this book helpful and understandable to the typical small-business owner.

We also must thank our amazing staff and partners at both of our offices, KKOS Lawyers, K&E CPAs, and Lifetime Paradigm. We are so grateful to have talented and dedicated team members helping us to deliver important tax, legal, and financial services that truly change the lives of so many.

THE DIFFERENCE BETWEEN WALL STREET AND MAIN STREET

This book is for business owners, or "entrepreneurs," as they are known. We are a different breed. We think differently, we dream differently, and of course, we operate differently. This couldn't be truer than when it comes to building and protecting our finances. **Our lives, our income, and our future, including retirement, largely revolve around our businesses.**

There is nothing wrong with this focus and perspective, but it's different—and Wall Street doesn't get it. Moreover, when it comes to the typical financial planner or "Wall Street" advisor, it basically boils down to these irrefutable facts.

If you:

§ Do not want to own a portfolio made up primarily of stock-based products,

§ Are not interested in using insurance products for retirement,

§ Want to use your business as your primary asset for retirement,

§ Self-direct your retirement account in nonstock investments, and even invest in some real estate,

. . . THEN, Wall Street advisors want NOTHING to do with you!

That's the truth, even though your advisor may sugarcoat their true feelings with words like "Let's review your estate plan and retirement structure" or "Let's look at your asset allocation and security needs," **no matter how they disguise that message, it's all code for "I need to sell you stocks, bonds, mutual funds, or insurance" or "I need to put your assets 'under management.'"** Either way, they just want to get paid for doing something with YOUR money.

Now, don't get me wrong, I'm not opposed to traditional financial products, services, or even paying for them, but the problem is that the number one asset for an entrepreneur is his or her business. So any financial products or insurance policy needs to "supplement" a broader plan. The reason being, deep down, most business owners plan on selling their business and somehow "retiring" on their business or on real estate, as we will discuss later in detail.

In the end, the "typical" financial advisor, broker, or insurance agent isn't equipped with the tools, nor are they motivated to assist in a plan centered on an entrepreneur's business or real estate portfolio.

With that in mind, I want to help. I know what resources and options you need to consider for financial security if you run your own business.

This book will speak to the soul of the entrepreneur!

An entrepreneur wants to know _how to use_ his or her business to create financial freedom, or what I often refer to as "flexibility." This is a unique discussion approached from a different perspective, with a different set of tools that a Wall Street brokerage "tow-the-line advisor" isn't even allowed to discuss. They work for companies that sell specific products and are, therefore, trying to maneuver your needs to fit their products, rather than the other way around.

I'm going to discuss these tools with you frankly and clearly and give YOU, the entrepreneur, the strategies to retire sooner and with more cash flow so you can maximize the true value of your business. Even for wage-earning Americans, financial planning isn't easy. For example, developing and maintaining a plan that incorporates saving and investing for retirement, protecting your assets, estate planning, and of course, minimizing taxes is very complex.

However, for the business owner, the complexities increase exponentially. He or she needs to incorporate all the issues that confront an individual, while also facing the day-to-day and strategic decisions needed to maintain and grow a business.

For those lucky ones who run a large business and have plenty of resources, they rely on consulting firms that can address virtually every need. Those resources are generally very expensive and, therefore, simply unavailable to the average small-business owner. **The result is that entrepreneurs often find themselves left without the support they need when, frankly, they need it the most.**

Helping small-business owners develop and maintain a solid financial plan is why I wrote this book. My goal is to provide small-business owners with the systems and strategies they need to achieve the financial independence they want. This book is about you and your financial freedom.

If you own or run a small- to midsized business or if you are a one-person startup, keep on reading. There really is a better, smarter, safer way to plan for your retirement, and I'm going to show you how.

PART

I

PERSPECTIVE

want to put things in "perspective." There are a lot of misconceptions about how an entrepreneur should approach wealth building and "who" they should work with and rely on.

Throughout the next four chapters, I will share critical concepts, belief systems, and facts about our current financial systems in the United States. I want to encourage you to look at your business and your approach to wealth building with a new set of eyes as we build the foundation for financial flexibility and freedom.

In Chapter 3, I will introduce the co-author of this book, Randy Luebke, a truly "independent" investment advisor. Randy's insightful comments in almost every chapter will shock and enlighten you as to the realities of trying to build wealth with a Wall Street "mindset." It's critical that in this conversation we have an "insider" that can explain the truth about Wall Street financial products, as they will be necessary tools on our path to financial freedom. However, Randy will help me explain which ones to steer clear of and which ones can actually help us as business owners.

As an entrepreneur, you have to look at financial freedom with a different perspective from what Wall Street tries to force upon you. Not every financial product peddled on Wall Street is in your best interest as a business owner, so we need to "Create a New Perspective." See page 2.

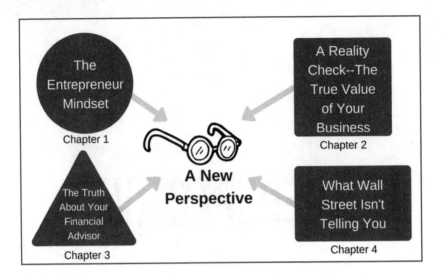

Figure I—Creating a New Perspective

THE ENTREPRENEUR MINDSET

If you call yourself an "entrepreneur, there's a good chance you had a lemonade stand or a newspaper route as a kid. Perhaps you tried to sell something door-to-door, invented something, or at least tinkered with a product or service that you dreamed of selling all over America, or even the world. **At a bare minimum, you still have a burning desire to work for yourself and to create something from nothing.**

This describes me. I love entrepreneurship, but I also know we're different from most other people. Not richer or poorer. Not smarter or more talented—and certainly not better people than the average wage-earning Americans. **We're just different.**

We have a passion and a drive—we want to take the initiative to do something on our own, but this also makes how we approach savings, wealth, and retirement different, too.

I have been fortunate to meet with more than a thousand entrepreneurs every year in one-on-one consultations discussing wealth. In fact, I have interacted with tens of thousands of small-business owners from all over the country as I teach workshops and meet with business clubs and associations. During these countless exchanges, I've learned that there are a number of common personality traits amongst entrepreneurs and their entrepreneurial mindsets. Some are good traits, and others are not.

Good and Bad Personality Traits of Entrepreneurs

First, it's worth noting that successful entrepreneurs are not necessarily born with all the good personality traits to succeed, but they develop them as their passion grows. Conversely, the bad traits, also noted below, tend to dissipate as entrepreneurs become consumed, or even obsessed, with their future business endeavors.

Good traits of entrepreneurs include:

§ dreaming big
§ loving what they do
§ an extraordinary drive compared to others
§ having determination and a "never give up" attitude
§ believing that their business is going to make them rich

Do these qualities sound familiar? These are all factors in creating success as an entrepreneur. As fellow entrepreneurs agree, this is what motivates us, gives us purpose, and drives us to not give up.

Common "Bad" Belief Systems or Characteristics of Entrepreneurs

Here are a few characteristics that we as entrepreneurs don't like to talk about. They can be the "Achilles' heel" or "kryptonite" for an entrepreneur. Fortunately, most can be mitigated or at least minimized.

Kryptonite traits of entrepreneurs might include thinking that:

§ Cash flow, while rarely steady, will work itself out, even with the ups and downs.

§ The demand for my product, service, or industry will always be there.

§ I should reinvest every dime I can back into my business because it's my best investment.

§ I'll be able to retire on my business.

I am convinced that these "bad" characteristics and overall mindset are what holds so many entrepreneurs back from financial independence and freedom. The result is stress, inconsistent cash flow, no constructive retirement plan, and oftentimes, finding themselves in serious debt. But, we don't give up, do we? **Determination is generally a good thing, but it can also be blinding us and stopping us from stepping back and looking at the whole forest.** We are simply stuck in the trees oftentimes making short-sighted decisions.

Freedom Versus Flexibility

Part of having an entrepreneurial mindset is being able to understand the difference between freedom and flexibility. The definition of "freedom" is generally misunderstood by those who are not entrepreneurs. The two questions commonly asked of entrepreneurs are: "Didn't you start a small business to be free?" or "Isn't it liberating to be an entrepreneur?"

I've asked thousands of students in my classes if they feel "free" as entrepreneurs, and they laugh as they glance around the room nervously. Then, I often hear these entrepreneurs state that they have "flexibility," not freedom. "We have the choice to work any 12 hours a day we want!" **That is flexibility. It can be our greatest strength if we can embrace it, use our agility and ability to make quick decisions, and cultivate better financial habits.**

I LOVE the entrepreneurial mindset, but many small-business owners need a little "tuning up" or "tweaking" that will give them much-needed power, strength, and wisdom to better succeed as entrepreneurs. The bottom line: You have the flexibility and power to make changes in how you approach and run your business!

A Better Entrepreneurial Mindset

As we consider the good and bad personality traits of entrepreneurs, we can change our mindset if we just tap into the control we have over our business and the flexibility to make decisions. **We can eliminate the incorrect belief systems that haunt us and create more financial freedom in our business and personal lives.** Below are three beliefs, or habits, that I encourage small-business owners to cultivate that will actually set them free financially.

1. *Don't depend 100 percent on your business for your retirement income.* It's important to step back and look at the big picture and the future on a regular basis. We need to realize that our industry, product, or service could disappear or dramatically decrease in sales overnight, or face increases in cost or competition through no fault of our own. Plan for such a possibility by diversifying your sources of income or opportunities.

2. *Remember the significance of cash flow.* They say, "Cash is King" and "Cash Flow is Queen," yet cash flow will almost always be sporadic or inconsistent in small business. That's OK. Don't bemoan this reality, complain, or be depressed. Instead, you should embrace it and plan accordingly. When you do have positive cash flow, you have to deploy it into other revenue-generating strategies, whether in the actual business or outside it. This is where real estate, retirement accounts (properly invested), building buckets of cash-flow-producing assets, and other small-business development options come into play.

3. *Know the true value of your business.* Your business has value, so you should never give up on making it more and more valuable. However, you need to understand that your business may not be as valuable as you think. Don't forget, your passion may blur

your judgment. You should know the value of your business (from an outside source) and start putting together a long-term exit strategy for your business early on. This means having a living, breathing *strategic plan* and being able to look at your business from a third party's point of view.

TIP FOR FINANCIAL FREEDOM

Change how you view your business.

As you embrace this entrepreneurial mindset, you will find financial freedom, independence, and flexibility. Independence to work when you want, flexibility to choose what you love to do, and having multiple buckets (or sources) to help you save for retirement will let you choose when to retire. **This new mindset works, reduces your stress, and puts you in control of your business!**

$ $ $

TAKEAWAY 1—Your business, while it may provide you with freedom or choice to pursue what you love, may not provide you with all the financial freedom you want and need.

TAKEAWAY 2—We as entrepreneurs need to recognize our good and bad personality traits that we inherit with business ownership. As we do so, we will be better able to enhance our good characteristics and address our bad belief systems and habits.

TAKEAWAY 3—You can create a new mindset. This will include a realistic expectation as to the value of your business and what type of retirement it may be able to provide. You can also start to approach your cash flow with a different perspective and start to use your profits to build other sources of income and assets that will truly help you experience financial freedom!

A REALITY CHECK—THE TRUE VALUE OF YOUR BUSINESS

If you're like me, you believe your business is your most valuable financial asset. Most entrepreneurs feel this way, and it's OK. You have worked hours upon hours and invested blood, sweat, and tears into your business. I get it, but is your business as valuable to others? Maybe, maybe not.

This chapter isn't about changing your perspective on the value or benefit of owning a business. **It's about understanding the value of the business to a third party so you can plan to retire on your business—or at the very least, have your business help you reach some degree of financial freedom.**

I'm sure many of you have a mature business model and structure well underway. You're creating monthly cash flow and hopefully a brand, a client list, a product or products, a website, and basically some equity or residual value. Some of you are just beginning to launch your concept or idea and/or making plans to build a business or real estate empire. Whatever the case may be, I want you to know the more you can see NOW about the capability or the capacity for your business to provide for future wealth, the better.

What Is the Dollar Value of Your Business?

Valuation, as it is called, is such an important topic and critical aspect to building financial freedom that I dedicated an entire chapter to the technical methods of coming up with such a value AND thus increasing the value of your business (see Chapter 19). **For now, I need to present an important concept I'll discuss again and again throughout this book: Your business is probably not worth as much as you think it is.** By understanding what the market, or a third party, will pay for your business, you can hopefully make modifications and changes in your business NOW so it will be worth more in the future. There are two reasons why you think your business is worth more than it really is: passion and potential. Let's explore those reasons.

Passion

If you're like me, you mentally elevate the value of your business because you have an emotional attachment. Just like your kids draw the best pictures and your house is the nicest on the block, your business is worth a fortune. You are biased, and you should be. You have poured blood, sweat, and tears into your business for years. You did this by working late nights, and on weekends, missing family functions, and skipping out on trips with your friends. You didn't take any income at times and everyone sacrificed. You took out loans, borrowed money, and invested your own hard-earned cash into your business. Why? Because your business needed you.

Such passion, dedication, and sacrifice create an emotional attachment to your business, and this will usually result in a perceived or unrealistic value. This is nothing to be frustrated or angry about. Your business *does* have value, and I want to build on that. **We just have to be able to look in the mirror and admit that we can be emotional about our business and a little less than impartial.** Face it . . . no one is going to think your business is worth more than you do.

Potential

The second reason why you think your business is worth more money is because you know your business has great potential! But do you and I spend as much time focusing on the future and development of our business model as we should? Probably not. I know I don't. The older I get, the better I become at strategic planning for my business, but when I sit down and think of the potential of my business, I always feel like I could do more.

So what are we to do? I realize we need to pay the bills, cover the overhead, try to support ourselves (and maybe a family) with our business profits, but just sometimes, once and a while, we need to implement better strategic planning *for the future sale of our business* by realizing more of that potential. It's not uncommon for business owners to think about what the business could, should, and would be able to accomplish with vision and planning. **It is, however, difficult to focus on the potential when we are knee-deep working "in" the business.** It's hard to find the necessary time to step back and work "on" the business. As a result, we *think* the business is worth more, rather than actually *making* the business worth more.

Building Value

While you may seek outside help in putting together an objective valuation of your business, you are still the person best able to see the potential and amazing future of your business. Because you have this unique and powerful perspective, you can build a three-, five-, and ten-year plan to improve the intrinsic, hard-core value of your business. Remember, the value of your business is more than the ability to create cash flow. It is also about your ability to make more money with your business next month and the month after that. This is how you create value.

Think about the organization of the business—not just how it's structured, but how it's *organized*. Could it run without you at the helm and make a profit? Are the accounting records in order? Do you have employee handbooks, manuals, and operational systems to help a buyer run your business without you? Why would I want to buy your business if it's not organized and can't succeed *without you?*

TIP FOR FINANCIAL FREEDOM

Processes—not persons—create value.

If you want someone to value your business at the same dollar amount as you, then the business CAN'T be only about you. The business has to have systems or processes! Yes, there will be managers at the helm, but is it organized and ready for a third party to hit the ground running? You are in the unique and powerful position to make that happen. You need to step back, "look at the forest through the trees," and do what is most important for your *business* in the long run—not just what will create the most cash flow next month.

Changing Markets, Industries, and Trends

Two major mistakes entrepreneurs make is thinking that their business model, product, or service will essentially be the same today, tomorrow, and forever, and that a customer's wants and needs will also remain the same. **You have to look outside and understand what buyers may be concerned with when "valuing" your business.** If there is a chance the market could change or the industry may go in an entirely different direction, what will happen to your business?

I know it's a scary thought, but this is what an appraiser or a buyer is going to think about before they sign the dotted line to buy your business. Buyers from outside of your business will want to consider numerous factors affecting your industry, including new technology, means of marketing, and the economy in general.

The excitement of owning a business and knowing there is no glass ceiling and unlimited potential must be balanced by the fact that we can be scared to death when it comes to our customer base, the industry, or simply collecting our accounts receivable to pay the bills next month.

Creating Value Outside of Your Business

Because of this unpredictability when valuing our business, and in order to build financial freedom, we need to take profits from our business and create other assets and sources of income. This doesn't mean you won't have your business as your number-one asset, it just means you can't reinvest every dime of profit back into your business.

I know what you are feeling and saying. I've heard it literally over a thousand times: "My business is my best and greatest asset. I should reinvest all I can back into my business where I get the greatest return on my dollar"—wrong!

If there is a change in the market forces, a change in your industry, a change in the laws or regulations, or even a terrorist attack or war, what would or *could* happen to your business? While a few major companies have successfully reinvested only in their business for years, way too many business owners have found themselves in great financial trouble (not to mention a ton of stress) putting everything into one bucket—the business asset bucket.

Don't be so naive that you think nothing could happen in the world to change your business model, product, or service. Think about the business owners in New Orleans who were hit by Hurricane Katrina. They did nothing wrong to minimize the value of their businesses, and yet the values went down. This is why we need to diversify—and I'm not talking about a stock portfolio. Your business can actually help you BUILD diversity. If you want to build "Financial Freedom," you can't have all your eggs in one basket. You need balance in all things, balance in your business, and balance in your assets.

First, take some profits, when you can, and invest in other income- or equity-producing assets. Invest in what you know. Invest in another business with which you have a strategic partnership or relationship. Invest in some real estate. Invest in precious metals. Invest in something that isn't dependent on the same market, industry, or customer base as your core business. Yes, you can even invest in Wall Street products and insurance, but only at the right time with the proper method that we will discuss later.

Now, I know you are busy, but you can't afford not to take a little time every week to think outside the box. Your business could very well be the goose laying some golden eggs right now, which is great. All I'm saying is to take some of those eggs and buy some cows, or buy a farmhouse down the road and rent it to a llama farmer, or even get out of agriculture altogether and take some of those golden eggs to set up an online fly fishing store in your spare time.

You owe more to your business, and to yourself, than having the pressure of paying all the bills and providing a retirement without diversifying. Do your business, and yourself, a favor by creating some cash flow somewhere else so your business doesn't have to be the superstar year in and year out. Let your business help you diversify.

§　§　§

TAKEAWAY 1—Entrepreneurs have an emotional attachment to their business, which often creates a perceived and unrealistic value of the business.

TAKEAWAY 2—You are in a unique and powerful position to build value in your business by taking time to create a strategic plan that will produce a greater core value for your business that others will also see as a value.

TAKEAWAY 3—A business, and the outside world around it, is intrinsically unpredictable. Therefore, we should not reinvest every dollar back into our business. Instead, it's important to peel out profits, when we can, to redeploy and invest in other income/equity-building ventures.

THE TRUTH ABOUT YOUR FINANCIAL ADVISOR

Wall Street doesn't understand the small-business entrepreneur. Your business is of no interest to them. Unless your business is driving billions of dollars in annual sales, you're just too small and inconsequential for Wall Street's big money strategies. Essentially, to the Wall Street advisor, if you aren't planning on going public or aren't able to provide a unique opportunity for a private equity firm to invest in you, they won't even talk to you.

What's worse is that the Main Street representative of Wall Street, for example your "local" stockbroker, insurance agent, or financial planner, says they care about you, but it's only a half-truth. I call them the Main Street representative because they are on the front lines working for one of the large Wall Street firms selling their products to "help" the average-income American or entrepreneur. But the half-truth is that they are captive to their employers.

Captive means that they can only recommend *their company's* **products or services, and if they don't, they get fired.** This isn't like the scene in the movie *Miracle on 34th Street* where the woman at the counter working for Cole's pulled out the Yellow Pages and recommended their competitor because that's what was best for the customer and where they could get the best value and price.

Do you really think your agent at State Farm is going to recommend a product at Allstate or Geico, even if there is a chance their rates are better? Or is your broker at Northwestern or Merrill Lynch going to recommend a different product or strategy at Edward Jones, or even a self-directed custodian like Pensco or DirectedIRA?com? Of course not! When it comes to our retirement portfolios, or insurance, the last thing you think you're going to get is independent advice that's *best* for you.

An Independent Advisor

I chose an amazing financial advisor to be my co-author for this book. His name is Randy Luebke, and he is truly an independent advisor who is legally required to give the best advice *for his clients*—not to give advice to enhance his own income. I was grateful he was willing to share his time, insights, and incredible wisdom to contribute to this book. Throughout the remainder of this book, you will see his sidebar comments from the perspective of an independent advisor without a self-serving agenda.

Randy is what is known as an Investment Advisor Representative (IAR), and he owns his own Registered Investment Advisory (RIA). While this designation and business arrangement is not a guarantee of independence (more on this to follow), without it he or any other financial advisor would find it difficult if not impossible to provide truly independent advice. In Randy's situation, however, it does mean he is *not* associated with a broker-dealer and he doesn't sell any proprietary mutual funds or other financial products. **You may not realize it,** but such independent advisors make up only 1.6 percent of all financial advisors in the country. Simply stated, he is only one of approximately 5,000 independent advisors out of more than 310,000 licensed financial advisors in the country.

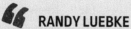 **RANDY LUEBKE**

> In Tony Robbins' book, *Unshakeable: Your Financial Freedom Playbook* (Simon & Schuster, 2017), he goes to great lengths to describe the lack of independent advisors in America and the misconception and misdirection promulgated by the financial industry that leads us to believe that most advisors are acting as fiduciaries on our behalf. They aren't! They can't—even if they wanted to. I believe this is truly the cancer in the financial industry, and no one is looking for the cure or even cares about it. In fact, you would actually be surprised to see more legislation aimed at reducing the rules and regulations that protect financial consumers.

Tony Robbins related his own frustration about trying to find independent financial advisors—"How are you supposed to tell which hat they're wearing at any given moment? Believe me, it's not easy. I've had the experience of asking an advisor if he was a fiduciary and having him look me in the eye and assuring me that he was . . . here was a person I thought I could recommend as a fiduciary, and he lied to my face."

Let me explain what this term fiduciary *really* means, as well as suitability.

Suitability Versus Fiduciary Duty

These two terms are rarely talked about by your rank-and-file advisors because they don't want to scare you away. Suitability means how appropriate the financial product is for the investor in a broad sense. Essentially, as long as a financial product is within your risk tolerance, and they think you can take the hit if it loses, then the advisor can sell it, and you can't sue them for the advice they provided you to buy it.

Fiduciary duty means that the advisor has a *duty* to recommend, and to do, what's best specifically for YOU—not for their employer. The type of advisor held to this standard is licensed as an Investment Advisor Representative, or "IAR," and they work for a Registered Investment Advisory, or RIA. **Now, you may think that your local advisor on Main Street is different, but they aren't.** In fact, the local advisor tied to a large brokerage firm or even a small independent shop that is supervised by a broker-dealer is contractually obligated to sell you their products and ONLY their products. Any recommendations to invest your money otherwise would likely be in violation of their employment agreement.

This would be what is referred to as *selling away*, the practice of recommending and selling assets to you that would move your money away from their employer's/broker-dealer's firm and investing your money elsewhere, like in your own business, for example. Even though investing in something other than the securities that the firm sells may be in your best interest, the Wall Street advisor cannot recommend it, or they could and would likely be fired.

 RANDY LUEBKE

Regrettably, it is more complicated than simply looking for IAR/RIA status. There are a few more questions you need to ask. This is because if the RIA is affiliated with a broker-dealer, they are once again being manipulated and recommending specific investments for which they are rewarded with incentives. Otherwise stated: they've lost their independence.

Moreover, if the IAR has established proprietary mutual funds or separately managed accounts, they again are highly compensated to steer you towards these highly profitable products, which is in their best interest and not necessarily in yours.

Frankly, the Wall Street advisors are generally good people caught up in a very bad system. My son in fact is currently attending college and loves to track individual stocks and do some commission free trading. He is enamored by the exchanges and financial industry. I'm okay with that and think it's great, but if he wants to advise others, I want him to be truly independent and focus on what's in the best interest of his clients.

Regrettably, many new stockbrokers drawn to the industry join large brokerages, banks, and advisory firms hoping to make their fortune but are held captive to their employer. **As a result, you are the target of their sales techniques instead of benefiting from their advice.**

The sad part is, you can't exactly blame them. It's like watching one of those wildlife videos where the lion kills a deer and then getting mad at the lion. You can't blame the lion. This is what they do. They hunt and they kill to eat and to survive. **Selling you Wall Street's financial products is what the Wall Street advisor does.** You can't blame them either. It's what they do to survive.

I'm so grateful that I was to come in contact and build a relationship with a truly independent fiduciary such as Randy Luebke. In fact, I'm honored to have him contribute to this book and have asked him to author a couple chapters in full on insurance products (Chapter 16) and what to buy from Wall Street (Chapter 17). Both of these topics I have no business writing on, and I hope you are as grateful as I am for some unbiased, nonself-serving advice on these critical subjects.

On the homepage of Randy's website, he uses the checklist created by Tony Robbins and his advice on how to find the right type of advisor. Robbins spent countless hours, and I'm sure thousands of dollars, to research and explain very powerfully in his book how

---

TIP FOR FINANCIAL FREEDOM

Find out who your financial advisor **really** *represents.*

---

important a fiduciary is to your success. Randy meets every one of these criteria to ensure that you get independent advice that is in *your best interest*. In our law and accounting firm, we only recommend advisors that meet this criteria for comprehensive financial planning.

§ § §

TAKEAWAY 1—Wall Street is not looking out for the individual investor or small-business owner.

TAKEAWAY 2—By far, most financial advisors are looking out for themselves. They work for large brokerages that sell products, and they are looking to sell you the products that will bring them the highest sales commissions.

TAKEAWAY 3—Only a Registered Investment Advisor (RIA) is truly an independent advisor with a fiduciary duty to look out for your best interest. Purchasing Wall Street products is oftentimes a good choice in your mix of assets to build financial freedom, but it's critical you search and interview to find an independent advisor.

WHAT WALL STREET ISN'T TELLING YOU

At this point, you hopefully realize that it's hard to find the right person in the financial industry to advise you. Regrettably, that's only half the battle. Frankly, we're just getting started when it comes to the corruption, in my opinion, permeating Wall Street.

It's the FEES!

This is at the heart of *why* you and I can't get independent advice from Wall Street. They are too addicted to the fees and the love of money. While making money is why we go to work or own our businesses, consumers need to know the truth about how this industry works and what is going on behind the curtain.

In the investment industry, there are two cost structures, or powers at work, that consumers know very little about. These two combine to undercut the average investor. This is why you *feel* like your retirement accounts and any such goal to use Wall Street products is a waste of time and money!

Problem 1: Annual Fund Operating Expenses (aka Fund Fees)

The fees buried in mutual funds are enormous and hidden from the average investor. We don't even know what they are nor could we figure them out. Why do I focus on the mutual fund as the problem? Largely, because most of us do not have the buying power or the time to research and invest in individual stocks. And we certainly can't be day traders and business owners at the same time!

In America today, there are more than 3,000 stocks on the NASDAQ and 2,800 stocks on the NYSE—not to mention another estimated 9,500 mutual funds and now thousands of Exchange Traded Funds (ETFs), with more created every day. The internal fees associated with this wide array of investments vary just as widely. By the way, I'm not bashing fees per se. Certainly, everyone needs to be paid, and no one is opposed to paying for value. **The problem is that most of these mutual funds charge a lot of fees and deliver very little value when compared to ETF's, where fees are very small. ETF's are not a panacea either.** There is no "free lunch" on Wall Street or with any investment. These fees taken by the mutual fund managers and companies can be off the chart!

Again, Tony Robbins, in *Unshakeable*, does a phenomenal job of investigating this issue, interviewing countless Wall Street insiders *and* outsiders to show what the average mutual fund can charge in fees. Based on the 2011 *Forbes* study titled "The Real Cost of Owning a Mutual Fund," Robbins summarizes that "If the fund is held in a nontaxable account like a 401(k), you're looking at total costs of 3.17 percent a year! If it's in a taxable account, the total costs amount to a staggering 4.17 percent a year!"

Once again, Robbins puts it best when he writes, "These expenses are a constant drain on your returns—the equivalent of a merciless vampire sucking your blood each night while you're asleep." **The result is that your "carefully chosen" mutual fund, selected by your advisor or broker, can barely exceed the market returns of a no-load index fund.** In fact, Robert Arnott of Research Affiliates reports that 96 percent of mutual funds failed to beat the market over a 15-year period in large part due to these excessive fees!!

Bottom line: We are doomed before we even get started when we trust in the investment advice of our so-called "independent advisor."

Problem 2: Administrative Fees (aka Plan Fees)

If you didn't think mutual fund fees were bad enough, let's add insult to injury and talk about the administrative fees of a 401(k) (the vehicle to hold your mutual funds). This is a cost thrown onto the backs of companies and business owners simply for the pleasure of being able to use a 401(k) structure, but of course, these costs will inevitably trickle down to the investor themselves as they always do in the process.

Yet, let me say adamantly that the 401(k) is amazing and an incredible opportunity and strategy if used properly. It can be the perfect vehicle to help reach more financial freedom or flexibility. The problem is that 98 percent of Americans are not the "driver" of this vehicle, but small-business owners could be if they knew who to ask for help.

 RANDY LUEBKE

Using the vehicle analogy, you're just in the front passenger seat as a spectator. Your broker or agent is in the driver's seat, and their friends, or financial products, are in the back seat. The broker tells you that you can "direct" your retirement, and can choose who goes in the back seat, but then they give you the caveat that it can only be "some of their friends." What's worse is that not only are you stuck with products in the back seat that aren't your friends, you have to pay all the fees that come with the vehicle AND the passengers.

It's no secret nowadays that there are an incredible amount of hidden fees and costs buried in your investments AND in the administrative costs of your 401(k) and almost every financial product peddled by Wall Street.

Again, Tony Robbins did the work for all of us exposing this scheme perpetrated upon us, stating, "You've got to hand it to these providers: They're truly ingenious when it comes to dreaming up different ways to siphon off the money in your 401(k)!" He goes on further to say, "Just to be clear, we're not referring here to the absurdly high fees that you're being charged by the mutual funds in your 401(k) plan. These are the additional fees that you're also being charged by the plan provider that's *administering* your 401(k)."

These 401(k) fees can be buried and disguised in so many unique ways it's hard to even find a range of what these fees can be. Moreover, the fees for such plans can be different from one company to another and one brokerage firm to another. **You also have to review a maze of paperwork and fine print to ever discover the true costs being extracted out of your hard-earned investments.** Suffice it to say that administrative fees can range from 1.6 to 7.75 percent or more, and again, that is on top of the actual mutual fund fees. It is truly sad when you consider the greed of Wall Street and their ability to extract more money out of the average American investor and entrepreneur.

Three Strategies Your Advisor Won't Talk About

Now, let me recognize that I have quoted Tony Robbins several times in this chapter, but also let me assure you that isn't going to be the case throughout the rest of the book. I think Robbins does a fantastic job in explaining the problems with Wall Street, the fees, the corruption, and the lack of independence they so claim. **However, Robbins stops there. His ultimate solution is to still approach investing in Wall Street, but to invest in no-load indexed mutual funds.** That's it! No other options for even the entrepreneur.

If I had the honor and pleasure to interview Robbins on my radio show and podcast, I would ask him why he doesn't discuss the three topics below. Also, keep in mind that you will never hear your advisor discuss these three strategies, at least voluntarily—and if they do, they will downplay, disregard, and outright discourage you from considering them. And yet, these three strategies will allow you to build for your future while growing your greatest asset of all: your business.

Strategy 1—Investing in Your Own Business More Aggressively

Remember, your business can be your most valuable asset, at present and/or potentially in the future. **We believe it will become the vehicle that drives you to your financial freedom.** Why not maximize its value cautiously and carefully?

You could be sitting on a gold mine or have a goose laying golden eggs to build other buckets of wealth. In Chapter 5, I will start laying the groundwork for optimizing your business more fully and feeding, or "funding," a diverse array of assets that will give you financial flexibility and ultimate freedom.

Strategy 2 —Buying and Managing Rental Real Estate—Even Passively

Real estate is such an important part of wealth building. More specifically, rental real estate has incredible tax benefits, generates cash

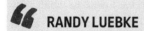

RANDY LUEBKE

I'm sure you have heard your investment advisor go on tirades or at least provide warnings of how terrible and risky rental real estate can be. "Remember the millions of Americans that lost almost everything in the real estate downturn in 2008?" What your advisor fails to mention is the percentage of millionaires who have built their fortunes in real estate. Even, the billionaire and industrialist Andrew Carnegie, over 100 years ago, declared that "Ninety percent of all millionaires become so through owning real estate. More money has been made in real estate than in all industrial investments combined. The wise young man or wage earner of today invests his money in real estate."

flow, and builds tax-deferred equity, and can even do so using leverage and the bank's money.

Warren Buffet, arguably the most savvy and successful investor in modern times, has consistently invested in real estate, and between 2010 and 2015 he purchased billions of dollars' worth of real estate and formed the residential real estate brokerage firm HomeSevices of America, held by Berkshire Hathaway Energy.

In the end, real estate should simply be included in your portfolio (and I'm not talking about a REIT). But, of course your so-called "investment advisor" won't tell you that. They don't get a commission for recommending you buy a building to rent back to your business operations, or a duplex where your child is going to college, or a real estate project next to your parents where you travel twice a year, or a few houses to rent in an upcoming neighborhood. Real estate can be such a sound investment strategy, and I have dedicated an entire chapter to this financial building block in providing financial freedom and flexibility (see Chapter 14).

Strategy 3 —Self-Directing Your Retirement Accounts and Investing in What You Know Best!

In the 2012 presidential campaign between Governor Mitt Romney and President Obama, America was shocked to discover that Mitt Romney had more than $20 million in his IRA account and asked, "How could this be? We can only put approximately 5k into an IRA each year. Romney must have done something illegal."

Essentially, Romney's response, which was later summarized in a *Wall Street Journal* article in January of 2012, was that of surprise and shock that Americans weren't also self-directing. Little did he know this is one of the best-kept secrets on Wall Street. The last thing the large brokers/dealers want you doing is taking over your IRA or 401(k) and investing in what you know best. If Wall Street was really looking out for your best interests, they would give you this option. Many times, you would be wiser to redeploy your 401(k) or IRA into investments that you have more information about, rather than the mutual fund options you are given by your "advisor."

Just as Randy mentioned above, the typical Wall Street advisor is allowing you to choose your rides in the car, but you can only choose from the advisor's friends. Hence, you really don't control who (or your investments) rides in the backseat. I want you to specifically direct who the passengers are in your investment "vehicle." That is the essence of self-directing. The following Figure 4.1 may better illustrate this metaphor.

Figure 4.1—Your Self-Directed Vehicle

If Wall Street cared about you, they would give you this option. Sometimes you would be wiser to redeploy your 401(k) or IRA in investments you know more about rather than a mutual fund. That's right, invest directly inside your retirement account maintaining the structure and continue to make annual contributions within your overall tax strategy. For example, here are just a few ideas of what YOU could do inside your retirement account without taxes, transfer fees, or penalties:

❙ Invest in a trust deed note and lend someone money to buy real estate, yet be in first position with the collateral to foreclose if they don't pay

- § Purchase a rental property and even borrow up to 60 percent from a bank in a nonrecourse loan. This can ensure cash flow going back into your retirement account with no personal guarantee with your own credit
- § Invest in a racehorse, ranch, or farming operation
- § Buy gold, silver, or other precious metals
- § Invest in small business, real estate development, or an online business, primarily owned and managed by someone you know personally and trust.
- § Start your own franchise owned by your 401(k) where you are still allowed to work in the business for a salary under the ROBS strategy.

These are just a few of the many possibilities, but you will never hear your broker, agent, or so-called investment advisor make the above recommendations. Since this is such an important concept in your overall strategy, I discuss the strategy of "self-directing" more fully in Chapter 13.

§ § §

TAKEAWAY 1—The hidden fees buried inside mutual funds is almost criminal. Wall Street will find ways to make more money and hide it from the average investor.

TAKEAWAY 2—Not only does Wall Street bury fees in its products, it also will find ways to create additional fees for using vehicles such as the 401(k). This is a structure that can help the small-business owner immensely but is abused by the Wall Street machine.

TAKEAWAY 3—There are three principal strategies you can utilize to diversify your assets and build your wealth: investing in and growing your business, buying and managing real estate, and self-directing your retirement accounts.

FORGE A BETTER, SMARTER, AND SAFER WAY

Like many of you, I have been searching and sometimes bumbling through my financial life looking for an "equation" that would bring it all together for me (at least financially speaking).

You might want to say, "Mark, what are you talking about? You are a CPA, author, attorney, and business advisor to so many people around the country! Didn't you figure this whole wealth building thing out years ago?" The answer is simply that it's been a process and only in the past three or four years has it really started to click.

I'll explain in the next chapter that Dave Ramsey, a national expert on financial planning for the common middle-income American, had a huge impact on me and our family's finances. But as I will explain, he ultimately didn't speak to me as an entrepreneur. I related to some of his initial concepts, but then as an entrepreneur, I just felt like I couldn't connect any longer. In my consultations with clients every day (who are predominantly small-business owners), I discovered I was taking some of the basics of Dave Ramsey's teachings, but then was adding what was lacking. I was "taking it to the next level" of planning that entrepreneurs were starving for. I then met another individual that truly filled in the blanks for me.

In the next chapter, I'm going to explain how I discovered the principles that brought it all together for me and summarize this *better, smarter, and safer* way of approaching financial planning. Then, in the four chapters that follow my introduction to this unique approach to financial planning, I'm going to lay out in detail the sequential steps that have changed my life financially.

It ALL STARTS with three important steps before you enter the Business Owner's Financial Landscape. These are foundational in nature and MUST be completed before you start investing. By working through this process, I am certain you will be on a better path to financial freedom. Here is a diagram to illustrate these next sequential steps.

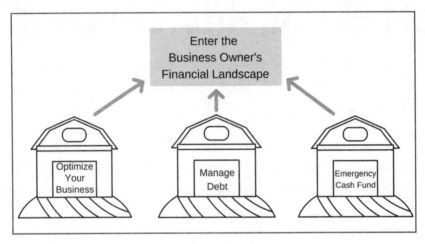

Figure II—Building a Foundation

THE LIFETIME PARADIGM AND THE 4 X 4 FINANCIAL INDEPENDENCE PLAN

Truthfully, I have been influenced by so many different sources that have helped me become a better investor, business owner, and ultimately a better advisor to you, my clients. In fact, in turn, I have been influenced by many of you. Participating in thousands of consultations, assisting so many people, but then also learning from the successes and failures of my clients has truly impacted me greatly.

I have even been shaped and guided by my incredible law and accounting partners, my employees, and my close family members. Their examples of thrift and wise financial decisions have had a big impact on me, and I try to pass those techniques and financial principles in my consults, videos, and presentations.

But I have to admit that Dave Ramsey at one point in my career was a huge influence in my financial life; **HOWEVER, his teachings and strategies seemed to only take me to a point, and then I was left wanting more.** Ramsey's theories ultimately didn't speak to me as an entrepreneur and encourage significant wealth building and using leverage to acquire real estate.

Frankly, it all started to come together when I met Randy Luebke. As I described in the last chapter, he really is one of the relatively few truly independent financial advisors in America—the 3 percent that actually advise their clients with strategies that are in *the client's* best interest.

For me, Randy picked up where Dave Ramsey left off. He brought ideas, strategies, and excitement to investing and building wealth *after* one is out of debt with reserves and maximizing their current resources.

I was so influenced by Randy that this is why I asked him to contribute to this book, and why almost every chapter has his mark or fingerprint on it. Randy introduced me to his incredible 4 x 4 Financial Independence Plan that spoke to my soul and brought it all together for me—financially speaking. It just clicked!

Four Sequential Steps

I like steps, checklists, and a process—something I can follow and that makes sense. If you're like me, we build confidence as we accomplish tasks and take baby steps towards the bigger goal or long-term vision. **Lets face it, trying to achieve financial security OR stability can be overwhelming. It doesn't happen overnight.**

Randy created four sequential steps that literally take an entrepreneur from start to finish on their quest for financial independence. Yes, there are a lot of details to each stage of the process, but I can get my "head around it," for lack of a better term, and they just make sense!

Here they are, simply stated:

Step 1—Optimize what you have
Step 2—Eliminate all reductive debt

Step 3—Establish significant cash reserves

Step 4—Invest for long-term goals and plans

Steps 1 to 3 are foundational and must be completed *before* embarking on Step 4. This focus on the first three steps will help you as an entrepreneur create more cash flow and operate debt free, and I'll explain later that not *all* debt is bad when building a business and buying real estate. **But this foundation is critical to build a strong and sturdy "house" of investments.**

Unfortunately, most financial plans don't address many of these steps that *must* be completed before investing. Instead, Wall Street advisors get a hold of an entrepreneur and focus on selling products like life insurance, annuities, or stocks and bonds (as I discussed in Chapter 3). **The result is that people end up with a bundle of financial products but lack a coordinated plan to fund their retirement.**

This creates a situation of vulnerability and, for many, a latent sense of anxiety in knowing that they are simply not prepared to retire. More importantly, they expose themselves to devastating financial consequences should they develop some serious health issue along the way. Unfortunately, they see no way to resolve this problem, and the traditional financial services industry, focused on selling their products, is simply not providing much help.

But not the Four Sequential Steps! They are focused on YOU and your success. We've also called them the sequential steps for a reason. They have to be done in order, and as you complete them one after the other, you gain confidence and momentum. So, allow me to outline them briefly for you, and then in the following four chapters, I'll dive into the details of each step and expand upon them.

Step 1—Optimize What You Have

Most people don't realize the power they have to take control of their finances and create the cash flow to fund their long-term plans (this is also discussed more fully in Chapter 6). *This step involves maximizing your business's profitability, continuing your education, cutting costs, and saving taxes.* The key to launching this step and continuing to live by its precepts is having a strategic plan and a team of advisors to help you make progress year after year.

Step 2—Eliminate All Reductive Debt

There are two kinds of debt: reductive and productive. Reductive debt is generally debt used to acquire "stuff," things that are consumed or depreciate in value and things that never provide an income. (This is discussed more fully in Chapter 7.) Think of bad credit card debt, which needs to be eliminated. On the other hand, productive debt is used to acquire assets that appreciate in value and/or do provide income. **In this Step, you will eliminate ALL reductive debt, build your credit, and utilize productive debt.** I like to refer to this step as almost debt management. You'll learn about the types of debt and understand that reductive debt gets in the way of growing your wealth. Productive debt nurtures and grows your wealth until you have financial freedom.

 RANDY LUEBKE

Reductive debt is generally expensive. Productive debt is generally cheap and helps you build your business or investments. This is why managing debt, as an entrepreneur, can be tricky at best. However, there is a path to using debt wisely and for your benefit.

Step 3—Establish Significant Liquid Cash Reserves

You need liquid cash reserves for two reasons: 1) when things go wrong, we need these reserves to help us weather the storm and avoid credit card debt; and 2) we need access to cash to take advantage of opportunities when they present themselves. (Again, this is discussed more fully in Chapter 8.) In fact, this second reason is important, and I can't over emphasize it enough. I *know* as an entrepreneur that opportunities are constantly arising. Maybe it's because we are looking and it's just our nature, but it's true—problems arise as a business owner, and opportunities jump right in front of you. Either way, you need reserves, and further, more *significant reserves* take you from living paycheck-to-paycheck to having 6-12 months of your earnings or monthly expenses available at all times.

RANDY LUEBKE

Most people do not have enough money set aside as cash reserves. In fact, most people live month-to-month or paycheck-to-paycheck. This is living on very thin ice because one little crack in your lifestyle could cause you to break through the ice and fall into some really deep cold water. It could be something as simple as a water heater breaking or something as devastating as a major automobile accident or losing your job. Whatever the incident is, it causes a financial expense and often a financial setback as well. If you experience an incident like this and have some cash to fall back on, then you will generally make it through this step even it if is a major financial storm.

Additionally, having cash reserves will also help you to take advantage of opportunities when they present themselves. This is when things go right. In fact, I would venture to say that if you have money in reserve, not only will opportunities present themselves, they will be created right before your eyes. More on this in Chapter 8.

Step 4—Start Investing and Building Different Buckets of Wealth

Once Steps 1 through 3 have been completed, it's time for you to work on this final step of the process. (This is discussed more fully in Chapter 9.) Most people jump to this step too soon (even though it may be with good intentions). Surely, this is the fun part of retirement income planning. Seeing your investments grow and provide great returns is rewarding at many levels. Still, without having all your investments working in concert it will be difficult to achieve the degree of financial freedom you are trying to obtain. Essentially, after presenting Step 4, the rest of this book is about building and enhancing those buckets of wealth and streams of income.

By following these four steps in sequence, you are much more likely to achieve financial success. Most people don't. As a result, most are financially unsuccessful. Most people invest their assets inefficiently, not optimally. Most people will have reductive debt and pay high interest rates for it. Most people don't have a significant liquid cash reserve. Yet, they try to save and invest in their company. **You won't be like most people anymore!**

The Four Essential Elements

Now, these four sequential steps come with four essential elements. That's why it's called the 4 x 4 Plan! When combined together the power you have as an investor, business owner, and wealth builder is unimaginable. **Every step of the process needs to be measured against the following four elements.** They provide perspective and direction to achieve your financial goals.

- § Independence Planning
- § Asset Protection
- § Estate Planning
- § Tax Planning

1. *Independence Planning.* This is the process of converting your earnings into investments that will provide you the income you need to live the life you want when you choose to no longer work. Everyone is at a different phase of their financial life. When one is younger, the focus is mainly on asset accumulation. The goal is to earn a living. **Then, as one's income grows, the goals evolve into saving and investing enough money to finance a lifestyle today and ultimately accumulate enough assets to finance a lifestyle that can be sustained in the future.** Generally, people refer to this as retirement. I prefer to refer to it as financial freedom or independence—when your

assets are sufficient to provide you with an income so that work is no longer a requirement. Instead, work is an option. Income planning is the process of taking you from where you are today to the financial independence you want tomorrow.

2. *Asset Protection.* Protecting what you have from those that would take it from you is asset protection. The takers can be creditors, relatives, the government, and others. Your assets not only include traditional things like stocks, bonds, and real estate. For many, their single biggest asset will be their ability to earn an income over their lifetime. This needs to be protected too. **The goal is simply to create barriers and boundaries that prevent and/or deter others from taking what you have earned.**

3. *Estate Planning.* We look at our financial lives in two phases: one while you are living and the other when you are not. I call this your life and your legacy. Think of it as asset protection once you are no longer here to physically protect your assets. The goal of estate planning is to ensure that what you have accomplished in your life will be passed on to your future legacy in a manner that you choose.

4. *Tax Planning.* Taxes are life's single biggest expense. Yet, like most expenses, paying taxes are a choice that you get to make. It's not that you get to choose if you should or should not pay taxes. It is simply a matter of making tax-efficient financial decisions.

> **❝ RANDY LUEBKE**
>
> The 4 x 4 Financial Plan offers a better solution. By following the steps we described and in the sequence we recommend, the odds of successfully implementing your financial plan increase substantially. I know this because not only have I seen the results again and again with clients all over the country, but also because they are truly based on sound financial principles. ❞

This is the principle of "The Net," which states, "It's not what you make, it's what you keep that matters."

A Lifetime Paradigm—A New Perspective on Retirement

Today, almost everything is different. Today, most retirees do not have a pension to provide a guaranteed income. Instead, it is more likely that they will have a 401(k) or IRA with no safety net to protect it from market downturns and no guarantee of lifetime income to protect the retiree. Social Security, while still available, is under tremendous financial stress. With Medicare generally the sole health-care insurance option for retirees, that system is also under financial stress. Volatility in the stock, bond, and real estate markets, huge mortgages, credit card debt, and low interest paid on savings all serve as serious problems for today's retirees.

TIP FOR FINANCIAL FREEDOM

Freedom is independence and security, not retirement.

Today's retirees need a new paradigm, a new perspective, and a new point of view to address the issues they face. In fact, I believe that today we need something so radically different that we chose to replace the word "retirement" altogether with the more appropriate concept of financial freedom, the very title of this book and set forth in the introduction.

 RANDY LUEBKE

I believe that today we need to stop thinking about retirement as we knew it in the past, and we need to intently and purposefully work on our financial freedom and independence over our lifetime. I call this "The Lifetime Paradigm" and a Better, Smarter, and Safer Way to plan for your retirement.

As an entrepreneur, a comprehensive financial plan takes a global perspective of one's financial situation rather than simply loading up on financial products. We want to focus on financial independence and developing and implementing a plan to achieve it. With this substantial change of perspective, now we can address all the issues facing us throughout our lifetime and develop strategies to avoid the problems that will develop and plans to help us to exploit the opportunities that present themselves. **While there are many ways to go about this, I believe that "the secret is in the sequence."** By this, I mean that while it is important to get things done, doing them in the *right sequence* is even more important as this increases the likelihood of achieving the desired outcome, which, in this instance, is your financial freedom and security.

$ $ $

TAKEAWAY 1—There are four sequential steps to achieving financial freedom, and we must follow them in order if we want to truly make progress and in the most effective and efficient manner.

TAKEAWAY 2—There are also four elements that complete the 4 x 4 plan and bring the whole process together. Every step we take and investment we make must be measured against these four elements.

TAKEAWAY 3—"The Lifetime Paradigm" is essentially a comprehensive financial plan with sequential steps to achieve a *Better, Smarter, and Safer Way* to reach financial freedom and enjoy our desired level of retirement.

CHAPTER

6

STEP 1: OPTIMIZE WHAT YOU ALREADY HAVE

All too often, I meet with clients that have grand plans for investing, or other projects for cash flow, but aren't optimizing what they already have. Many times, my clients are sitting on a gold mine, but they either don't know it or are struggling to exploit it and take it to the next level. It could be their business underperforming, a strategic relationship they aren't cultivating, or an underdeveloped real estate venture. **Bottom line: they aren't optimizing what they already have right under their nose!**

What I've oftentimes discovered is that they are simply missing two key tools that, if implemented properly *and* consistently, would help them quickly find the cash flow they need to get out of debt, build cash reserves, and start properly investing. **Those two critical tools for business owners are a *dynamic strategic plan* and a well-designed and *utilized management team*.**

This is why Optimization is the first sequential step in your financial plan, your paradigm, and your comprehensive plan to financial freedom. We can't start on Step 2, 3, or 4 until we have organized and/or optimized what we already have. This is almost a universal, or even spiritual, point of view. How can you expect to build financial freedom if your current house isn't in order?

I also can't go on without a reference to the Kevin Costner film *Field of Dreams* wherein the main character, played by Costner, had to build a baseball field in a cornfield in the middle of nowhere, on a prompting, on faith that "if he built it, they (the players) would come." I don't want to ruin the movie for you, but spoiler alert: the players ultimately came *after* he built the field. **As such, your financial freedom is only going to come after you build it (and by that I mean plan) and have your affairs in order.** You can't put new wine in old bottles, so get ready for success if you really want success to come!

Now, this process or my request of you may seem a little overwhelming or complicated at first, but the beauty of having a small business is that you can be agile and quick to change the course of your ship. You can make executive decisions and implement them rather quickly. Large companies can't do this. You are the captain of your ship and generally don't have to answer to anyone (except perhaps your family, backers/investors, or banker), and you can make things happen much faster than any Wall Street executive. Use this to your advantage—start with a plan!

Creating Your Strategic Plan

Let's face it; it's easy in a small business to become reactionary to the concerns or crisis of the day, and you will often feel like you are holding on for dear life. You can literally be living month to month financially *and* emotionally. I've been there. Heck, I think any honest business owner will admit to having had those moments, days, sometimes months or even years of living on the edge. **A strategic plan, however, can help you get from where you are to where you want to be.** This strategic plan will be designed by you (and by your team, which we'll discuss shortly) to help you succeed as a business owner and build wealth.

Not everyone knows about having a strategic plan when they start out; in fact, most people learn about it somewhere along the way. In fact, I learned after years of college, a master's degree, a doctorate, and consulting with thousands of clients that you can control your business through the proactive approach of strategic planning. This whole concept was introduced to my partner, LaDell Eyre, and me at a two-week business training retreat ten years ago. Yes, we took 12 days out of our busy schedules to try to get a grip on our business because we felt like the business was controlling us—not the other way around.

We had been operating our accounting firm, Kohler & Eyre CPAs, for close to five years and needed a solution to the stress of small-business ownership and a grueling tax season year after year. The solution, having a strategic plan, or "Strat Plan" as my partner likes to call it, is a living, breathing document that you will take with you everywhere you go. **You'll put your best ideas in it and then fine-tune it on a regular basis to coincide with carefully, well-thought-out plans.**

We learned that a strategic plan sets forth a timeline of specific tasks that need to be completed to make your business plan a reality. It's a specific list of objectives to reach specific goals.

Even experienced business owners can benefit from using a strategic plan as an integral part of their business. It is so difficult to manage all the loose ends and chaos that can occur when running a small business. A strategic plan will help you overcome these hurdles. Such a plan is essentially a checklist of things that need to be completed in the next month, three months, six months, and 12 months. **It takes your business to the next level when you are trying to decide where it is most effective to spend your time.** It also takes the guesswork out of what to do next.

Anyone that has owned their own business knows that success can often turn on one simple principle: self-discipline. When you own your own business, there is usually no one leaning over your shoulder making sure you are putting in the hours you need and focusing your energy on the right tasks. A strategic plan can give you a regular road map to keep you focused and help you set goals and then follow a strategy for achieving them.

> ## ❝ RANDY LUEBKE
>
> Without exception, when a new client starts working with me and we start to evaluate everything they have done financially up until now, what I find is a hodgepodge of investments, plans, and strategies. I refer this as "Plan du jour." Along the way, most people have joined in, signed up, gotten started with strategy after strategy. Now they have this cacophony of plans that, rather than playing beautifully together, often do nothing to support each other. At worst, they conflict with each other and/or the client's goals. The solution is to simplify, organize, and systematize, which will ultimately optimize their financial goals and strategies into one unified and manageable system. Think of this like packing a car when you go on a long trip with the family. **If you were to grab one suitcase and place it in the car, then randomly pack your golf clubs and so on, in the end, you may or may not get everything you want loaded up.** Instead, you lay out everything you want to pack for the trip in one place. Determine if you really need all that stuff. Eliminate some of it. Maybe pack some things inside of others for more efficiency. Then, you systematically pack everything in an organized manner into your car. You still may not get it all in of course. So what! What will get into the car is what is most important first. Whatever is last, if it doesn't fit, can likely be left behind anyway. Simplify, organize, systematize, and the result...you optimize! ❞

In a partnership, it doesn't have as much to do with self-discipline as it has to do with trust and accountability. **It is so important for partners to meet on a regular basis to discuss, strategize, decide, assign, and then document every decision they are making as**

partners. It is so easy to forget who is doing what and why you decided on a certain course of action in the business. During difficult times, as well as successful times, the strategic plan is oftentimes the glue that can hold a partnership together.

There is a lot of debate as to whether or not a weekly plan is helpful or more time-consuming than it's worth. I have found that simply reviewing my monthly strategic plan is more than sufficient and keeps me on task each week. The following shows you how to get started.

1. Put Your Vision in Writing

Sit down in that special place where you feel like you can think clearly, which could be anywhere from your home office to the mountains, the beach, the park, or the local library, and create your "ideal scene." What does your life look like now and what do you want it to look like (at least within your business) one year, three years, five years, and even ten years from now? You and your management team need to know what you're planning for. A plan without specific goals is like taking a trip without a destination.

A strategic plan actually works in reverse. For example, let's determine what that realistic picture for your business three years from now looks like. Now, where do you have to be at least 1.5 years from now, and even one year or six months from now? Your goals, objectives, and the steps you need to take will become much clearer. It's like taking a trip across the country. You can see your final destination and then look at milestones that you will reach along the way.

2. Create the Necessary Sections for Your Strategic Plan

The sections of your plan should correspond with the goals you've set for yourself to reach. The following sections, I feel, are the bare essentials of a good strategic plan and what you should consider each time you sit down to plan:

- $ Personal training and education
- $ Organizational or management issues
- $ Legal and tax planning

- $ Product or service development
- $ Systemization
- $ Employee and vendor relationships
- $ Marketing tasks (based on your marketing plan)

3. Create a Timeline for All of the Action Items to Occur

Don't stress about this step. All objectives and tasks to complete from the different sections above can be coordinated into an overall timeline. Don't set up a checklist for each category. Put them all in one master timeline that should be broken into 3-month, 6-month, and 12-month periods.

Sometimes, it is important to set up weekly or monthly tasks that need to be completed when you first get started.

4. Share It with Your Board

It becomes "alive" when you share it and someone is holding you accountable. I discuss the importance of your Board of Advisors or Board of Directors below.

5. Revisit Your Strategic Plan Regularly

As I stated above, I suggest you update your plan monthly and at the very least redraft it every three months. Also, you should be carrying it around with you everywhere you go. Review it constantly and stay disciplined. Make sure you are adding notes to your plan whenever you have a brilliant idea. Don't say to yourself, "I need to do that next quarter when I review my plan." Write it down now!

6. Manage by Statistics

Your numbers and reports, even if you are only keeping track and reporting to yourself, will consistently tell you if you are headed in the right direction. Don't get discouraged. Make changes as needed. **Being a business owner means constant change.** Don't be afraid of change; expect it, embrace it, and become accustomed to it.

Once you have this living, breathing document and you *own* it, you need help to implement it. You need support, outside voices, and someone to hold you accountable. This is where your Wealth Management Team comes into play, and it's more than just a board of directors.

Building a Wealth Management Team

It's sounds ostentatious or a little over the top, doesn't it? But it's actually very easy to do and will pay off enormously. In fact, you probably have most of the people in your contacts on your phone that will play a role on this team. You just may not have organized it properly yet *and* specifically requested and assigned the people on the team their duties and role they will be playing.

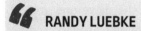 **RANDY LUEBKE**

When building your Wealth Management Team, keep in mind that your team can only perform to the level of its weakest player. As you evaluate your current team of advisors, always keep this in mind. While I would certainly never encourage you to drop and replace weaker team members with stronger ones over and over, you do need to make changes if a team member is holding you back. I grew up in the '60s, and one of my favorite bands of all time was and still is the Beatles. None of these guys were absolutely the greatest musicians individually. There were many, many better guitar players than George Harrison and John Lennon. Ringo was outplayed by scores of other more technically proficient drummers, and Paul and John may have been the number-one song-writing team of that era. Alone, none of them would have been all that great as they proved in the years after the band broke up. Yet, together, however, they were a phenomenon that we may never experience again. Build a team, develop your team, and make changes if absolutely needed. The bottom line is you won't do nearly as well on your own as you will with a great Wealth Management Team supporting your efforts.

Now, keep in mind that this team is far more than a board of directors or advisors. Your board is just *part* of the Wealth Management Team and will indeed play an important role, but I need you to think more broadly than that.

First, let me explain why I emphasize this step of having a Wealth Management Team, and frankly it comes down to what I said at the beginning of the chapter—Optimization. **THIS team will help you succeed and optimize and grow and build that financial freedom you are seeking.** Next, let me explain another reason why this team concept has proven itself as a critical piece of the equation.

In the world of the super-rich, or the "one percenters" as they are called, they utilize what is called a family office. It's actually pretty cool. The family office is where both the family business and wealth are monitored at a real office with managers that have one goal: to preserve and build the family wealth. They employ managers to make it happen, and what they pay them is far outweighed by the growth and protection to the family wealth. However, you don't have to open a family office or put some high-powered employees on the payroll to make this happen; simply design your team, give assignments, meet regularly, and hold *each other* accountable.

Because of the importance of this team and its members, I want to discuss the characteristics of your Wealth Management Team members before getting into their individual titles. Also, keep in mind this list of people will includes the professionals you hire, like a lawyer or accountant, as well as your board members or even your credit repair person. They all need to give you **honest, unbiased** advice that can help you make **proactive, decisive** decisions. Let's talk about those four words emphasized in the preceding sentence. These are the qualifications for ANY of your team members.

§ *Honest.* Have people on your team that will tell you the cold, hard truth. They are your cheerleaders, but they'll tell you what you *need* to hear in a kind way. Avoid "yes" men and women who will tell you only what they think you *want* to hear.

§ *Unbiased.* Remember the point I made earlier? Any advisor who works directly for a Wall Street brokerage or insurance company doesn't have a fiduciary duty to recommend or tell you what's best for your business or retirement. The point is that anyone on your team needs to be in a position to give unbiased advice that may not always be in the advisor's best interest but is in YOUR best interest.

$ *Proactive.* I use this word because when you have regular meetings with a team like this, your goal is to be more proactive in your business and financial life rather than reactionary. This means that you do not wait for something to happen and then hold a meeting; it means meeting before a crisis or major problem arises. We need to have a short, mid- and long-range vision and plan. By meeting with a hand-selected board, you will be forced to consider all your goals and objectives on a regular basis.

$ *Decisive.* When you put together a team to advise you, they will have a number of ideas, some of which may even conflict. Be very clear about which ideas are best to meet your needs. Being decisive, and sticking to your decisions, is a sign of strong leadership and puts the wheels of change in motion. There will then be pressure to follow through and perform. You will be accountable to a group of people invested in your situation and goals. They will want to help you take action and may even create action items for you to accomplish.

Wealth Management Team Circle

To best explain the key people that will play a role in your quest for success, I created the most comprehensive diagram I have ever seen on the topic. The reason why it needs to be this complex and dynamic is because there are people that you will meet more regularly than others, and they will also have different duties within different teams. Figure 6.1 on page 50 is a visual representation, and following are descriptions of the circles.

$ *Inner Circle.* This is just that. These are the advisors on the "inside" that you will generally pay for technical advice and direction on major decisions that truly require skilled expertise.

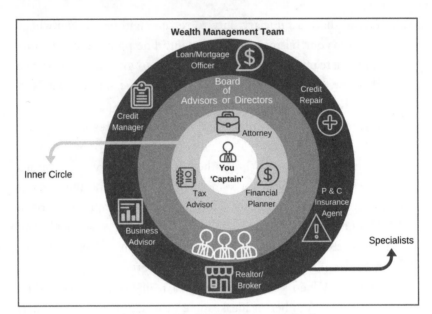

*Figure 6.1–*Wealth Management Circle

You will also meet with them more regularly. Sometimes, you'll meet with them as a group, while other times you'll meet them individually. They will certainly know each other and the role they play on the team serving your needs first and foremost. Yes, they will cost you per hour, but they will also have a fiduciary duty to look out for your best interest.

§ *The Board of Directors/Advisors.* This is your team that you will meet with at least annually and hopefully twice a year to report on your progress and get big-picture advice and direction. (Also, take a tax write-off for the meeting.)

§ *The Specialists.* These are just what they sound like: specialists you call in and meet with as necessary to accomplish special tasks.

Team Captain

Before I discuss the titles of roles of any specific members of the team, I need to talk about the "Captain." Every team needs, and I mean NEEDS, a captain. This person can and should be you. It is your business and your vision. Although you can, and will, rely (heavily at times) on specific advisors, friends, or family members, the buck stops with you. **You need to serve as the leader of the team**—a coordinator, a facilitator, someone who sees and understands the big picture and someone who has the knowledge and understanding of how the various pieces of the plan fit together. No one else can do it but you, and frankly, it's too expensive to pay someone to play this role and it's too risky since they may not see your vision clearly.

I have worked with too many clients that feel they can delegate the vision of their business to someone else and that this other person will do the same job as they would and care just as much about the details. They won't. You're the captain of your ship. Own it!!

Board of Directors or Advisors

In many ways, this is the most critical portion of your team. I love to discuss the board and the importance it plays in the life and success of an entrepreneur. This board concept is an important tax strategy, legal strategy, and business strategy.

First, from the point of view of a tax strategy, the existence of a board creates the opportunity for an excellent tax write-off. **We all should be holding regular board meetings, if not quarterly, at least annually.** This is an opportunity to deduct some travel, dining, and entertainment with your board as you discuss the status and condition of your business and, of course, plans and goals for the New Year. Now, I'm not saying you can write off ten days in the Cayman Islands, but you can certainly write off a couple days of travel getting to and from your meeting.

Next, it's an excellent asset protection strategy because you should be having regular board meetings to substantiate your "corporate veil," and this goes for even LLCs. **Don't think because you have an LLC you can skip all these legal formalities.** You should have a corporate book where you keep your minutes from your regular meetings. If you are ever in a lawsuit, you want to be able to pull out your corporate or LLC records and show the court you have properly maintained your entity and had regular meetings and kept records.

Finally, probably the most important reason for a board of directors or advisors is the very purpose of this chapter, and that's the business purpose. **Having a board will help guide you, give you encouragement, and at the least follow up and hold you accountable for your goals.** The board should be people you trust for a straight answer but won't beat you up in the process. They could be family, friends, or even mentors you look up to in the business world. Bottom line, this is a critical piece of your Wealth Management Team.

Meet Your Team Members

Let's go through some examples of the team members in the inner circle and specialists in the outer circle. During this process, keep in mind this is my unique perspective on these team players. I am simply presenting a basic structure of what I use or have seen, over the years. Frankly, it's your team. **You own it and design it!** You may consider your accountant a specialist and not in the inner circle, while you may place your realtor, a specialist in my diagram, in the inner circle of your team. It's up to you. Place the value on the person or title as you see fit.

> § *Financial Planner* (Inner Circle). The primary role of this person is to create a coordinated and comprehensive financial plan. The essential elements of a financial plan work independently, yet they all affect each other. So the role of the financial plan and the financial planner is to provide the framework for the big picture with enough detail that the other team members will be able to play along. The other team members will bring their expertise and advice in to the plan. Keep in mind that this is NOT a financial planner or advisor working for a brokerage—it is someone truly independent and who has a fiduciary duty to

organize your finances and make sure they are running in accordance with your financial plan.

⑧ *Business Attorney* (Inner Circle). A person who's been formally trained in the law, especially one whose profession is advising others in matters of law. The will understand business entity structuring, asset protection, and how they are affected by taxes in general.

⑧ *Tax Advisor* (Inner Circle). A financial expert with advanced training and knowledge of tax law. The services of a tax advisor are usually retained in order to minimize taxation while remaining compliant with the law in complicated financial situations. Tax advisors can include enrolled agents, certified public accountants, and tax attorneys.

⑧ *Business Consultant* (Specialist). This person provides an analysis of the existing practices of a company and makes recommendations for improvements. These professionals frequently specialize in business management and strategic planning.

⑧ *Realtor/Broker* (Specialist). A person who works in the real estate business and is a member of the National Association of Real Estate Boards as a Realtor. They will help you with rental property acquisitions.

⑧ *Litigation Attorney* (Specialist). Litigation attorneys, also known as "litigators" or "trial lawyers," represent plaintiffs and defendants in civil cases and manage all phases of the litigation process from investigations, pleadings, and discovery to pretrial, trial, settlement, and appeal.

⑧ *P&C Insurance Agent* (Specialist). A person or firm that sells property and casualty insurance offering suitable policies. They will help business owners with auto, business, home owners, and even health insurance.

⑧ *Credit Repair Advisor* (Specialist). Credit repair is the process of fixing a bad credit report, if for whatever reason, its deteriorated in the first place. It may be as simple as fixing mistakes with the credit agencies. A credit advisor can help accelerate your credit report or even obtain business lines of credit..

§ *Loan/Mortgage Officer* (Specialist). Loan officer representatives of banks, credit unions, and other financial institutions that find and assist borrowers in acquiring loans. Business owners will need sophisticated loan officers to help get competitive loans.

§ *Property Manager* (Specialist). An individual or company responsible for the day-to-day functioning of a piece of real estate. Property owners typically hire property managers when they are unwilling or unable to manage their rental properties themselves.

The property manager's responsibilities might include supervising and coordinating building maintenance and work orders, doing light handyman and cleaning work, resolving tenant concerns and complaints, advertising, showing and leasing vacant units, collecting and depositing rent.

§ *Bookkeeper/Accountant* (Specialist). A bookkeeper is usually employed by a small- to midsize company to record its transactions, such as sales, purchases, payroll, collection of accounts receivable, payment of bills, etc. A very small company might use the services of a bookkeeping firm that employs bookkeepers. Typically, this will be a person or company proficient in accounting software.

TIP FOR FINANCIAL FREEDOM

It is absolutely critical to have a team of specialists to help you succeed.

Meeting with Your Management Team Regularly

You should be holding a meeting at least twice a year. I know it will take time and some costs to put together, but it will be far more worthwhile than you can imagine. The meeting can take place via conference call, videoconference, or in person. Have an agenda prepared and disseminated in advance, and remember that you, as Team Captain, run the show.

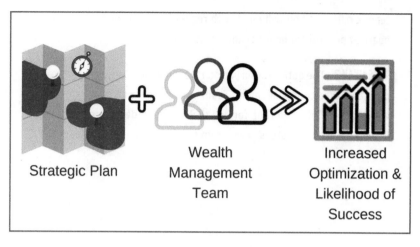

Figure 6.2—The Optimal Combination

Remember, it's the *combination* of BOTH the strategic plan and the Wealth Management Team that will truly increase your optimization at every point of implementation in your financial plan AND increase your likelihood of ultimate success. See Figure 6.2.

The goal of the meeting is to update your strategic plan and make sure you are executing it and progressing towards your ten-year goal. You need advice as much as you need encouragement and someone to hold you accountable to the plan. As Nike says, Just do it!

$ $ $

TAKEAWAY 1—Having a strategic plan is essential to optimizing what you already have and the success of your business. It can take you from where you are to where you want to be by laying out actions necessary to meet your goal(s).

TAKEAWAY 2—You need to put together a Wealth Management Team that consists of a "circle" of people. You need honest people, well-versed in their areas of expertise, who can give you unbiased opinions and answers whether they think you want to hear them or not. The core group in this team circle, that you will meet with regularly and depend upon, is your board of directors or board of advisors.

TAKEAWAY 3—The optimization you start to implement through a strategic plan and Wealth Management Team will immediately start to create wealth, cash flow, and time for you that you're in desperate need of to implement the other steps in your comprehensive financial freedom plan.

STEP 2: DEALING WITH DEBT AS AN ENTREPRENEUR

The plague of debt to the entrepreneur is all too common. As an entrepreneur, I have certainly had my battles with debt over the years. Frankly, I know the cycle all too well. We try to maintain a certain lifestyle, and not even extravagant at that, but with the ups and downs of cash flow in our business, credit ends up being the buffer. Debt can grow quietly and quickly right under our noses. It truly can be like a thief in the night and steal our business from us when we least expect it.

Throughout this chapter, I want to discuss the concepts of good debt versus bad debt, or reductive debt versus productive debt. Frankly, debt can be used for good to build our business and wealth. **Debt can be an amazingly useful tool when we grasp** the concept of proper leverage. *Conversely, we can get sucked into bad debt that doesn't do us any good at all.* We can get into a personal debt crisis that is suffocating, stifling, and truly sucking the life out of our businesses and ourselves personally.

Thus, the purpose of this chapter is simple, short, and to the point: get out of bad debt ASAP, stay out of debt, and understand how you may have got here in the first place so it doesn't happen again!

Good Debt Versus Bad Debt

As entrepreneurs, it's important we know the difference between good debt and bad debt. It's generally OK to get into good debt as long as we know the difference. **We can accomplish amazing things with the bank's money and leverage.** But it's important we are clear about the different types of debt.

Good debt comes in the form of loans, a mortgage, or lines of credit that can be used to the benefit of the company. I call this productive debt. When a business can calculate returns that will surpass the debt and the cost of interest, that business can then use debt to their advantage. **Good debt is, therefore, working for you!** Productive debt also includes getting a mortgage to buy your personal residence and certainly a rental property that creates cash flow. Leverage is *not* a bad thing if it can create wealth without too much risk.

Conversely, bad debt, for our purposes, is debt that you cannot leverage when growing your business. I refer to this as reductive

 RANDY LUEBKE

Debt is like a power tool. It can help you to quickly and easily rip through a 2 x 4, or it can take off your fingers. It certainly makes more sense to use a power tool to saw through a board instead of, say, trying to chew your way through it like a beaver. That said, learn how to use this tool safely, and treat it with respect.

debt, and it is simply used to buy stuff. **Consider it the same thing as personal consumer debt or the plague of credit card debt.** Otherwise stated, it's money that isn't working for you in any productive way. Typically it's used to buy things you cannot really afford, and when that happens, it will never produce a good outcome.

With that said, I certainly recognize that a line of credit is common in a successful business to smooth out the ups and downs of cash flow. However, in the months when times are good, the novice entrepreneur oftentimes doesn't take the extra cash to pay off debt and/or the credit line. Growing the business or enjoying the fruits of our labors can be a strong temptation.

Why Entrepreneurs Get into Debt

I believe there are three primary reasons why entrepreneurs get into debt. I know this because I have experienced all these instances myself, or it's from the experience of meeting with thousands of business owners during my career and identifying the plague of debt over and over again. **Yes, I understand there can be a myriad of circumstances that could cause you to get into debt—life happens!** However, if you and I can at least identity the main reasons or causes, we can do a better job recognizing the tell-tale signs of debt creeping into our lives. Let's explore those signs:

1. *The ups and downs of cash flow.* Do I really need to say it? Small business can be a roller coaster of ups and downs in income. When the cash is rolling in, there isn't anything more exciting and exhilarating. However, business owners oftentimes under-estimate the dramatic ups and downs and don't foresee the months of terrible cash flow. For W-2 employees considering entrepreneurship, this is the very fact that scares them to death. But for some reason, we as entrepreneurs are undaunted, and what do we do? **We turn to credit cards to smooth out the ups and downs of cash flows so we can provide some type of economic balance for our family or personal life.**

Of course, we are also risk takers as entrepreneurs and presume we can easily pay off the credit card next month, but we don't. Thus, the crisis begins.

2. *Putting too much pressure on our business.* This took me years of being in business *and* working with thousands of business owners to actually recognize and *then* to be able to put in words. **Many times, an entrepreneur will start trying to live on the income from their business *before* their business is able to sustain them.** Entrepreneurs quit their day jobs and work hard to build the businesses, but they don't realize they're just not ready to pay the monthly salary that the entrepreneur needs to live on. **The business needs reinvestment and time to mature. It needs reserves and time to create consistent cash flow.** Don't do this to your business. Maintain a second job or another income in your family relationships to give the business some breathing room. Before you know it, the business will be able to cut you the monthly check you need to live on.

3. *Being overconfident.* Yes, this can be a weakness. Sometimes entrepreneurs can be using productive debt and believe they are being wise and cautious. However, in reality, they are over-extended a little too much. Productive debt is good debt as I described above, but too much productive debt can be as problematic as reductive debt. Typically, it goes like this: the entrepreneur has a couple of great years of earnings and decides to expand and increase debt to grow as quickly as possible, but they also change their lifestyle to their new income level. Now comes the downturn in the economy, a change in their industry, or the loss of a couple large customers. With the resulting major drop in profit, things get pretty rough financially. Pretty quickly, the situation can snowball out of control, and the entrepreneur could be at risk of losing the best. **Sometimes, a slower, more pragmatic approach to growth and a conservative level of productive debt could have kept them out of harm's way.** Yes, even good debt can be bad when things go wrong.

If you are experiencing any of these tendencies or situations and things appear to be headed in the wrong direction with your debt, it's important to get help immediately. Don't be embarrassed. Ask for help from your Wealth Management Team. **Your key inner circle advisors should be informed immediately, and they will most certainly help get you on a path of debt redemption (as I like to call it).** In fact, start with an intervention. If you don't get help and the cycle of consumer debt continues for a considerable time, it can deteriorate one's health and even relationships with family and friends.

Getting Out of Bad or Reductive Debt

The best of us have been in debt before and know how debilitating it can be. The purpose of this book and these four sequential steps is to make a financial plan that *includes* getting out of debt. Getting out of debt and learning how to stay out of debt is Step 2 for a reason! **It is absolutely critical to your long-term success and plan for financial freedom to expunge all reductive or bad debt out of your life as quickly as possible.** Your Wealth Management Team is a key part of this process and will and should be a huge support to you.

Implementing a debt snowball is critical. You have probably heard about this type of strategy of spreadsheet or analysis that can fast-track you to getting out of debt quicker than you ever imagined. **You will be shocked at the self-confidence and sense of relief that comes**

> ❝ **RANDY LUEBKE**
>
> Bad debt or reductive debt is sexy. It's seductive. It makes you feel good for a while because of the things it buys you. It's an illusion! Car loans, student loans, credit cards, whatever. Good debt will improve your life and leverage your returns. Bad debt will take you down. If that debt did not purchase something that is making your money, get rid of it now, before you move on to saving and investing. ❞

over you when the debt snowball starts to kick in. You'll start to see credit card bills disappear from your mailbox, and the air will seem crisper, water will appear clearer, and food will taste better—yes, life will be enjoyable again!

Now, the concept and procedure behind the debt snowball is simple.

1. Create a simple plan.
2. Stick with it.
3. Celebrate your success.

First determine how much of one's monthly income can be consistently committed to eliminating reductive debt. Then we focus that excess money on the smallest debt first, eliminating that debt as quickly as possible. This focus on paying off that one small debt provides us with even more money to pay off the next debt, snowballing the payments on the next larger debt, until it is paid off as well.

To create your debt plan, start with making a list of ALL your reductive debts. Be sure to include all of them and list them in order, beginning with the largest debt at the top of the list and ending with the smallest debt at the bottom. It does not matter whatsoever what the interest rates are on these debts are because we are going to eliminate them so quickly that, unless you borrowed this money from "Uncle Louie the Leg-Breaker" and you are paying some outrageously crazy interest rate, we don't care. The fact of the matter is that with this plan in place, you are going to pound away your debt so aggressively that the cost of borrowing will seem relatively insignificant.

Then, list the minimum payment next to each debt on your list. Again, I do not care which payment is the largest or has the highest interest rate. It does not matter. **The goal of the debt snowball is to increase the size of the snowball as quickly as possible.** Therefore, paying off the smallest debt first will allow that payment to roll up into the next payment and so on.

Now, the tough part. You need to commit as much as you possibly can to apply to these debts. This needs to be painful. Seriously, the amount of money you are going to commit to eliminating this debt has to stretch you. Save money anywhere else you can, then, as you start to eliminate your debt, you will truly feel the reward, and the lifting of that psychological weight off of your shoulders will feel amazing!

Often, I advise my clients to reduce or even stop making contributions to their retirement savings until their debt is gone. This is a bit counterintuitive and can increase your level of pain and discomfort. Good! More pain, right? In all seriousness, it is far more important to eliminate these debts and earn a guaranteed return on your interest savings than it is to put more money into your 401(k). (However, you may want to evaluate this strategy in the context of employer matches, etc.)

Now, you are ready to implement your plan! You simply take the amount of money you committed to your debt plan each month and add that extra cash to the payment of the smallest debt. You continue to make the minimum required payments to all your remaining payments. Soon, your smallest debt will be fully repaid. **Now, the snowball increases in size as all the money you were sending to that small debt is now applied to the next larger debt along with its normal regularly required payment.** You continue making these increased payments to that debt until it is eliminated as well. Then, you repeat this process over and over until all your debts are gone.

With your debts gone and the habit you developed of making these payments, you may find that the once very painful payment from your cash flow to eliminate these debts is not all that painful. With that in mind, now you can continue to pay that now giant snowball amount into your retirement savings, and in a very short while, you will be not

---

TIP FOR FINANCIAL FREEDOM

Business owners have to master the proper use of debt.

---

only making up for lost time but also you will be free, once and for all, of the burden of having bad debt. In all likelihood, you will never see yourself in that situation ever again. Congratulations!

Staying Out of Debt

Obviously, the best way to get out of bad debt is to avoid getting into such debt in the first place. I know this is a terrible thing to say, but it's actually a very important point. If you are reading this chapter, you are either in debt now or know the dangers of debt and want to be vigilant to never fall prey.

Thus, if you want to get out of debt and *stay* out of debt, it necessitates planning in advance. Let's talk about some of these habits and good practices now so you come out of this step a new business owner. Here are some core business practices that will help you stay out of debt in your business as you grow and expand:

- § **Constantly minimizing expenses. It's OK to be frugal. Make sure to read** *The Millionaire Next Door: The Surprising Secrets of America's Wealthy* by Thomas J. Stanley Ph.D. and William D. Danko Ph.D. (Taylor Trade Publishing, 2010). Put it on your reading list!

- § Hiring employees only when you can afford to do so and expanding your business when the sales come in the door—not in advance, hoping for the growth.

- § Avoiding wasteful spending, and always consider the opportunity costs when making financial decisions. This means learning how to weigh your business choices since opportunity costs exist with every financial choice you make.

- § Don't overextend yourself even with productive debt. Be cautious and try to grow on the profits of the business as much as possible.

- § Have ample cash reserves to deal with emergencies and potential downturns in your business. I discuss this in detail in the next chapter—Maintaining Proper Cash Reserves.

As an entrepreneur, when you find yourself in a situation where your debt is working against you and no longer working for you, then you need to make that debt disappear . . . quickly, which means cutting expenses—sadly, even personal living expenses if necessary. **Notoriously optimistic entrepreneurs will almost always believe that things will pick up and that, at that point, they'll be able to pay off debt. Don't succumb to this mentality.** It is flawed and ultimately ends in disaster.

In my experience, it's a rare circumstance that sales explode and magically resolve the debt problem. The entrepreneurs that make it out of these situations will take quick action to cut their expenses and focus all resources on paying down the debt. In sum, staying out of bad debt should not have to be reactionary; it should be part of your operating plan.

§ § §

TAKEAWAY 1—There are two types of debt: good debt, which you can use to the advantage of your business, and bad debt, which is a burden and can destroy your business.

TAKEAWAY 2—Entrepreneurs can get into debt for a variety of reasons. It's important we understand how it can happen and be vigilant to keep bad debt out of our personal and business lives.

TAKEAWAY 3—The best way to get out of bad debt is to cut costs in our business, without damaging it, and start a debt snowball to tackle our various creditors.

STEP 3: MAINTAINING PROPER CASH RESERVES

Cash is king, and the benefits of significant *and* liquid cash reserves will change your economic future more than you can imagine.

The expression "cash is king" has been around a very long time. It appeared in news and publications prominently in the '80s and has come to be a favorite phrase used by thousands of financial gurus, advisors, lawyers, and accountants over the years.

I think my dad may have even taught me the concept (he was a successful entrepreneur in the medical industry for years). But it truly didn't take hold in my personal investment life and have deep meaning until I had already been a lawyer, an accountant and a business owner for years. Sometimes, we don't really understand the importance of cash and expenses until we own our own business.

As I mentioned in Chapter 5 regarding the 4 x 4 Independence Plan, I was reminded of the practical importance of this by Dave Ramsey. I love the revolutionary steps and concepts that he teaches in his Financial Peace University. I was blown away with the simplicity and genius of his first step: that of saving $1,000 in a separate bank account for emergencies.

Of course, there are many reasons for this strategy and why it's the first step in his program, but most importantly, it sets the foundation for having a financial cushion in your life. Dave Ramsey has explained it so many times in his teachings as a buffer between you and life's happenings. **But frankly, it's just the beginning for an entrepreneur.**

This is where Dave Ramsey helps millions of people around the country, but again he stops short when it comes to expanding this strategy for the entrepreneur. This is where Randy Luebke made a huge impact in my life and took the concept of reserves to the next level. During his many years in the financial industry, Randy learned two very important lessons about cash and passed them along to me:

§ Having *enough* cash to help you weather the storm during the bad times, when things go wrong.

§ When opportunities present themselves (and they will), if we don't have sufficient cash reserves to exploit these situations, huge returns can pass us by. In other words, when things go right or when things go wrong, having available cash will allow you the best opportunity for a successful outcome.

Cash Reserves Means CASH Reserves

It's important to mention right from the outset that both Randy and I strongly believe that credit cards and Home Equity Lines of Credit (HELOC's) are **NOT** cash reserves!

Yes, I know the counterarguments all too well. We have very dramatic conversations with clients that fight back on the idea of setting up a cash reserve fund. They say that they don't want it or need it. They do not want cash in their checking or savings account earning no interest. Instead, they always want it invested. Their comeback is most often, "If I really have a need for cash, I have $50,000 of unused credit cards or $100,000 of an untapped Home Equity Line of Credit (HELOC) to get me by." We agree that using debt may work in some business situations, but once you bring your personal assets into play, you run much higher risks. Remember that with debt comes the obligation to repay, and that's what can make things go from very bad to really ugly over a short period of time. **The idea of cash reserves is to have actual, available cash!**

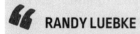

RANDY LUEBKE

They say that "money can't buy you happiness," and I agree. However, having money/cash in a very safe place that you can go to when needed can buy you a lot of peace of mind.

Additionally, many people rely on their credit when times are good, only to find it unavailable when things turn bad. Credit cards as well as HELOC's can be frozen or the amount of credit available can be reduced by the lender at their discretion and often at the worst possible time. Moreover, one of our primary strategies is to stay out of consumer debt. That is why we stress having actual cash reserves.

Significant Versus Liquid

I often see people with far too little, and limited, cash reserves. They may have enough money set aside to get them through a month—possibly two or three. But that's not really enough, and as an entrepreneur you definitely need more.

Randy's personal advice to me was astonishing when I thought I already owned this concept and was fine. Furthermore, I was a follower of Dave Ramsey's teachings, so what more could Randy teach me about reserves that I didn't already know? Randy's direction to me, and to *all* of his clients is that we need to have *significant* liquid cash reserves on hand. *Significant* **reserves mean that you have a substantial**

amount of money in reserve, not just a few bucks to get you by. Of course, this is a subjective amount because everyone's lifestyle and needs are different.

How much you need in your personal situation will depend on a number of factors, for example, the reliability of your income, the amount of risk you maintain, your monthly business overhead, your personal living expenses, the needs of your family, your tangible assets, and even your age, just to name a few. You want to be able to stay afloat and have cash flow when times are tough due to loss of a job, an economic downturn, etc. You also want to be able to utilize the cash when you want to put a down payment on a house that you want to buy before someone else beats you to it. **Remember, cash reserves are not only for emergencies; they are equally important for potential opportunities.**

Liquidity is the engine behind the reserve, and if you have significant reserves, but they aren't quickly accessible, what's the point? In fact, you have missed the point altogether, and you'll be back in the debt cycle relying on lenders to help you get out. Liquidity means being able to get to your money when you need it. *That's why some people call their cash reserve an emergency fund, while others call it an opportunity fund.* It is readily available if there is an emergency or an opportunity.

The Three-Bucket Cash-Reserve System

In order to have both liquidity and significant cash reserves, it takes more than just plowing cash into a bank account. It's a unique structure called the "Three-Bucket Cash Reserve System." This system not only ensures that you will have enough readily available cash that is safe and secure, but it will also allow you to earn a fairly decent overall rate of return on your money as well.

What I also like about the Three-Bucket System is that I could do it in stages. Once I got started, the reserves became such a comfort and strength that I truly wanted more. If I dipped into my reserves at all, for anything, good or bad, I was extremely anxious to get the money back into the system. I was addicted to the security and flexibility it offered me. We start with the first bucket to build some confidence, momentum, and yes, better habits, and then we can graduate to the other buckets. It's easier than you can imagine once you get started.

Bucket One: One Month's Personal Living Expenses

Of course, this one month's amount is going to vary dramatically from one person to another. Moreover, monthly living expenses can also fluctuate dramatically from one month to the next depending on what's going on in our lives. This unpredictability is what causes some people to stop right here and give up dead in their tracks. Don't do it. To help calculate this amount and create a new mentality to saving and spending, I'll define essential living expenses below. Also, the simplest approach is to take your total expenses for the year (as best as you can estimate them) and divide it by 12. This monthly average accounts for the ups and downs in monthly expenses. Save that average amount each month and get the bucket going. This money should be in a separate bank account, or even a separate bank from your other accounts (if your self-discipline is lacking a little). Here's the statement you may have trouble with: *don't worry about interest rates or investment factors.* People are so trained to chase interest rates that they hesitate to simply have money available. Interest rates on liquid accounts are very low these days. Sure, 2 percent beats 1 percent, BUT just having available cash is more important. Just make sure it is accessible and liquid in the event of an emergency.

Bucket Two: Two Month's Living Expenses

This is an additional two month's of take-home pay in your savings and is on top of your first bucket. **Thus, you will now have a total of three months of living expenses in reserve**. Again, you can use an average of what this expense may be, and I encourage you to be generous. Fault on a little extra, rather than less. You won't regret it. There is an ingenious way to slowly build these accounts by depositing the distributions from your business into savings *first* before paying your living expenses (note the section on false security below). This bucket will be in a savings account similar to bucket one. Again, don't worry about interest or rates of return. This bucket has a far bigger purpose and benefit.

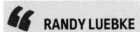

RANDY LUEBKE

It would be great, wonderful, and awesome if you could create the perfect budget, stick to it, and set up the exact, correct, ideal amount of money in reserve. However, having something is better than nothing—way better. So if you don't have any savings today, get started saving something, anything. Conversely, do not overfund your cash reserves. Your money needs to make money to help you to achieve financial freedom. My point is that doing nothing is unacceptable. Regardless of the details of your situation, do not overlook or underestimate the power of doing this step correctly.

Bucket Three: The "It Depends" Reserve

At this juncture, with one month's essential expenses pouring into the checking account monthly and two months net take-home pay in your savings, now we need to think about how much more money is enough to keep in your third cash reserve bucket. The amount of money you keep in this bucket will vary widely from person to person or family to family. That being said, it needs to be a significant amount. In fact, as an entrepreneur, this bucket will need to be much bigger, like six to nine months. This bucket may be funded with cash value life insurance. Yes, believe it or not, insurance can provide two or three ancillary benefits. There will be a death benefit, and the cash asset will be protected and guaranteed no matter what happens to your health.

Whatever your dollar amount needed to be to fill all three buckets, they need to be completely full BEFORE you save and invest for your retirement. In order to succeed in this process of the 4 x 4 Financial Independence Plan, and specifically the *four sequential* steps, these buckets need to be taken seriously.

What Randy and I have found is that our clients will fall into one of two categories at this juncture. There are those who have woefully underfunded their cash reserve accounts and those who have way too much money in their cash reserves. Obviously, both categories have their issues, and either way, you will have to make whatever adjustments are necessary. It's important to step back and look at how you define the amounts of money in your buckets. You need to know what your living expenses truly are, how much you are actually saving and how much is necessary to cover your living expenses.

Personal Living Expenses and Lifestyle Expenses

Again, the key figure that drives the amount in your cash reserve buckets is your monthly living expense. It's critical this number is close to accurate or as realistic as possible. However, we can sometimes look through rose-colored glasses and choose a budgeted amount that is too low or too high depending on our personality or temperament.

For most people, budgeting is painful. It's like dieting or exercising but worse because if you are spending too much, you really don't want to know about it. You just want to move on with your life and hope that somehow things work out. On the opposite side of those ignoring their budgetary problems are those who simply want to spend it all. Who wants to stop too much of a good thing? Frankly, I'm guilty of being on both sides of the equation. **The solution to this quandary is implementing what is called "False Scarcity."** This approach breaks down all of our expenses into just two categories: essential expenses and lifestyle expenses. To do this, you need to recognize that not all the things you spend your money on are equally important.

Essential Expenses

These are for food, shelter, clothing, and health care. That's it. That's pretty simple, right? Food may be a little difficult to document 100 percent accurately, but you can keep receipts of all your food purchases, including dining out, for a few weeks to get a general idea of how much you spend in a given week on food. Next, you include how much you spend on rent, or if you own a home, how much your mortgage payment, property taxes, and insurance come to each month. Clothing is typically not something you buy regularly. Look through your closet and estimate how many items you have purchased in the past two or three months and roughly what the cost was for these items. This may help you guesstimate how much to put down. Health care, for most people, is fairly simple as the primary health-care expense is the cost of insurance, average monthly out-of-pocket expenses, and/or contributions to a HSA (Health Savings Account).

Lifestyle Expenses

These are expenses that need to be identified specifically and for which you need to save. We won't buy things on credit except for productive debt, and thus, expenses to increase our lifestyle will only be incurred once our Three-Bucket System is in place and we are well on our way to investing in the fourth sequential step. **Give yourself some silly money, or spending money, for small items in your essential expense line. If you don't, you'll go crazy and fail.** We need to embark on this savings system with moderation and realism. Some families that are more frugal will accomplish this feat more quickly. Those that tend to be big spenders will need a little more time. Bottom line—find your essential expense monthly dollar amount separate from lifestyle expenses. Get to work and remember that close IS good enough.

The Transfer System and Creating a "False Scarcity"

First, let's discuss the transfer process. As entrepreneurs, we are typically transferring the money we need to live on from our business account to our personal account. Sometimes, this is a constant and repeated transfer throughout the month as needed. Once you have your cash reserve buckets set up, you will transfer money from the first cash reserve bucket and then replenish it from your business as needed.

The beauty of the transfer system is to ONLY transfer from the cash reserve bucket to your personal account the amount that you think you need for living expenses, and maybe just a little for lifestyle expenses. Moreover, I want you to make just a couple transfers during the month. The goal is to create this feeling that money is scarce. This will prevent, or at least help you cut down on, spending too much on lifestyle expenses. **With this method, you only see a limited amount of money in your personal account and thereby train your mind to believe that is truly ALL you have for the month.** Even though it's not true and there is more money in the business, you aren't going to go and transfer it. By being self-disciplined, you will create a false sense of scarcity that the business doesn't actually have more money to transfer (even though it does).

False Scarcity will evolve as you can only spend what you have transferred to your personal checking account from your cash reserve buckets. If you spend all the money you have allocated for your essential expenses, then you have spent too much. In sum, your business profits and any wages from a spouse or a side job will go into your bucket system of savings *first*. Then, your monthly essential expenses amount is transferred from your savings into your checking account. DO NOT deposit your business revenue, any earned revenue, into your personal checking account directly. This process repeated over time is what creates false scarcity.

Adjusting Your Monthly Transfer

After two or three months, it will become clear how much you need to maintain in your checking account to ensure that you can cover your essential monthly expenses. Think of it like the gas guage in your car and the goal is to pull into the gas station on the last day of the month on empty. Fill up your tank once a month. Drive around and try to refill your car on the last day of each month. Now, you can see why you don't have to necessarily be 100 percent accurate with how much you are spending on any one of these essential items, although, you will develop an awareness of how much you are spending over time. Regardless of what has to happen each and every month, you will either have gas left in your tank (not the best outcome) it will be empty (the best outcome), or you are going to need to add more gas to your tank during the month (the worst outcome).

To summarize, as you start to recognize your needs from your wants and build these reserves, you quickly become addicted to the feeling of security rather than the feeling of consumption. **The media, advertisers, and corporate America want you to be a consumer; in our plan, to find your freedom, you will become a saver.**

Ironically, by becoming a saver, you will experience more wealth, more freedom, and more security. It's a more natural and desirable feeling to be secure. Deep down, being a spender, without checks and balances, creates a feeling of insecurity and is irresponsible.

Freedom and wealth will start to permeate your life as you start to build cash reserves.

$ $ $

TAKEAWAY 1—Understanding the need for cash and having cash reserves with liquidity are cornerstones of your financial future.

TAKEAWAY 2—The Three-Bucket Cash Reserve system is a means of ensuring that you will have readily available cash that is safe and secure.

TAKEAWAY 3—The most important takeaway from this chapter is that you want to become a saver rather than a spender. Saving money in cash reserves will allow you to sleep at nights knowing you have cash available. It will also allow you to seize investing opportunities when they are right for you.

STEP 4: INVESTING YOUR PROFITS AND BUILDING BUCKETS

At this point, you are ready to start working through various phases of investment options. You are out of bad or reductive debt, and you have your six-to-nine month emergency fund with plenty of liquid cash available for problems or opportunities. Most importantly, you have started to better optimize your business for success by implementing a more comprehensive strategic plan and organizing a Wealth Management Team including a board of directors or advisors to assist you on your path. Because of these steps you have taken, if you haven't already started to see growth in the profits in your business, I'm confident you will—and soon. So now, it's time to plan for the next phase of investing.

I really feel that one of the most important takeaways of this entire book, and the foundation of Step 4, is that we as entrepreneurs need to harvest profit from our business and redeploy it more strategically. For some reason, we get deceived into thinking our business is our greatest and *only* asset supporting our retirement, and thus, we drive all of our profits back into our business month after month, year after year. This is NOT a wise strategy and certainly won't help you on your path to financial freedom.

A key step in this process is changing our perspective as I stated earlier and to quit having tunnel vision in regards to our wealth building, relying wholly on our business. We need to start creating other buckets of assets, investments, and streams of income. **Stated otherwise, let your business fund your financial freedom plan—don't make the business itself the plan.** This is a major change in the mindset of an entrepreneur (hence Chapter 1 of this book), and now this is the point in the book where we start to talk about these other investments that will be funded and supported by your business.

We as entrepreneurs need to *diversify our assets,* and frankly I hate to even use the word diversify. This is because of the Wall Street connotation, and I need to be clear that I'm not talking about your stock portfolio. I'm talking about diversifying ALL of your assets and possible streams of income.

Phases of Investing

The first point I want to make in this process of investing is that we are all at different phases in our lives. Regrettably, I wish I could just lay out the 5, 10, or 15 steps you need to take and the order in which to do it. For example, start a Roth IRA, buy a home, fund your Health Savings Account, start a 401(k), buy insurance . . . the list could go on and on. **But the truth is everyone is different, and the phase OR the strategy you implement is going to depend on a lot of variables.** How old are you? Single or married? Your income? Do you have children? What part of the country do you live in? What have you already started to fund? What are your goals? What type of risk taker are you? The answers to all these questions will place you in a different phase of investing than someone else.

To try to help those who read this book or to introduce this book to others around the country, we have developed the Business Owner's Financial Readiness Challenge™ (take it at www. eguidetofinancialfreedom.com). This is a questionnaire in which the answers will help indicate where you are on a spectrum of investment options and in the Business Owner's Financial Landscape™ (more on this below). **It will help guide you generally as to what investment strategy you might want to consider next.** Of course, no written quiz will be exact or completely able to design a comprehensive financial plan for someone, but it certainly doesn't hurt to get a rough idea of where to start.

As Randy and I considered the best way to teach this concept and present the chapter, we literally turned to the actual conversations we have had with entrepreneurs every day in our practice, and we both realized that we use the word buckets quite a bit. You may or may not like the analogy, but we feel it is at least clear. All of us should be able to understand the concept of phases, and we added the words buckets into the dialogue to further build a visual as to what your investment path may look like.

But we needed a "landscape" to discuss the unique path each person may take on their way to financial freedom. Thus, we created the Business Owner's Financial Landscape™. Figure 9.1 on page 80 is a diagram that serves as a discussion point to start building a frame of reference for these *phases* and *buckets* an entrepreneur can pass through.

This landscape also creates an outline for the rest of the book, or at least the next eight chapters. A lot of these buckets need some explaining, and, as I discussed earlier, a new perspective by entrepreneurs. **The new perspectives on these topics will accelerate your progress to financial freedom!** Now, I KNOW this all sounds very cliché! In fact, as I was writing this section of the book, I almost started to roll my eyes.

But then, I literally thought back to three conversations I had with clients this past week. Each one centered on these VERY issues

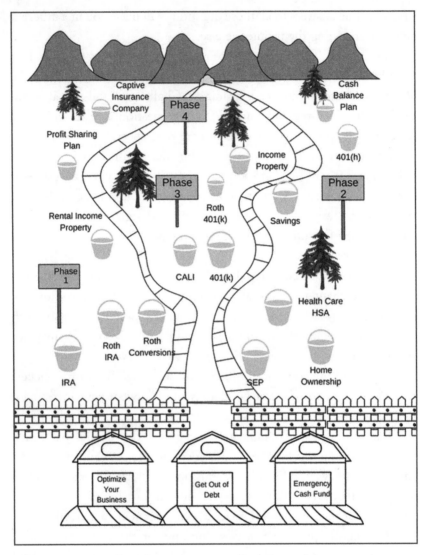

Figure 9.1—Business Owner's Financial Landscape

of creating income and reducing stress in their business. In fact, one client asked me point blank, and I share this word for word: *"Mark, I'm out of debt and have a little money set aside for emergencies.* ***What should I invest in next?*** *I just don't know where to turn."* This client felt lost because they didn't trust a banker or Wall Street advisor, let alone a wild search on the web.

That question is WHY I wrote this book and partnered with an independent financial advisor to do it! Entrepreneurs are desperate for sound financial advice that makes sense with them as a business owner and not as a W-2 employee.

So in the chapters to follow, I am going to discuss the serious topics of:

§ Selecting health care options
§ Buying a home
§ Creating IRAs and 401(k)s
§ Self-directing your retirement accounts
§ Reviewing insurance options/strategies
§ Investing in Wall Street
§ Purchasing rental property
§ Implementing Social Security strategies
§ Investing in vacation homes and timeshares

Some of you may think that a few of these strategies or investments are no-brainers, for lack of a better word. However, I caution you to not jump so quickly to that conclusion. **Based on your situation, you could be in a phase of life or part of the country that lends itself to a different approach or strategy from the next business owner.** Otherwise stated, don't think they are a perfect investment for you or anyone.

The Perfect Investment

I realize many of you may be asking what the "perfect" investment is for you. I know because I asked the same question of my financial advisors time and time again. However, does it really exist? In a nutshell, the PERFECT investment would have the following characteristics:

§ 100 percent safe
§ 100 percent liquid
§ 100 percent return on investment (ROI)
§ 100 percent tax-free
§ 100 percent passive

Doesn't that sound great? An investment that has no risk. One that is liquid so you can turn it into cash at any time without any fees or penalties. An investment that provides awesome earnings that are all income tax-free. In fact, while we are at it, you should even get a tax deduction just for investing in such a wonderful vehicle. Why not, right? Then, you don't have to do anything. You can just invest your money and passively watch it grow!

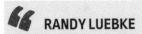

RANDY LUEBKE

Unfortunately, no investment is perfect. In fact, every investment is a compromise. You must be willing to give up something to get something else. If you want safety and liquidity and are unwilling to take any risks, then you may be best putting your money in a checking or savings account. You can run any investment you are considering through all the characteristics and find that you are always giving up one thing to get something else. A safe investment usually means you are sacrificing your ROI, a tax-free investment may mean that it is not liquid. A risky investment usually comes with a greater upside, but you may not sleep as well at night.

Regrettably, this perfect investment doesn't exist. This is important to keep in mind as you read the rest of this book and consider your other investments, assets, and streams of income to choose from. **Thus, what better reason to have a bunch of assets and different types of investments, each with their own purpose,** *including* **your business?** When we can bring them all into concert and coordinate

---

TIP FOR FINANCIAL FREEDOM

Search for the proper mix of investments, not the
"perfect" investment.

---

them together, that is when we start to experience more and more financial freedom!

$ $ $

TAKEAWAY 1—Entering the Financial Landscape and investing does not take place until after you are fully optimizing your business with a new strategic plan, all reductive debt is paid off, and your emergency funds are in place.

TAKEAWAY 2—As an entrepreneur, you don't want to reinvest all your profits back into your business; instead, you need to redeploy profits when possible into other assets and strategies for streams of income. Once you are making more money, you can then expand upon your buckets and strategies into additional phases that involve investing for your additional needs.

TAKEAWAY 3—Unfortunately, you will never find the perfect investment, and even your business isn't a perfect solution for your financial success and freedom. Hence, it's important to stay diversified with multiple assets and strategies in place to supplement your income and build wealth.

PART

III

DEPLOYING YOUR ASSETS STRATEGICALLY

I t is now time to start on the process of deploying the profits from your business into various other buckets and resources that will start to create other sources of revenue now or sometime in the future.

As I have stated repeatedly already, one of an entrepreneur's greatest downfalls is relying too heavily, or even solely, on their business for their retirement and financial freedom. This is extremely dangerous, and it's critical for a business owner to redistribute their wealth little by little into other various buckets of assets and streams of income.

Please take the time to read all the following chapters, *even if you don't* plan on implementing that particular strategy quite yet in your overall plan. It's important you have an understanding of where you've been and where you are going—not just where you are now. Be open to options that don't fall directly in line with your business. This is your opportunity to truly build your financial freedom!

UNDERSTANDING THE LIMITATIONS AND POTENTIAL POWER OF SOCIAL SECURITY

On August 14th, 1935, President Franklin D. Roosevelt signed the Social Security Act into law. With that signature, the United States started what would become one of the biggest and longest lasting experiments in social welfare known to mankind. Now, over eight decades later, Social Security has become deeply ingrained in our society and is providing benefits to more than 62 million people, and that number is going up every year.

As an employee or as an entrepreneur, Social Security benefits can play a significant role in funding your retirement. In both situations, the taxes collected today to fund tomorrow's Social Security benefits are significant. Thus, it is important to understand the role of Social Security and how it impacts you directly, as well as how it affects your business so you can make better choices and decisions when you address it.

Now, as I have said previously, many entrepreneurs see their business as their primary retirement tool. **Regrettably, they often view Social Security as their second source of retirement income.** This may be shocking (or not), but too many entrepreneurs don't fund retirement accounts (which we hope to change to any degree possible by writing this book). As a result, for better or for worse, it is critical that entrepreneurs understand some key strategies about Social Security.

The Concept and Reality of Social Security

Social Security benefits are a big deal, and most people do not fully comprehend the value of their Social Security benefits. Today, a married couple with a strong work history who maxed out their contributions into Social Security during their working years will typically receive between $800,000 and $1,000,000 in benefits paid to them from Social Security over their lifetimes. Looking at it from another perspective, a couple receiving a combined benefit of $4,000 a month, or $48,000 a year, would require a retirement nest egg of nearly $1,600,000 earning 3 percent to generate that level of income during retirement adjusted for inflation. That's a big deal!

Of course, the underlying concern and debate is whether or not these benefits will actually be there in the future, but that's a topic for another day. All we can do for now, and what we recommend to our clients, is two things:

1. Use your business as the primary tool to building wealth with multiple strategies (the purpose of this book).
2. Assume for now that Social Security will be there, and understand what you can do to take the best advantage of this benefit (the purpose of this chapter).

W-2 employees will literally have no choices on the contributions side of the ledger, meaning as an employee, they will be taxed with

FICA for what they earn up to the Social Security income limits. Today, those limits cap out to some degree at around $120,000 of income. This means that a W-2 employee earning $120,000 a year will pay the same amount of Social Security taxes as a multibillionaire real estate mogul would pay.

As a self-employed business owner, however, you have tremendous flexibility and opportunity to fine-tune this system and do some amazing tax planning! You have many more choices and options than the average wage-earning American. Thus, you want to be vigilant with your tax planner to stay on top of these strategies.

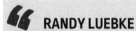

RANDY LUEBKE

What I have discovered in developing hundreds of Social Security plans is that the contribution made into the plan as well as the timing of the benefits received vary wildly. Depending on your current age, income, health, and family history of longevity, making smart choices and wise decisions about your situation is very important. Yet, although it's complex, there are financial advisors with special knowledge in this area that can put together a creative and well-thought-out plan that could end up to be thousands in retirement dollars.

Optimize Your Contributions Now

Notice I said the word optimize and not maximize. The key strategy *during the phase of paying into the system* is to adjust your Social Security wages to the lowest level possible in order to maximize your benefits for later—yes! **There is a sweet spot to planning your contributions.**

As an entrepreneur running an operational business, you are going to pay into Social Security whether you like it or not. Those contributions will either be through Self Employment Tax paid on a Schedule C or through a K-1 as an LLC. However, the beauty of an S corporation is that you have the autonomy to control *how you* pay those taxes and *how much* you pay.

I have been writing and speaking about the S corporation strategy with entrepreneurs for almost 20 years. **It's an excellent strategy to save on FICA taxes AND plan for your future Social Security benefit at the same time.** If anybody tries to tell you the S corporation strategy is high risk or going away sometime soon, get a second or third opinion. You will quickly discover they are on an island with their conservative or archaic approach to tax strategies.

It's beyond the scope of this chapter and book, but I encourage you to study this incredible, yet simple strategy in my other book *The Tax & Legal Playbook: Game Changing Solutions for Small-Business Questions* (Entrepreneur Press, 2015).

However, for purposes of Social Security planning, here is the point: check your Social Security benefits statements annually to be certain that the amount of FICA taxes you paid are reflected in this report, AND see what the calculation is for your potential benefit. **Your financial advisor that understands the intricacies of Social Security can also meet with you to calculate the optimal salary level to get the maximum benefit at retirement age.** Of course, your age and your lifetime contributions are going to play into this as well as other factors.

Bottom line, salary planning is still an art, and I mean that in all senses of the word. Your CPA should be trying to peg the proper salary out of your S Corporation to keep the IRS happy and pay the least amount of FICA, but then in turn, your financial advisor should be chiming in regarding the proper range of salary for future Social Security benefits. **Don't take this payroll planning lightly or discount its importance.** It can truly save you thousands in taxes annually and deliver you thousands more on the back end in Social Security if you do it right!

What About My Spouse and His or Her Payroll Planning?

One might presume that the spouse of an entrepreneur (assuming they don't have their own employment or business) should also be on payroll in the business of the entrepreneur. In fact, one might

RANDY LUEBKE

There are really three issues to consider as it relates to your Social Security planning: it's expensive, it's really insurance, and it's out of your control. First, it's expensive because at today's Social Security tax rate of 15.3 percent, two married wage earners making $100,000 each will be required to put $30,600 into the Social Security kitty. This leads me to my second point. Social Security is insurance. It's not a savings account like your 401(k). There is always a possibility that you could pay hundreds of thousands of dollars into this fund and never collect a penny. My third point, "it's out of your control," is equally important as the choices and decisions that affect your Social Security contributions and the benefits you ultimately may receive are completely in the hands of our lawmakers in Washington. They can raise the taxes and lower the benefits, and you have nothing to say about the matter, no recourse whatsoever. What can you do? What should you do? You should think strategically and plan carefully. One the one hand, you cannot count on receiving Social Security benefits, especially if you are younger. On the other hand, Social Security benefits are significant, paying out close to $1 million in benefits to many families over their lifetime. If you are a W-2 wage-earner, you are just going to go along for the ride. You will pay what is required, and you will receive what is provided. If you are self-employed, however, you have tremendous flexibility and options. Take advantage of them.

think it obvious that the spouse's payroll should be the same as the primary owner of the business so as to ensure the spouse would have the same Social Security benefit. **You would be wrong to make this presumption.**

Now, of course, not every entrepreneur and marriage will be the same, but what turns this presumption on its head is the rule that if a marriage has lasted for ten or more years, regardless of a future separation (death or divorce), both spouses will be potentially entitled to the same Social Security benefits as the spouse with the majority of earnings under the business.

If you think about this rule/law, it makes perfect sense. The spouse that may have been the caregiver in the home shouldn't be penalized and receive a lower benefit because they didn't take a formal paycheck for all their work in the marriage.

From a tax perspective, I see clients rush to put a spouse on payroll in their older years before they sell the business or retire, but it frankly can be futile to make up for years of payments into the system for the primary entrepreneur. Reason being, it is highly unlikely that the taxes of the lower-earning spouse will provide enough benefit to justify this expense. **In other words, sometimes you are better off maximizing**

❝ RANDY LUEBKE

The risk here is obvious in that no one knows if or when changes could be made to the current Social Security claiming options. There are lots of unknowns. Therefore, I REALLY like the strategy of relying on the primary wage-earner's Social Security account when a couple has been married for at least ten years and they are both in their late 50s. As the changes made in Washington are slow to occur, a couple with these demographics can be fairly confident that this strategy will work for them. The savings in not paying Social Security taxes that will likely never provide a substantial benefit can then be redirected to something that will provide a guaranteed benefit like life insurance, asset-based long-term care insurance, or adding to one's retirement savings plans. Again, this strategy is relatively complicated to design and model and a bit risky due to potential legislative modification to the Social Security rules. That said, the savings are substantial, and in the right circumstances, implementing this strategy can yield tremendous financial benefits to offset these issues. ❞

the contributions to bolster one spouse's earnings record as they will both jointly benefit from it. Any Social Security taxes paid by the other spouse are, essentially, wasted money.

When You Are Ready to Claim Social Security

Presently, the earliest age at which one can claim Social Security benefits is 62 years old. If you are within ten years of this mark, then the first rule is to strategize.

TIP FOR FINANCIAL FREEDOM

Do not, and let me repeat, DO NOT rush to start claiming Social Security.

You have options, and by claiming Social Security too soon or by making poor decisions, it could cost you hundreds of thousands of dollars. Now more than ever, it is important for you to understand your options and make the best choices among them.

There are a myriad of potential claiming strategies and scenarios. Moreover, the choices and decisions you make about your Social Security benefits are generally permanent and cannot be undone. The following are some basic guidelines for claiming your benefits:

1. *Delay claiming YOUR benefits.* Yes, you've been paying into Social Security your entire life. You're concerned that the government may renege on the promise to pay, and of course no one knows for certain how long they will live. There are so many reasons to want to start receiving benefits as soon as you are eligible. **However, if you claim benefits at the earliest possible date, you are going to receive a significantly reduced payment.** That reduction is permanent with very few options available to you to fix this problem should you change your mind. At minimum, you should generally wait until Full Retirement Age (FRA) as defined by the Social Security Administration to

receive your benefits. At FRA, you will receive 100 percent of the benefits you are entitled to receive. **Moreover, you can earn an unlimited amount of other income, and there is no reduction in those benefits.** If you can afford to wait and delay receiving your Social Security benefits beyond your FRA, you will automatically receive a substantial increase in payments.

2. *Delay claiming your SPOUSE'S benefits.* The significant increase in Social Security benefits I just discussed for you can have a trickle-down effect with your spouse's benefits as well. If your spouse is younger and/or had a lesser earnings history, then by delaying YOUR benefits you are not only going to create a bigger payout for you, but the benefits also pass down to your spouse, and it will provide a larger and permanent benefit throughout your spouse's life as well.

3. *Spousal benefits.* If you were previously married and you are now a widow, widower, or divorcee, then you may be entitled to receive benefits under that spouse's earning records. Often, you can claim a survivor or spousal benefit and earn delayed credits on your own earning record simultaneously to supercharge the income you may receive over your lifetime. **A spouse, past or present, can be a tremendous opportunity to maximize your benefits.**

TIP FOR FINANCIAL FREEDOM

Develop a specific and targeted Social Security plan.

The fact is that I could go on and on with suggestions, ideas, and strategies to consider. Thus, the reality is that you need a Social Security plan: one that not only will help you to determine the optimal claiming strategies, but one that will also help you to determine the optimal contribution strategy as well. Again, Social Security is expensive, it's insurance, and it's out of your control. **Ignoring it and going along with the government's plan will generally not be**

in your best interest. Take charge. Be in control. Make informed choices and decisions. It's well worth the time, effort, and expense.

⑤ ⑤ ⑤

TAKEAWAY 1—As an entrepreneur, you have more choices and options to strategically plan your Social Security contributions. No matter your age, understand that there is a strategy that you can employ, and you should be talking about with your tax planner.

TAKEAWAY 2—If you are generating ordinary income in your business, it's critical you avoid as much as possible the dreaded self-employment tax and consider using an S Corporation. Learn about the S Corporation option. If your tax advisor isn't recommending it OR downplaying it as too risky or not beneficial to you—get a second opinion!

TAKEAWAY 3—Don't start claiming Social Security the minute you turn eligible. Consider your options, and meet with an experienced advisor to put together a Social Security plan. It could create hundreds of thousands of extra dollars for you during retirement.

THE ROLE OF YOUR PERSONAL RESIDENCE

Your primary residence is a huge part of your financial picture and needs to be discussed—so much so that I felt it deserved its own chapter. At first blush, it may seem like a simple topic, but the strategy for your home can actually get quite complicated. When do I buy a home? Should I pay off the mortgage? Do I utilize the equity in some fashion? Tax strategies, second mortgages, the list goes on and on.

Here's the bottom line. Owning your personal residence should be a primary goal early on in your wealth building process. **It will save you taxes, build equity, and enhance your financial freedom as you drive down your monthly housing cost in the process.** When you rent, it can seem like you're throwing money down the toilet. You're not building equity, and you certainly don't get a tax write-off when paying rent, compared to buying with a mortgage and being able to write off mortgage interest.

However, many argue that we need to keep it in perspective and realize it's not an investment, but an asset. Think about it: your home won't make you money per se like a rental property or mutual fund; your equity could be invested elsewhere if you didn't own a home. Conversely, you can create a target for a creditor in a lawsuit if you have too much equity in your home, and the equity can essentially just be sitting there and not making any money. That's where it starts to get complicated and becomes a heated debate.

Do I Rent or Buy?

As I stated above, the ultimate goal is to buy your personal residence and, frankly, as soon as possible. In fact, I would argue that if you really want to build financial freedom, 95 percent of entrepreneurs should be headed in the direction of buying. However, there are certainly instances when renting might make sense.

For example, you might need to rent if you are saving up for a down payment to buy. Maybe you live in a high cost of living area, like a major city, and renting is far more affordable. I've seen many situations where the down payment for a home or condo in an urban area is clearly out of reach, and those dollars could be better spent buying rental properties out of town and creating cash flow. **Sometimes, it can be necessary or wise to rent while acquiring rental properties, buying a lot, or building a home.**

In other instances, we can be recovering from losing a home in an economic downturn or from buying too much of a home we are unable to afford. There's a list of personal financial problems that could put us in a situation where it's better to rent for a while. **I've sometimes referred to this as "circling the wagons financially" and conserving funds in order to refocus on our financial goals and to get back into the right home ownership situation.** Whatever the reason may be for renting right now, don't beat yourself up; stick to your long-term financial plans. If there's a possibility in the foreseeable future to buy, then set your goals and sights in that direction, and don't give up until you get there.

Should I Have a Mortgage in the First Place?

Let's face it, rarely are most people going to buy their first home for cash. It just doesn't happen unless maybe you are a drug dealer and have Saul Goodman laundering your cash. For the rest of us, it's absolutely necessary to get a foot in the door of home ownership. But is it really a bad thing? Yes, we may want to pay off the mortgage as we continue down our path of building wealth, but I don't think we should shy away from a mortgage, and the following is why.

Leveraged ROR on Your Capital

Debt creates leverage, and leverage can work for you or against you. Either way, it is always working. If you pay cash for $100,000 home and it goes up 10 percent, the new appreciated value is $110,000—a 10 percent Return on Investment (ROI). Now, use just $10,000 of your money to purchase the same $100,000 home. Again, the home's value goes up by 10 percent. With only $10,000 of your money invested, you end up with a 100 percent ROI instead. That is the power of leverage. Leverage works to the advantage of the borrower more than to the lender, which is why I say that not all debt is created equal.

Tax Deductions

The deductibility of interest paid on your mortgage has been on the books for a very long time, and it can have a direct and positive impact on your tax return. For example, let's say you are making mortgage payments of $1,000 a month, and $700 of that is mortgage interest. At the end of the year, that's $8,400 in mortgage interest. If you're in a combined Fed and State tax rate of 25 percent, you just saved over $2,100 in taxes, and that's close to saving you effectively $200 a month off your mortgage payment each month. If you were renting for the same amount, that adds up to be a big deal. Millions of Americans take advantage of this write-off each year, and regardless of Washington's appetite for money, for now and into the foreseeable future, mortgage interest is here to stay and a great tax strategy.

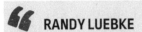

RANDY LUEBKE

Today especially, people are concerned about inflation. Most people concerned with inflation like to consider gold or silver as an inflation hedge. While it is true that these metals will generally increase in value during inflationary periods, the truth is that debt is a MUCH better hedge against inflation. **First, understand that debt, especially mortgage debt, creates bonds**. When bonds are issued, the terms of the bond are set in stone by contract. If you've ever obtained a mortgage loan, you will remember that huge stack of papers you signed. You may not have realized it, but you were signing a contract and the terms of that contract were locked in via your signature. Therefore, the principal (the amount you borrowed) and the coupon (that rate you agreed to pay for that money) are fixed, and for that moment of that day, those terms represent the market's value for the bond. Tomorrow is another day, however, and things may change tomorrow or the next day or the day after that. **During times of inflation, interest rates rise. When they do, then the value of the bond must decline as the components work in opposition of each other**. However, just because interest rates on current loans have increased does not mean the borrower (you) has to pay a higher rate. Remember, you locked in the terms of the loan when you signed the contract, and Wall Street accepted those terms when you gave them your money. So your "safe" bond could lose money if inflation goes up, but you keep paying the same interest rate. **The lesson here is that inflation benefits the borrower and punishes the lender**. If you really want to create a hedge against inflation, borrow all the money you can afford under a fixed-rate contract, and pay it back as slowly as the contract will allow.

Debt Is Not a Four-Letter Word

OK . . . yes, technically "debt" is a four-letter word, but not a bad/ swear word. As previously addressed in Chapter 7, there are two kinds of debt: bad debt and good debt, or what's referred to as reductive debt and productive debt. Reductive debt is debt that is generally used to buy the "stuff of life," the things that are used up, consumed, or lose value over time. Productive debt, on the other hand, is used to acquire things that produce income and/or increase in their value over time. **An example of productive debt would be a loan used to finance your personal residence.** You are using debt and leverage to build equity, save taxes, and reduce your monthly cost of living—if not now, certainly in the future. Don't be afraid of productive debt and a mortgage to buy a home—if buying wisely, it's a good decision to use leverage and a mortgage 99.9 percent of the time.

Should I Refinance My Mortgage?

Before we talk about methods to pay down your mortgage quickly, we should talk about refinancing. Many people think if you can save a couple points with a lower interest rate and get a good deal on the fees to "refi," it's a no-brainer. Slow down, Tiger. It's important to understand why you need to be wary of refinancing when you are simply trying to lower your interest rate. Fundamentally, lowering the rate on your mortgage will save you money. **However, refinances are not, in general, free.** In fact, the costs of an appraisal, title insurance, recording fees, etc., can easily cost $4,000 or more.

Your loan officer may increase your principal balance to cover those costs so that you don't have to reach into your pocketbook to pay them. Then, to help you justify the transaction, they will show you how much lower your new mortgage payment will become. The advanced mortgage professional will then divide those savings into the cost of the mortgage and proudly announce that your break-even will be in 18 months. *Wow! You save all that money each month, and 18 months later, you've saved enough to recover from the costs, and you get to save that same amount of money every month until the loan is paid off.* But that is the problem.

Oftentimes, the bulk of the monthly savings is the result of extending the term of your mortgage and not due to the interest savings. **Your once 20-year payoff debt has now been reset to 30 years, and at the end of the day, you may end up paying more for your new and improved lower interest rate loan than you would have had you done nothing and not refinanced.** The lesson you should learn here is be sure to do an apples-to-apples comparison when considering a refinance. A good loan officer should be able to easily crunch those numbers for you so that you can make an intelligent and informed decision.

Do I Pay Off My Mortgage Early?

Now, we have reached the topic many of you have been waiting to sink your teeth into. As my entrepreneurs start building wealth and financial freedom with more cash flow in their life, inevitably the question arises: "Should I pay off my mortgage?" **The easy answer is yes, and there are all sorts of methods to do so.** In fact, I have worked with some excellent companies to assist my clients with guidance and support throughout the process. One in particular is Sweep Strategies in Honolulu, Hawaii. They have helped hundreds, if not thousands, of islanders pay off their mortgages early with strategies that are used worldwide but are less common in the U.S.

However, the real question is, what do you do with that equity in your home once you pay off the mortgage? For some, their life's goal can and should be to pay off their mortgage. **Their home may be a central part of their retirement plan as they rely on a meager retirement plan and Social Security.** Having their home paid off could be critical, if not a lifesaver, in their situation. In fact, this is really a Dave Ramsey-type strategy and what he teaches to so many Americans that are in desperate need of this message. I think it's a fantastic message and goal for a certain demographic or cross-section of Americans.

But for many of my clients, the home is just a piece of the equation, and they are generating income and wealth in several

THE BUSINESS OWNER'S GUIDE TO **FINANCIAL FREEDOM** ▪ l03

areas. **When this is the case, paying off the home and sitting on the equity could be a poor financial decision.** This is because they have the financial resources and depth to their plan that utilizing that equity could be very wise and powerful. So in sum, YES! Pay off your mortgage, but have a plan as to why and what you are going to invest in when you get close to that Holy Grail of paying off your mortgage.

With that said, here are four methods to consider utilizing to pay down your mortgage in a cost-effective and efficient manner.

1. Shortening Your Term

If you really want to pay off your mortgage faster, then get a shorter mortgage right from the start or during a refinance. In the past, you could always refinance your home and switch from a 30-year loan to a 15-year mortgage, for example. **Now, you don't need discipline to stay on track with your accelerated mortgage plans. Instead, you will have the threat of foreclosure to motivate you.** Moreover, with every accelerated payment, you increase your risk of foreclosure and increase the lender's desire to foreclose as you rapidly increase your equity stake in the property. Heck, if you really wanted to go for it, you could get a 15-year loan and send an extra 1/12 payment along with your regular payment every month and knock off that debt in ten years. **In fact, today many lenders will let you choose the term you want and will create a customized loan repayment plan.** Perhaps you are going to retire on your birthday when you turn 65 years old and that is 88-months from today. These lenders will create an 88 month mortgage to meet your goal. No discipline needed here. No flexibility either.

2. The Biweekly Mortgage (Not a Payment Plan)

Another popular method, one much less complex than the HEAP method (see page 105), is the biweekly mortgage. Generally, a mortgage payment is made once a month, or 12 times a year. With a biweekly mortgage, you make a payment every other week. The payment is only half of the full payment, however, as there are 52 weeks in a year, meaning you are actually making 26 half-payments

CHAPTER II ▪ The Role of Your Personal Residence

or the equivalent of 13 full mortgage payments over the course of a year. Once again, you accelerate the principal reduction, saving you the interest expense. **This method will generally pay off a mortgage in two-thirds of the time it would otherwise take if the payments were made on the monthly plan.**

Be aware that many lenders will not accept payments more often than once a month, and even fewer lenders will apply the additional payments received mid-month to the principle during the month they are received. Additionally, in the modern mortgage world, the loans are regularly sold, changing to whom those payments are due. The opportunity for errors is just too great to justify the savings. Therefore, I would rarely recommend deploying this strategy. **Alternatively, you could simply divide your mortgage payment by 12 and add that additional amount to your monthly mortgage payment.** That way, your lender receives just one payment from you each month, and even though you are sending them a little more than you are required to send them, the lender can generally process these payments without issues. The net result is that you end up making 13 full payments over the course of the year.

3. The HEAP Method

The Home Equity Acceleration Plan (HEAP) method has been around for decades under various names: The Wealth Accelerator,

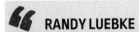 **RANDY LUEBKE**

Having equity, as in owning your home, comes with a greater risk. Paying off your mortgage can result in seriously exposing yourself to a loss in the event of a lawsuit. After all, if there is little or no equity in the property, then a creditor will have no desire to own the real estate. But maintaining large amounts of equity in your real estate should not give you great comfort; it should give you great concern instead and a reason for an asset protection plan.

The Banker's Secret, The Sweep Strategy (as I referenced above), and others. Essentially, once you get under the hood with all these methods, they will boil down to the same thing: using a home equity line of credit (HELOC) in conjunction with your primary mortgage to more effectively manage your cash flow.

There is no magic to this process. All you are doing is making better use of your cash flow and paying simple interest under a HELOC. The net result is that without refinancing your current mortgage and without changing your lifestyle expenditures, you will end up paying off your mortgage way ahead of schedule. **In fact, I've seen many examples where the HEAP method would pay off a 30-year mortgage in just seven to ten years.**

The process works like this:

1. Obtain a HELOC of any size, as long as it allows for interest-only payments and that the interest charged is compounded daily. These elements are critical for the system to work correctly.
2. Direct your paychecks into the HELOC rather than into your checking account.
3. Spend less than you deposit each month.

Essentially, that is the process, and it may seem magical, but it really comes down to self-discipline. This is why having someone coach you or hold you accountable until it becomes a habit for you can be a huge help. There is no software wizardry. This is simply making better use of your cash management. **You stop lending your money to the bank for free.** You borrow their money to reduce your debt. You temporarily reduce your overall debt with your paychecks. Most importantly, you spend less than you earn. Again, I recommend some support with this strategy. It can be a little challenging to work with your bank and change your methods of spending to make it happen quickly; however, it really does work and is amazing at that.

4. The Single-Payment Acceleration Plan

This is my last payment acceleration rabbit trick, but I have to admit it a pretty good one. It's very simple to implement; however, getting

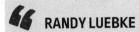

RANDY LUEBKE

Is there an emotional strain having a mortgage? For those of you who studied history, you know about the Great Depression of the '30s. There were many similarities to the recession of 2008. In 1929, and for the next decade, many people lost their farms to the bank when they lost their jobs and could no longer afford to make their mortgage payments. Similarly, many people lost their jobs during the 2008 Great Recession, and they had to give up their homes to the bank. When times of tremendous financial hardships like this occur, rest assured that the emotions attached to these serious and long-lasting negative circumstances become ingrained in the minds of people for decades—perhaps even for generations. **Looking back to 2008, I recall that many people were overleveraged and lost their homes because they could no longer afford them.** Those with small mortgages or no mortgages at all did not have to bear that financial strain, which meant, for many, they were able to remain in their homes and ride out the storm. So, what is the answer? It really depends on your risk tolerance and your overall financial wealth and portfolio. If your home is your single most valuable asset, safe-guarding that equity should be a priority. If you have other buckets of wealth, then leaving that equity just sitting there could be an irresponsible move. Do a self-assessment with your trust advisors to determine what strategy fits you best.

your head around the concept may be a little difficult, so please hang in there with me. First, remember the issues with refinancing I covered above. It may not always be the best decision, and we have to be wary of trading a lower monthly payment for a longer term. Nonetheless, remember the concept of refinancing because if you are self-disciplined, you can turn the tables on your banker.

Let's say that 20 years ago, you borrowed $300,000. Now, your balance is only $200,000, and your loan will be paid off in ten more years. Yes, that is how the math works. It takes a very long time to pay down the mortgage initially. Then, the principal reduction accelerates automatically and pays the remaining balance off in a relatively short period of time. Let's use this concept to our advantage. Instead of getting a new 30-year mortgage for $200,000 and restarting your amortization schedule, let's get a new $300,000 mortgage instead. What? Am I crazy? Crazy like a fox maybe because here is the plan.

Refinance any mortgage for the amount you originally borrowed, in this example, $300,000. **Then, along with your first regular mortgage payment, make a one-time principal reduction of the difference.** In this example, I would include an extra $100,000 with my regular first month's payment. Guess what happens? With that one-time payment, you have just reset your payoff for ten years again (or wherever you were in the payment schedule on any loan). **Then, all you need to do is continue making your monthly mortgage payments as required and you will not extend the term of your loan whatsoever.** The only discipline required is to make one big payment. Just do that once-in-a-row, and you will be good to go. The interest savings will be real. You don't have to worry about extra payments or biweekly, HELOC, whatever. It just works.

In sum, you can see that your personal residence and all the financial issues related to it can become a little complicated. Don't take the common perspectives about home ownership for granted. With a little study on many of these topics above and a consultation with your professional advisors, you could dramatically increase your wealth without a lot of effort.

$ $ $

TAKEAWAY 1—Make home ownership a priority if you don't already own your personal residence. Renting is certainly acceptable when necessary, but your home should be one of your primary assets.

TAKEAWAY 2—Having a mortgage with a home is okay, and it doesn't have to be a major priority to pay it off immediately. There are tax and asset protection benefits to having a mortgage, and it can be an excellent hedge against inflation.

TAKEAWAY 3—Once you start building more financial freedom, cash flow, and wealth, implement a method to pay down your mortgage as quickly as possible. Determine the best method to approach the equity in your personal residence. Hold it sacred and consider a HELOC and invest to build more wealth—but remember it depends on your situation!

HEALTH CARE—THE HIDDEN TIME BOMB

We can't have a discussion about financial freedom without including the topic of health care. The cost of health-care related expenses, from insurance to prescription drugs to out-of-pocket copays, is out of control and can eat up our wealth as fast as we make it.

Then, we have the future costs of health care as we get older that we simply ignore because it just seems either too far away or too complex or even painful to think about. Long -term care and the related costs can consume your nest egg before you know what hit you.

There have to be some solutions, right? Is there something we can do as entrepreneurs to hedge against these huge financial risks that we are facing at the beginning of each year and then into our retirement years? As I write these words, the debate over health care is raging in Washington and on the news. **But we can't depend on or hope for some magical legislation that is going to fix this.** There ARE some things we can do to prepare and insure ourselves against catastrophic health-care costs during our lives.

Once again, as entrepreneurs, we will have to adapt and adopt. If you get nothing else from this book, get that. It's our ability to make smart changes quickly and decisively that will allow us to continue to follow our dreams and, frankly, help to make the world a better place for everyone.

Health Care 101 and the Heart of the Solution

As a primer, understand that the current state of health care is a combination of providers, suppliers, facilities, insurance companies, attorneys, and their customers (aka us). Right there, you can see the diverse set of interests and needs. From the business side, that is everyone besides us, their primary need is to earn profits. Fundamentally, there is no issue with that premise as businesses need to be profitable to survive and grow. Profits allow companies to invest in themselves, which in turn, delivers better products and services from which we ultimately benefit.

What we as the customers of the industry want is fairly basic as well. **As consumers, we want the very best health care available at the very lowest cost.** The question is: can these two goals coexist? My response is yes, of course, that is how and why a capitalist country like the United States has helped to create more wealth for more people than at any time in the history of mankind. I believe that the essence of the problem we face with health care today is that there is a disconnect between us, those that want and purchase services and the providers and suppliers. That disconnect is the "insurance" system, which has placed itself right in the middle of everyone to serve as the gatekeeper. **The result is that no one, neither the consumer nor the provider, has accountability for the costs involved.** Therefore, as entrepreneurs, this is also where the opportunity lies.

TIP FOR FINANCIAL FREEDOM

*We can insure ourselves with several unique structures
and slowly but surely eliminate health care costs as a
risk in our plan.*

I'm certainly not going to try and "fix the health-care system" within the pages of this book. However, what I am going to do is once again help you to make the best choices and decisions when it comes to spending your health-care dollars.

HSAs, HRAs, and the 401(h)

I have a simple goal when it comes to health care that I summarize in one sentence (called "kohlercare"): **I want to make sure my business owners get the correct insurance that fits their needs, while also being able to deduct all their insurance premiums, write off ALL their medical expenses, and build up a bucket of wealth to pay for health-care expenses for the rest their life—tax free!** Simple, right? Well, it can obviously be a little tricky, but I have a roadmap for you. Obviously, the topic of choosing the right insurance and deducting your insurance costs is beyond the scope of this book (see *The Tax & Legal Playbook* for those details and more). However, in this chapter, I want to summarize the three bedrock strategies to writing off all your health care and building that tax-free bucket: the Health Savings Account (HSA), Health Reimbursement Arrangement (HRA), and 401(h).

Health Savings Account (HSA)

The Health Savings Account is one of the most powerful pieces of a well-designed health-care strategy. It includes saving money, saving taxes, building a tax-free bucket for health care, and most importantly, taking control of your own health-care strategy. You save money because in order to have an HSA, you have to have a high-deductible health-care plan. Well, chances are, you will have a lower premium with a higher deductible and save money.

Also, you save taxes because you get a tax deduction when contributing to your HSA—it's right on the front page of your tax return. At the same time, you build a tax-free bucket of money in an HSA, just like an IRA. The money can be invested, the growth is tax-free, and withdrawals for health care are also tax-free.

Finally, you take control of many health-care decisions because you can pay cash out of your HSA. Imagine that! No insurance company between you and your health-care provider where you can control your care and negotiate for lower prices. Even the doctors win! Now, let's hit the nuts and bolts:

1. *The Tax Deduction.* Your HSA contributions are deductible from your gross pay, or business income, on the front page of your tax return. This gives you a powerful tax deduction and can potentially even put you into a lower tax bracket. The tax deduction has been hovering between $3,000 to $4,000 for singles and $6,000 to $7,000 for families, adjusted for inflation each year.

2. *The Deadlines.* There are two important deadlines. First, you have to enroll in a high-deductible health insurance plan (HDHP) before December 1st in the year you want the deduction. So for example, if you want the write-off in the current year, make sure you have the right type of plan in place by December 1 of that same year. Second, you can make the contribution and take the deduction up until April 15th *following* the year you want the deduction. For example, you can open the account AND make the contribution before April 15 and get a write-off for the prior year.

3. *Tax-Free Growth.* The funds grow tax-free and aren't a "use it or lose it" plan. The HSA account grows and builds for your future health-care needs. Investments aren't counted towards contributions either. Win big on investing with your HSA and still "pass Go" every January and make another contribution.

4. *Tax-Free Withdrawals.* You can also spend the money tax-free on qualified medical expenses. This could be deductibles, dental, eye care, chiropractic care, acupuncture, and even hotel and lodging while at the hospital. The list is quite exhaustive

and comprehensive. Moreover, you can start taking out money immediately, and there's no waiting period. **Just change the way you normally approach your health-care spending.** For example, stop at the bank and make a deposit in your HSA on the way to the doctor. Then, pay the bill out of your HSA visa. You just generated a write-off the same day. Check out IRS Publication 502 for a list of the hundreds of medical expenses you can pull out of your HSA tax-free.

RANDY LUEBKE

Health-care expenses, ugh! After taxes, health-care expenses are likely to be your next biggest expense over your lifetime, and that is only if you stay healthy. Get sick, and you will become even more ill over the costs of care. The only thing worse than paying for health-care costs is paying for them with after-tax dollars. If health care were expensive already, then why would you want to increase those costs by another 20, 30, 40 percent or more and pay for them with after-tax income? Stop doing that! Implement as many of the pre-tax solutions as you can, and keep your costs of care as low as possible.

5. *Self-Direct Your HSA Investments.* You can even "self-direct" your investments inside your HSA. This means you aren't simply stuck with a mutual fund option provided by your bank. You could invest in a restaurant, real estate, or even Super Bowl tickets. If you want to self-direct, just place your HSA funds with a custodian that allows for self-directing rather than with your local bank. See the next chapter regarding the concept of self-directing and investing in what you know best.

6. *An HSA Can Help Pay for Your Retirement.* After you turn 59½, there is also the option to withdraw the money for non-health-care expenses and then pay federal income taxes on it. The HSA then acts much like a traditional IRA since the

HSA holder pays ordinary income taxes on nonmedical-related withdrawals, with the added perk that you don't have the mandatory disbursements usually required by traditional IRAs. This protects you from the concern I often hear, "What happens if I don't need the money for health care?" The simple answer is, don't worry—you can use it like an IRA in the future.

7. *How to Set Up an HSA?* Remember, the insurance is completely separate. Get the right type of insurance that qualifies you, and then DON'T CALL your insurance company for a Health Savings Account—they don't administer them; they just sell insurance. Once you have the insurance, the easiest way is to open up an HSA at your local bank. You can sometimes even do it within minutes online. No major paperwork. Just check the proper boxes, sign the form, and make a deposit. Most bank HSAs will then give you a Visa card to pay for medical expenses right out of your HSA. However, if you want to let the money ride and invest the HSA and not pull out money for medical expenses immediately—for example, to self-direct (see item 5 above), then you would open up your HSA with a self-directed IRA custodian.

The HSA is one of the most under-utilized tax strategies by Americans today. President Trump in his 2017 Inaugural Address even mentioned the HSA by name and stated it needed to be a larger part of any changes to the health-care legislation. It's a fantastic tax savings strategy as well as a powerful tool to help pay for current and future health-care costs. Everyone should at least consider the HSA as an option when purchasing insurance and saving for taxes.

Health Reimbursement Arrangement (HRA)

Millions of Americans are unaware of the power of an HRA, or Health Reimbursement Arrangement. In fact, many don't even know that it exists. If you have more than $5,000 a year in out-of-pocket medical expenses, such as co-pays, deductibles, prescription drugs, dental care, eye care, chiropractic, etc., then chances are you could benefit from an HRA. In fact, legislation that went into effect for small-business owners in 2017 allows you to write off up to $10,000 of medical expenses *before* insurance premiums *and off the top* (not like itemized medical expenses).

Chances are you aren't getting any sort of a tax deduction for these extra medical expenses, and just imagine if you could deduct 100 percent of these medical costs. Even further, imagine the power of this strategy if you have significant medical costs in your family and you could deduct 10k or 20k of medical costs—it could be life-changing!!

Now, many Americans take advantage of the HSA, or Health Savings Account, **but this is completely different—and keep in mind, not everybody qualifies for an HSA.** You must have the right type of insurance. Yet, if you have a lot of medical expenses, you probably aren't using an HSA type of health plan. Hence—the HRA could be the perfect plan for you!!

What Are the Rules?

- § An HRA can only be used by small-business owners. It is an employee benefit to reimburse the medical costs of the employee, *which could be you!*
- § If you're single, you will need to utilize a C Corporation to employ you with a W-2 and provide the HRA.
- § If you're married, you can probably implement an HRA simply through the use of a Sole Proprietorship, keeping the cost down.
- § For those of you already utilizing an S Corporation, you'll need to use the C Corporation or Sole Proprietorship described above.
- § You'll need to implement an HRA plan document and procedure for reimbursement, which can actually be affordable, self-administered, and simple to do.

Figures 12.1 and 12.2 on page 116 are some diagrams that explain what your structure may look like.

What Are Some of the Benefits?

- § There is no need to have a high-deductible insurance plan like with an HSA. In fact, you don't have to have insurance at all.

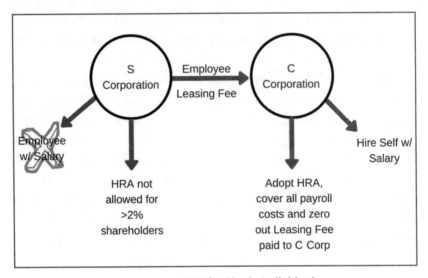

Figure 12.1—HRA for Single Individual

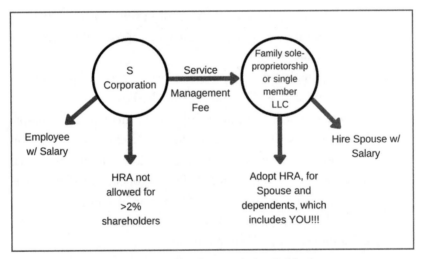

Figure 12.2—HRA for Married Individuals

§ It can be self-administered and is relatively inexpensive to implement ($400 or less).

§ You can write off all the medical expenses up to the plan limit, which you set!!

- § The same medical expenses apply for the HRA as for itemizing and HSAs.
- § The payments under the HRA to the employee are not subject to payroll withholding taxes.
- § You can even deduct long-term care insurance premiums through an HRA that aren't otherwise deductible for average Americans.

In summary, remember you must have a profitable small business to implement the HRA, you should have medical expenses of at least $4,000 (or more) a year to justify the additional administrative cost of the structure, and you should get some professional advice regarding your situation. **Run the numbers, and make sure your tax advisor understands the documentation and reporting requirements.** The HRA isn't particularly expensive or difficult to implement, but this is something the average person shouldn't try to figure out on their own. Get some technical support and guidance if you think the HRA is a potential strategy for you.

401(h)—The Trifecta of Retirement and Health-Care Planning Benefits

The 401(h) is similar to the 401(k) but different in some significant ways. Not only do you get a tax deduction upfront, followed by tax-deferred growth on your investment, but you can withdraw 100 percent of your money tax-free as long as you spend those withdrawals for medical purposes.

The 401(h) is an add-on to a defined benefit plan. It is part of the Super(k) mentioned in Chapter 16. The 401(h) allows the participant to contribute a significant amount of money annually to ultimately create a pool of money for you to access at retirement simply for health care and even long-term care costs. How much can you contribute? That is very difficult to define as it is based on your age, your income, and the ages and incomes of all the other employees in the organization. That said, the contributions can range from somewhere around $25,000 to $50,000 a year, which is significantly more than the amount of money you could contribute to a traditional HSA-type plan.

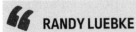

RANDY LUEBKE

For those who earn substantial income and believe that they have run out of options to reduce their tax burden, the 401(h) can be a welcome solution with a powerful set of tax-free benefits waiting for them at retirement.

The Cost of Health Care During Your Retirement and the Role of Long-Term Care Insurance

Do you think that you may have some health-care expenses as you grow older? Obviously yes, and they can add up quickly! Health care during your retirement is not free. The cost of Medicare premiums, deductibles, and co-pays can be quite a shock, especially for those who have been working for a company that provided much of the cost of their health care through premium health insurance plan coverage subsidies.

RANDY LUEBKE

One analysis I provide to my financial planning clients is called the "Retirement Health-Care Expense Estimator." This analysis estimates the cost of health care throughout the 25 years or more of your retirement. One thing that everyone will agree on as it relates to health care is that the costs continue to rise. They increase not just due to inflation. They also increase due to the complexity of the procedures and, as you age, the frequency with which you need them. In general, a healthy person can expect to pay about approximately $250,000 on health-care related expenses during your retirement. And that is if you are healthy! If you experience poor health, your expenses can soar.

The long-term health-care insurance industry will tell you that 75 percent of seniors will experience a long-term care need during their retirement. That is a very high percentage. In fact, it is so high that you may as well assume that you will be one of the three out of four people who will have a need for it.

What they don't tell you is that not every one of those unfortunate 75 percent will experience prolonged, financially catastrophic issues. Most people will end up passing away after a relatively short period of time, or they will minimize their costs by receiving care from home.

What are the solutions?

1. Rely on a family member to care for you.
2. Pay for care from your savings.
3. Receive welfare.
4. Have long-term care insurance.

Relying on family members would seem to be the logical and most affordable solution. Maybe dad has a stroke but mom is still healthy, so she can take care of him, right? I agree that for a time mom can do this. However, if dad requires more and more care, mom may become unable to provide the care needed both physically and emotionally. Perhaps there is a nearby son or daughter or another relative that can help. You can only imagine the problems that can, and do, evolve as such a situation develops.

While on the surface relying on family makes sense and often times initially even works out, more often, the caregivers become tired, frustrated, and angry with the other family members who just send money, periodically call, or come to visit on holidays. They have no idea what the day-to-day strain can be like when providing care. **You can see, from all sides, it is not likely to have a good outcome.** There is also the fact that illnesses, and their effects, may necessitate the care of professionally trained people.

At this point, paying for your care is the next option. Again, if you have a spare $2 million to $3 million in liquid reserves earmarked for health care, then you are in great shape. However, think about dad spending even $100,000 a year for care and having to withdraw those funds from his 401(h). That means that an additional $25k to $35k must also be withdrawn to pay the income taxes. Even a $1 million 401(k) won't last that long, and as it is dwindled down, so is the potential income it was supposed to produce to support both mom and dad during their retirement. This can lead us to the third solution: welfare.

Medicare is the health insurance provider for nearly everyone living in America over 65 years of age. Medicare provides no long-term care benefits. **Medicaid does provide those benefits, but unfortunately, the only way to qualify for Medicaid is to be broke.** Intentionally becoming broke was not part of anyone's retirement plan, yet for many, this ends up being the only option available to cover the costs of care.

Finally, there is long-term care insurance, and frankly, I do NOT like it for the following reasons:

§ Long-term care insurance is expensive.

§ Pre-existing health issues may prevent you from getting it.

§ The premiums can increase or benefits can be reduced at any time.

§ You may live a long and healthy life and never develop a long-term care need.

Without going into all the details for each of the reasons I've mentioned above, rest assured that they are real, and they are the primary reason I have not encouraged my clients to purchase traditional long-term care insurance. **Fortunately, within the past few years, a number of alternatives have been developed.** These plans, called Asset Based Long-term Care Insurance (AB-LTCI), may be the best solution ever developed to assist people should the need occur.

Asset-Based Long-Term Care Insurance

As the name implies, this strategy is based on the asset within life insurance and NOT long-term care insurance that operates like medical insurance. The idea is that while everyone should set aside some money for long-term care expenses, even if you did have the money, would you really want to set it aside in what must be a very safe and relatively liquid investment? Maybe a CD that pays next to nothing in interest? I really don't think that anyone who was smart enough to have an extra $1 million to $2 million in savings is going to be keen on that idea. **What if you could, however, deposit that money into an account where, overnight, it became worth 50 percent more?** What if you passed away and never needed to spend that money on your health care and it could then be passed down to your heirs, all 150 percent of it, income tax-free? Well, this is how AB-LTCI works.

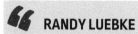

RANDY LUEBKE

In the American health-care system, we get sick and then have someone help us get better. It's backwards, of course, but it is our system. The goal is to help you recover and move on. When you don't get better, however, it can cause severe financial distress that can be as devastating as the illness itself. Rule #1: stay healthy. Eat right, exercise, rest, and enjoy life. All good. Then, before you become ill or get hurt, create a health-care insurance plan. Our health-care system may or may not be the best on the planet. Regardless, do what you can to make the most of it, and protect yourself and those you care about most against the financial consequences that could occur as well.

It's safe; it immediately increases the value of your money significantly; if you change your mind, you can have your money back; and if you need it for care, it's there. **Furthermore, if you don't use it, or use a portion of it, then you can pass the remaining funds on to your heirs.** The insurance company can never increase your premiums or reduce the benefits you were promised, and you can purchase one policy that can cover two people who don't have to be spouses.

TIP FOR FINANCIAL FREEDOM

Don't ignore planning for your long-term health care.

Again, regarding some of these topics, it's not the purpose of this book to go into every detail of every strategy, and health care is clearly one of these topics. There is just *so much* to cover, with intricacies and nuances that need to be tailored to each business owner's situation. However, I want to make sure you are at least introduced or reminded as to the benefits of these tools at your disposal.

§ § §

TAKEAWAY 1—We need to take control of our own health-care situations, stay informed, and try to build structures and procedures that help us insure ourselves.

TAKEAWAY 2—Determine if an HSA, HRA, 401(h), or even a combination of strategies is best to maximize writing off health-care expenses and saving for health-care costs with tax-free methods.

TAKEAWAY 3—Don't ignore long-term care needs and hope something works out for you in the future. Take an active role in making a plan, and consider an AB-LTCI as an option.

SELF-DIRECTING AND STRATEGIC USE OF THE IRA, SEP, AND 401(K)

It was critical that this book include a chapter on self-directing. This is the concept that speaks to the heart of an entrepreneur and helps investors build their wealth faster and more wisely. Simply put, self-directing means taking control of your retirement account and investing in what you know best—not in Wall Street products, but real estate, notes, tax liens, small business, and even race horses or concert tickets.

It's actually amazing what your retirement account can invest in. However, this is another strategy that Wall Street doesn't want you to know. As I discussed in Chapters 3 and 4, your standard financial advisor has no interest in you investing your retirement account in what they call "alternative investments." **I** call it investing in *what you know*, and it may mean your broker doesn't get a commission in the process.

I also want to emphasize this strategy for entrepreneurs because many small-business owners disregard and ignore the benefits of using a retirement plan to build and protect wealth. They view a retirement plan as stagnant, untouchable, and useless, if not a complete loss of funds that they could use in their business.

Self-directing is the strategy that blows open the opportunity for entrepreneurs to change their entire outlook and perspective towards retirement accounts.

CASE STUDY

My partner and I recently met with a land developer in a major western city, and in that meeting, he explained the dramatic impact our advice had on his life over the past four years. When we first met, he had the traditional land development business: putting partnerships together, buying land, and constructing new buildings, or buying and selling projects in older developments making improvements along the way. He was very successful and frankly was on his way to making millions. However, he was also paying hundreds of thousands of dollars in taxes. Well, during our meeting four years ago, he learned that he could do the same developments with IRA or 401(k) money! He could literally sell his lackluster stock portfolio in his retirement accounts, create and fund LLCs without paying any penalties or taxes, and start developing land with his retirement accounts. At our recent meeting he shared his Roth IRA was now worth over $5 million! That's right, his Roth account, which he'll never pay taxes on the distributions he starts taking when he hits 59 1/2. That's something unfathomable to accomplish on Wall Street with your broker in the same four-year period. THIS is the type of power an entrepreneur wants to know about when it comes to retirement accounts. Your business doesn't have to be your only asset providing for your retirement anymore!

Self-Directed Retirement Account Basics

A self-directed retirement account could be an IRA, Roth IRA, 401(k), Roth 401(k), Pension Plan, SEP, or even an HSA or Coverdell or College IRA. Any of these accounts could be moved from a traditional brokerage to a custodian or structure that allows you to invest in what Wall Street calls alternative investments. These other investments could include real estate, promissory notes, precious metals, and private company stock.

The usual reaction I hear from investors is, "Why haven't I ever heard of these self-directed IRAs or self-directed 401(k)s before? Furthermore, why have I always been told that my retirement portfolio has to be in a bunch of mutual funds or stocks?" **The answer is quite simple: the large financial institutions that control most of the U.S. retirement accounts don't make enough money off the self-directed industry or strategy.** They just point you in the direction of products that generate sales commissions and excessive fees (see Chapter 4).

What your stockbroker or captive financial advisor won't tell you is that under current law, a retirement account is only restricted from investing in the following:

§ Collectibles: such as art, stamps, coins, alcoholic beverages, or antiques
§ Life insurance
§ S corporation stock
§ Any investment that constitutes a prohibited transaction (discussed below)
§ Any investment not allowed under federal law (e.g., a marijuana dispensary)

What this means is that you have far more control than you ever imagined over your retirement accounts. You have the potential to get a tax deduction in your business to fund your retirement accounts AND THEN invest those retirement accounts in a more creative fashion to build your financial freedom. This is one of the key buckets we are trying to build with the profits from your business, so that you are more diversified in your wealth-building process.

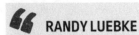

RANDY LUEBKE

When instructing clients about self-directing, I oftentimes suggest they use the concept of "opportunity shifting." This means, that instead of making every business deal or investment in your own name or company, every once in a while, shift an opportunity to your retirement account. **Essentially, let your retirement account do the deal—not you!** This allows you to potentially defer any and all taxes, OR you may be able to avoid any taxes altogether with the use of a Roth IRA or Roth 401(k).

Avoiding Prohibited Transactions

When self-directing your retirement account, you must be aware of the prohibited transaction rules. This is typically the topic your standard financial advisor will jump on and warn you about in order to scare you off from self-directing. Your advisor (looking out for your best interest—*that was sarcastic*), may also tell you to avoid self-directing because you could get audited, have penalties, or lose your retirement account altogether. Don't listen to them! **Yes, there are rules to follow, but investors have been using the self-directing strategy for over 30 years and have made billions of dollars doing it.**

The general rules regarding prohibited transactions are found in Internal Revenue Code 4975 and the Employee Retirement Income Security Act (ERISA). These rules don't restrict what your account can invest in but rather *whom* your IRA may transact with. In short, the prohibited transaction rules restrict your retirement account from engaging in a transaction with a disqualified person.

The rationale behind the prohibited transaction rules is that the federal government doesn't want tax-advantaged accounts conducting transactions with parties who are close enough to the account owner that they could be designed to avoid or unfairly minimize tax by altering the true fair market value or price of the investment.

Disqualified persons include the account owner, his or her spouse, children, parents, and certain business partners. For example, your retirement account could not buy a rental property that is owned by your father. The IRA must hold the property strictly for investment. **The property may be leased to your cousin, friend, sister, or a random unrelated third party, but it cannot be leased or used by the IRA owner or the aforementioned prohibited family members or business partners.** Only after the property has been distributed from the retirement account to the IRA owner may the owner or family members reside at or benefit from the property.

Of course, this short section can't do the topic justice, and anyone self-directing an account is well advised to speak with a tax advisor or lawyer that thoroughly understands the topic. This does not mean getting advice from your IRA custodian or 401(k) administrator. **If you get audited or make a mistake, you pay the penalties and taxes, and no custodian or administrator will stand behind you.** Their fine print always instructs the investor to get their own personal advisor—someone that is licensed and carries malpractice insurance to ensure the advice they give you is correct.

The Special Purpose LLC Structure

Using an LLC for your retirement account projects is becoming more and more commonplace. Many self-directed retirement account owners, particularly those buying real estate, use a Limited Liability Company (LLC) as the vehicle to hold their retirement account assets. This structure has become popularly known as an IRA/LLC, which could mean an LLC with any type of retirement account as an owner or part owner. I love these structures, because they give more control and autonomy to the retirement account owner to access money quickly to make investments. The account owners can often simply write a check, which is why these accounts are frequently called checkbook IRAs.

In a typical IRA, your custodian holds your investment in their company name for your IRA's benefit (e.g., property is owned as ABC Trust Company FBO John Smith IRA). The custodian then receives the income and pays the expenses for the investment at the account owner's direction and instruction. If it's a 401(k), your trustee

RANDY LUEBKE

In a self-directed retirement plan, you are allowed to invest in anything that isn't illegal, prohibited, a collectable, shares in an S Corporation, or life insurance. That's it! Every other investment opportunity on the planet becomes an option to you. Wall Street brokers will not tell you this because they are prohibited from advising you to invest in anything that would cause you to move money away from their firm—a practice called selling away. If they do suggest you invest your IRA funds in real estate, for example, they will likely be in violation of their employment agreement and, because they are not licensed in real estate, they may also be in violation of the law as well. Just because they cannot tell you to do this does not make it a bad idea. I recall seeking this type of advice before I became a licensed advisor. My Wall Street advisor was a great guy—honest and smart. When he presented me with my financial plan, I asked him, "where's the real estate component?" as I had specifically told him I wanted to invest in real estate. He pointed out proudly that he had allocated a percentage of my "diversified portfolio into alternative investments including REITs" (Real Estate Investment Trusts). I told him that REITs were nothing more than a security that invests in real estate. I wanted to invest in real estate directly and not have someone else do it for me. I wanted the profits and, more importantly, the control. He looked at me like a puppy dog, tilting his head from side-to-side as he had no idea whatsoever about what I really wanted. Even if he did, he would have been unable to help me.

of the plan, which could be you, holds the investment in the name of the 401(k) and the employee account name. All cash flow and profits from the investment then go right back to the 401(k) allocated to the employee's account. However, the LLC provides a lot of ancillary benefits, such as easy access to the money and asset protection for you from the operations of the LLC.

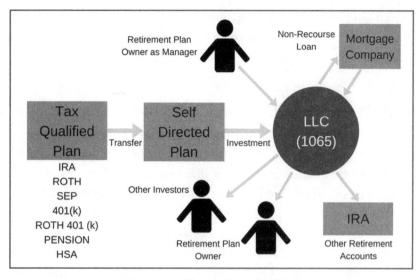

Figure 13.1—Illustration of IRA/LLC

You also have low expenses for an IRA/LLC as there are no custodial fees. The IRA/LLC can be managed by the retirement account owner, who then directs the LLC; the LLC takes title to the assets, pays the expenses to the investment, and receives the income from the investment. For the rest of this discussion, when we reference the "IRA/LLC," this is an LLC that may be owned, in part or wholly, by an IRA, 401(k), or any type of retirement account. Figure 13.1 shows an example of what an IRA/LLC structure may look like.

It is also important to note that there is a lot of misunderstanding and misdirection in the self-directing industry regarding the role of the account owner as also the IRA/LLC manager. The truth is that there is a lot of flexibility and allowable duties the IRA owner can perform as the IRA/LLC manager, such as making investment decisions, writing checks, and hiring property managers or vendors to complete the day-to-day activities/duties of the IRA/LLC operations.

Of course, there are other considerations and several restrictions to the IRA owner as the manager, such as not receiving compensation or personal benefit from the IRA/LLC. Please be sure to consult an attorney before establishing an IRA/LLC and not just trusting a document prep company or letting a custodian or nonlawyer take you through the process. **If you go that route, you'll be on the hook if something goes wrong.**

Possible Tax Bite: UDFI and UBIT Taxes

There is always a tax bite it seems, right? Well, there are two types of taxes that can blindside a self-directed retirement account owner. It's important that an investor enters their projects with their eyes wide open and evaluate if, and how much, these taxes might impact them.

The first is called unrelated business income tax (UBIT). This tax doesn't apply to retirement accounts with passive investments like rental real estate or capital gains or on dividend profits from a C corporation (i.e., what you get from publicly traded stock owned by your IRA) as those types of income are specifically exempt from UBIT tax. **However, anything that creates ordinary income will trigger the tax—and it's serious.** The UBIT tax rate is 39.6 percent once you have $12,000 of annual net profits.

A few examples of businesses that create UBIT are ones selling goods or services or a real estate project doing a development or rehabbing more than three properties a year. Being subject to UBIT tax isn't the end of the world. There are some structuring options to minimize the tax, such as a C corporation "Blocker Company," which can cut the tax rate in half in many instances. You will need to review the possible impact of the UBIT tax with your tax professional.

The second tax is the unrelated debt-financed income (UDFI) tax. **This tax only applies if there is acquisition debt on the sale of the asset held by the IRA.** It's the same rate as UBIT, but it only applies on the debt ratio of the asset. For example, if you sell a property worth $100,000 and the debt remaining on the property is $70,000, then the debt-to-equity ratio is 70 percent. Next, calculate the amount of profit on the property. Assume you purchased the property for $60,000, and the adjusted basis is $50,000. Your profit would be $50,000, and 70 percent of that profit would be subject to UDFI. That's $35,000 taxed under the UBIT tax table and paid on a Form 990-T.

TIP FOR FINANCIAL FREEDOM

The primary strategy to avoid UDFI is to move your assets from a self-directed IRA to a self-directed 401(k). UDFI does not apply to a 401(k)!

Avoid the Naysayers

Now, is self-directing for everyone? Absolutely not. If you listen to Jim Cramer on the TV show *Mad Money*, he will tell everyone that they are crazy to self-direct. However, this is the typical Wall Street approach to this topic: "Let us invest your money. We know best—not you!"

If you believe your financial advisor is more knowledgeable than you and/or you don't have the time to get more engaged in your retirement plan investments, then certainly stay away from self-directing. However, if you want more freedom and feel you have some great ideas on how your IRA could be making more money, then look into self-directing.

Bottom line: you have to be more engaged in your retirement planning. You know this, you probably feel guilty about it, and it's time you do something about it. Study more and get engaged. Whether you decide to self-direct or stay with your financial advisor, you will be informed—and pleasantly surprised at your many options, and the potential you have to succeed in this area.

Additional Resources

For more up-to-date resources and information on how to open your self-directed IRA with a new account or rollover visit www.directedira. com. To open your own self-directed Solo 401(k), in which you can be the trustee and manage your own 401(k) bank account and investments, visit www.navbrs.com.

Finally, please note that my law partner, Mat Sorensen, is the nationwide legal authority on this topic and author of the best-selling book, *Self Directed IRA Handbook: An Authoritative Guide for*

Self Directed Retirement Plan Investors and Their Advisors (SOKOH Publishing, 2013). To learn more about his book and pick up a copy, visit www.sdirahandbook.com.

§ § §

TAKEAWAY 1—Self-directing your retirement plan means investing your retirement account in what you know best and moving your retirement vehicles like an IRA, 401(k), SEP, or pension away from your financial advisor into a structure that gives you more control.

TAKEAWAY 2—Consider an LLC owned by your retirement account to save administrative costs, give you more control quickly and easily over your account, provide asset protection, and partner with other accounts or investors. You can even use your debt to leverage or expand the investments within your retirement account.

TAKEAWAY 3—Understand the rules regarding UBIT and UDFI taxes, prohibited transactions, and what role you can play as the owner in managing your IRA/LLCs. There are just a few rules that are easy to abide by, and you will still have the flexibility you have never dreamed about with your IRA.

TAKEAWAY 4—The primary goal here is to consider another bucket to fill from the profits of your business. You can even get a tax deduction to fund these self-directed accounts and then invest in creative ways that can get you unbelievable investment returns.

TAKEAWAY 5—Invest in what you know, and build more options for your retirement!

WHY RENTAL REAL ESTATE, AND HOW TO DO IT RIGHT

Real estate, particularly rental real estate, is one of the most important "buckets" to deploy a portion of the profits from your business. Real estate has a variety of unique investment characteristics that can not only hedge against the ups and downs of your business and industry, but can also generate wealth and cash flow that can change your entire perspective about your business—in a good way.

I have said it repeatedly that an intense and focused entrepreneur can reinvest too much of their profit back into their business. That passion is what makes an entrepreneur tick, and often successfully, and that's not a bad thing, but certainly that overcommitment to reinvesting can go too far and risk too much. **Rental real estate can be the weight that provides harmony to your investment portfolio.**

Over my career, I have met successful entrepreneurs that are well balanced and wise with their business and overall asset mix. They have found the right mix between reinvestment and redeployment of their profits. Their financial maturity amazes me and do you know what common characteristic they all share? **They all own some degree of rental real estate.**

Because of this observation and the ongoing success in my own life living this principle, I started recommending years ago that all my clients purchase at least one rental property a year—no matter how inexpensive—for the tax planning and wealth-building benefits.

The Art of Buying Real Estate

First, understand from the outset that your reasons for not buying real estate shouldn't be lack of capital, credit, or know-how. Each of these things can be acquired through time, energy, and partnerships with others who are stronger in the areas where you are weak. Most importantly, as a business owner, the profits from your business can, and should, be the seed for a different bucket of wealth you can rely on.

Let's go through a checklist of reasons why buying rental real estate can be a life-changing experience and strength to your primary business:

§ The tax write-offs are incredible when you treat your rental property as a small business. You may get to use those deductions against your ordinary income, but if not, they will carry forward until you sell the property.

§ The value of the property will grow tax-free until you sell, and you may be able to use other strategies to delay or avoid the gain entirely.

§ The vast majority of rental properties allow investors to create tax-free cash flow based on the amount of write-offs related to the property.

§ You can leverage your money to buy more investment properties and thus increase your **Return on Investment** (ROI). That's something you can't do with stocks, bonds, or mutual funds.

§ You can involve family members as employees, travel to check on your rentals, and take these expenses as valid business deductions.

§ You can enjoy average appreciation and growth that outper-forms Wall Street and a variety of other benefits.

 RANDY LUEBKE

Just like people, real estate comes in all shapes, sizes, and colors. Just like people, real estate is complex. It is the combination of this diversity and complexity that effectively keeps Wall Street away from investing in it directly. Sure, Wall Street offers their REIT's. If you are wealthy and qualify as an Accredited Investor, you may have access to limited partnerships and private offerings that involve real estate. TICs, or Tenant in Common products, are security instruments that own real estate. What is in common with all Wall Street real estate investments is that someone else besides you is in control. Now, I get it; this can be a good thing too. With control comes responsibility, and it takes time and expertise. All that being said, again, there is no perfect investment. While real estate may be called a "passive investment" by the IRS, anyone who actually owns real estate knows that it is the polar opposite! **Real estate is a great investment for anyone who is willing to put in the time to learn about it**—someone who is smart enough to make informed choices and good decisions. However, if you think you can buy a piece of real estate and just make a bunch of money without putting in some work and effort, you are going to be sorely disappointed. Instead, you want to jump into real estate with both feet and your eyes wide open. Embrace the diversity. It allows you to pick and choose from an almost endless array of real estate investment options. Exploit that complexity. Make it work for you. Let it stop others from getting into the game, but do not let it stop you.

It's interesting, but I have often said that rental real estate can serve as a forced retirement. Once purchased, a rental can create a sense of urgency to maintain and improve the property, and "being stuck with it" will motivate us to push through the bad cash flow at times. **I say this because Americans are generally terrible at saving money.** We may try to save a few dollars in our IRA or 401(k), or even in an after-tax account, but let's face it: on average, our savings rate is pretty pathetic.

Rental properties, however, are something we can identify with that makes sense. We can identify with them as another business and not an intangible investment in a brokerage account somewhere. For whatever reason (perhaps because they are tangible and you can actually visit the property), rentals give us a greater sense of commitment.

Is Real Estate for Everyone?

I certainly want to acknowledge the risks of buying real estate; this type of investment requires commitment and isn't for everyone. It's important that investors get properly educated and not rush into the process.

Is there risk involved in buying rental property? Certainly! Is it sometimes hard to manage rental property, both locally and from a distance? Yes. But knowledge is power and will reduce fear. **I encourage all my clients to find inspiration and guidance from other successful real estate investors, while making sure they are cautious, careful, and conservative.** I also urge them to focus on cash flow and the numbers—never just appreciation.

I know it seems that at times there can be so much misinformation in the marketplace regarding real estate investing that it makes this whole process seem daunting—that it's too expensive, too difficult, or only for rich people. **Please know that I have had clients buy dozens of properties all over the country on a meager budget with creativity and determination.** And, despite the risks, I still feel strongly that buying real estate can be one of the most secure paths to creating tax-free cash flow in today's economy and a major reserve of equity for retirement.

Four Benefits of Owning Rental Property

As previously mentioned, **a good rental property strategy will not only build immediate cash flow and provide a long-term retirement strategy, but it can also create some incredible tax benefits if you plan wisely.** Figure 14.1 is a diagram that I have used countless times in presentations and lectures around the country to help identify these four benefits.

1. *Property appreciation.* I'm not advising a "fix and flip" strategy. You should plan on keeping your rental property for at least seven to ten years. As such, appreciation is one of the key benefits in your ROI. In fact, the National Association of Realtors© has reported that real estate nationwide has averaged more than 6.74 percent appreciation annually during the past 50 years. This rate of return outperforms the S&P 500 and most Wall Street investments. I realize that not all property in every market experiences this type of growth, but this average is definitely something to consider. Don't discount the power of property appreciation.

2. *Mortgage reduction.* This is an often-overlooked benefit to owning rental property. If you purchase wisely, the property should be at least breaking even in cash flow if you have tenants. The renter is essentially paying the mortgage for you. This principal reduction within the mortgage is an ongoing tax-free benefit,

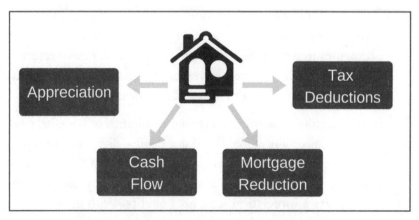

Figure 14.1—The Four Benefits of Rental Real Estate

along with appreciation, that you can calculate and count on over time. Keep this in your spreadsheet as you calculate your total ROI.

3. *Tax savings and deductions.* It's no secret that rental properties lose money on paper. But with the power of depreciation, the fact that you get to deduct the mortgage interest that your renter is essentially paying for you, and the additional deductions you can take for travel, property taxes, HOA fees, repairs, maintenance, home office, supplies, cell phone, etc., the tax benefits add up very quickly! **However, how you are classified as a real estate investor is absolutely critical.** The IRS may classify you as passive, active, or professional, unless you take proactive steps to understand and elect the best classification for your situation on your tax return. Be careful as you work with your tax advisor because the benefits vary widely.

4. *Cash flow.* **Simply stated, good rental property creates cash flow; bad property does not.** Purchasing good cash-flow property causes the other benefits to fall right into place. If the economic downturn and the drop in real estate values have taught us anything, it's that we must analyze and purchase property based on cash flow above all else. **Cash flow is essentially your rents less the direct costs of the property known as PITI** (**P**rinciple and **I**nterest payment, property **T**axes, and **I**nsurance). As good cash flow, the property should at least exceed PITI or more. Cash flow is a key part of your ROI when you analyze a property. You will take into account all your cash expenses to determine what your cash-on-cash rate of return is as you try to minimize cash expenses related to the property. Conversely, you'll want to maximize your tax.

Savvy investors realize that these four quadrants, or benefits, work together and can produce double—if not triple—digit rates of return on their leveraged rental properties. **Your overall ROI analysis of any property will include cash flow, the mortgage principal paydown, property appreciation, and tax benefits.** With these benefits and the substantial ROI, it's no surprise that the wealthiest and most

" RANDY LUEBKE

Oftentimes, and I mean REALLY often, after someone invests in real estate, they regret it. They become frustrated with their property manager, the tenants, whatever. If all the activities don't get them, when they start to analyze their numbers they can become even more frustrated, especially when that wonderful real estate investment is losing money. I agree, we do not invest in anything to lose money; however, real estate is different. Often, while on the surface it may appear as though someone is losing money, when you dig under the hood, you find that it is providing you with an excellent profit.

Mark has provided you with a nice overview of the four different returns one receives from real estate. The problem is that only one of them, cash flow, is obvious to the investor because you can see the rents coming in each month, and you write the checks to cover the expenses. Once you add back the principal reduction, the appreciation, and the depreciation, you start to see the whole picture. If you don't see a great return when you put all four of these together, it's important you realize you have more options than just selling. That's the beauty of real estate. **"**

successful people in America hold rental property as a large part of their portfolios.

All this should be enticing, and as you do your due diligence, you can learn more about investing in real estate by networks with successful investors. Through networking, you can learn how they succeeded. As is the case with most aspects of life, especially investing, there are always some potential pitfalls that you want to know about in advance to avoid.

How to Avoid the Common Pitfalls of Real Estate Investing

Learning to invest in real estate is just like any other business or career. It takes time to get good at it. **You'll make mistakes, and that's OK.**

It doesn't mean real estate is bad or in turn that you are bad at real estate. Too many people get frustrated very easily and give up, and this is not only the case with real estate.

Study and learn as much as you can about the process, the industry, and the areas in which you are interested in investing. As I have watched clients create, as well as lose, rental real estate fortunes, I have learned common themes and strategies that have helped more succeed with fewer mistakes. Here are six concepts I encourage you to consider when investing in rental properties.

§ *Have a master rental property analysis spreadsheet.* This is an Excel spreadsheet to analyze any and all possible deals. That's right— **you're not going to buy the first rental property you see this year.** Run every property through the gauntlet of your spreadsheet. Own your spreadsheet. Know every column. Start with the Fair Market Value (FMV), money down, improvements, and mortgage/carrying cost—then move it through rental income, expenses, and wrap it up with a cash-on-cash ROI figure. If, after putting the numbers into all the columns the ROI is not good, or is not in your favor, move on to the next property. **Base your decision on the key factors generated by your spreadsheet.** This is why you took fifth-grade math—embrace it. Figure 14.2 on page 141 demonstrates what a basic spreadsheet analysis would look like. Of course, they can be basic or quite elaborate, and you will want to tailor one to your individual needs.

§ *Remember, you are buying "numbers."* **Too many investors get emotional about their purchase and can even envision themselves living in the rental property they are analyzing. This is a terrible mistake.** In these situations, the investor often over-improves the property, investing far too much time or capital and blowing their ROI out of the water. **Don't think your rental property needs granite countertops; instead, realize you aren't buying a property, you are buying numbers.** What do your dollars get you in "dollars and cents"? Remember, it's not about your personal wants and needs; it's about how much you can make off the property.

Rental Property Analysis

Monthly Operating Income	Property
Average Monthly Rent per Unit	$ 800.00
Total Rental Income	-
% Vacancy and Reserve	5.00%
Total Vacancy Loss	40.00
Other Monthly Income (laundry, vending, parking, etc.)	
Gross Monthly Operating Income	760.00

Monthly Operating Expenses	
Property Management Fees	80.00
Repairs and Maintenance	40.00
Real Estate Taxes	50.00
Rental Property Insurance	30.00
Homeowners/Property Association Fees	
Utilities	
Pest Control	
Accounting and Legal	
Monthly Operating Expenses	200.00

Net Operating Income (NOI)	
Total Annual Operating Income	9,120.00
Total Annual Operating Expense	2,400.00
Annual Net Operating Income	6,720.00

Loan Information	
Down Payment	10,000.00
Loan Amount	70,000.00
Acquisition Costs and Loan Fees	2,500.00
Length of Mortgage (years)	30
Annual Interest Rate	5.000%
Initial Investment	12,500.00
Monthly Mortgage Payment (PI)	375.78
Annual Interest	289.90
Annual Principal	85.88
Total Annual Debt Service	4,509.30

Cash Flow and ROI	
Total Monthly Cash Flow (before taxes)	**184.22**
Total Annual Cash Flow (before taxes)	**2,210.70**
Cash on Cash Return (ROI)	**17.69%**

Figure 14.2—Basic Rental Property Analysis

CHAPTER 14 § Why Rental Real Estate, and How to Do It Right

Pouring a lot more money into the property to get a higher rental rate can backfire.

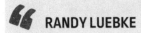
RANDY LUEBKE

The first thing I do with my clients when evaluating their current real estate holdings is to create a detailed "Schedule of Real Estate Owned." It's not enough to know how much your rents are, your mortgage payments, and a few other numbers. You need to see ALL the numbers: the purchase price, the current value, the current rent, maintenance costs, mortgage expenses, and so on. At first, accumulating all this information in one place may seem like a lot of unnecessary work. It's not! Getting all your facts and figures together in one place so you can see them, monitor them, and evaluate them all make you a better investor. It's similar to an airplane pilot. I'm sure that you've peeked into the cockpit of a plane and viewed what appears to be hundreds of dials, buttons, guages, and gadgets. Do you think that the airline pilot wants to look at a bunch of useless junk and clutter during your six-hour flight, day-after day after day? Or, do you think that the pilot may feel that having all of this information available at their fingertips is a good idea and that it may provide some useful insights as to how to make more informed decisions about managing the plane?

§ *Do your research.* Let me say that again: do your research and then do it again. I see so many new investors buy the first rental they see. Take your time. Also, don't look at a property as to "why shouldn't I get this?" —look at it as to "why should I get this property?" **Make the numbers prove it to you. Don't assume you're going to buy it unless you find something wrong with it.** I love a positive attitude and glass-half-full approach, and thus, this has been one of my greatest learning experiences. I have trained myself over the years to be a lot more skeptical—at least when it comes to analyzing rentals.

- *Buy local IF you can.* Let me repeat the words "if you can." That's the key. **Don't get hyperfocused on buying local so you can check on the property.** It's OK if you don't buy local. It's far more important to buy QUALITY rental properties (good bones, reputable location, ease of upkeep, etc.) RATHER than LOCAL. But if you are living in an area where there is a strong rental market with legitimate returns on investment (that aren't dependent on putting down a fortune) then consider yourself lucky. Gain some experience, put in some sweat equity, and shop till you drop!

- *Learn to manage your property manager.* Yes, unless you are a full-time real estate investor and one tough SOB—get a property manager. If you don't have the temperament to be tough and start eviction proceedings three days after a tenant is late, have a personal intervention with yourself. You may not be cut out to be a property manager even if the property is local. You may not have the time, skills, or system to be your own property manager. **Be a realist. Your time could be better spent looking for other rentals, doing the books, or running your business.** So with that said, always—and I mean always—have a budget in your rental property analysis for a property manager (approximately 10 percent of gross rents). Even if you have visions of grandeur and start managing, you want the budget to stick in a property manager.

- *Bundle.* I recently met with a client that had five properties in four states. They were great properties, but seriously. Look at the inefficiency (and headaches) of registering an LLC in four states, doing four state tax returns, having four different property managers, four different trips to at least occasionally check on your rentals, and four different rental markets to understand and follow. Perhaps when you have 25-plus rentals and you can afford to make your full-time job managing your rentals and property managers, then you can tackle four or more markets. **For now, purchase rental properties in just one or two markets, or "bundle" as it's called.** Using this type of "bundling," your property managers can handle a few properties at the same time. You will also save travel time and expenses. **Plus, you can familiarize yourself with a few good locations rather than having properties scattered all over the place.** You can also be more efficient with your tax and legal planning and save a lot of time and money by bundling.

Protecting Yourself from Your Rental

Owning your rentals in an entity (typically an LLC—Limited Liability Company) is just one of many asset protection strategies for protecting your personal assets from liability arising from your rental activities. However, I don't recommend relying upon an entity alone as your sole asset protection strategy. **Instead, I recommend a multi-barrier approach that creates as many impediments as possible between you and any would-be litigant.** This would include a good lease agreement, proper insurance, operating as a responsible landlord, and maybe even an umbrella insurance policy.

You certainly don't have to set up an LLC for each rental you purchase, but at least have one. You could even risk having multiple eggs in one basket—meaning that you have several valuable rentals in one entity, risking them with each other. HOWEVER, don't risk your personal assets by owning rentals in your own name or trust. I realize you have to think twice in expensive LLC states, but at least explore your options for an entity structure. It's always in your best interest to have personal assets that litigants, in a very litigious society, cannot easily go after.

TIP FOR FINANCIAL FREEDOM

Once you have a rental property an LLC is critical for protection.

---

§ § §

TAKEAWAY 1—There are four significant advantages to owning rental real estate: property appreciation, mortgage reduction, tax savings and deductions, and cash flow.

TAKEAWAY 2—You need to determine if real estate is for you—it's not right for everyone. If you choose to go this route, you need to set up a Master Rental Property Analysis spreadsheet and list all real estate possibilities on the spreadsheet to analyze.

TAKEAWAY 3—As is the case with any undertaking, you need to learn a lot about what differentiates a good rental property from a bad one. You also need to learn the tricks of the rental trade (such as how to find and hire an experienced property manager) and the potential pitfalls, such as the inefficiency of having properties spread out across various states or regions. You cannot just jump in, buy real estate properties, and figure it all out later. Start by taking a trip around the learning curve.

VACATION PROPERTY AND TIMESHARES: STRATEGIES AND PITFALLS

Have you ever taken a vacation that was amazing? Maybe you visited a location so unique and so wonderful that you knew you would want to return again and again. Maybe it was that place at the beach or the slopeside condo where you could ski. Whatever and wherever it was, you just had to go look in the windows of one of the local real estate shops to see how much a little piece of heaven would cost you. The next thing you know, you are talking with a realtor. Shortly thereafter, you find yourself signing a contract to purchase a beach house, cabin, or condo—a "vacation home."

Fast-forward a few years. Now you've spent a fortune refurnishing, remodeling, and stocking your second home.

You're starting to realize that now you need two of everything, and that somehow things seem to break when you are gone for a while even though no one's been using them. You realize how much you are spending on airfare or how long the drive to this place really is when you've made the same trip 30 times. You also realize that you stopped exploring other new and exciting places you once planned to visit because it's been cheaper to stay at your vacation home than to rent a condo somewhere else. Plus, you feel guilty that your place is vacant 90 percent of the year.

What you once thought would be "the" place for you and your children and grandchildren to gather and create memories seems more like a very expensive, money-sucking, problematic place where you spend most of your time fixing what's broken and cleaning it because no one does that as well as you do. After all, doesn't everyone want to go on vacation to be a handyman and cleaning crew knowing you've paid for everything in between?

Let's face it. For most people, I've done a pretty accurate job of describing what ownership feels like when you've purchased a second home. It's great in the beginning, but once the reality hits, it's just not that much fun. You've tied up a lot of money. You continue to pay even more. Face it. A second home is really a very expensive toy that you will eventually get tired of playing with, especially when it continues to break and cost you money to own.

For Those in "The Market"

If you are considering a vacation rental, I want to make a few suggestions and give some cautionary points. First, please keep reading below as I give options to those already in a pickle, for lack of a better word, with a vacation home. I will discuss the particulars of making a vacation rental profitable. But nonetheless, here are a few important considerations:

- § Before buying a vacation rental, assume the worst when it comes to rental income. I'm not saying they can't be a bad investment for cash flow OR that you might even break even with the operational costs or mortgage—HOWEVER, **you should be at least willing to live with bad cash flow; otherwise, it's probably not a good idea.** Ask yourself the hard question: could you afford it if the real estate market crashed or if the economy took a nosedive and rents disappeared? You need to be able to live with that answer. My wife and I bought a vacation rental for investment in 2006. How do you think that went? That's right, hard questions and hard answers.

§ If you're OK with my last point and still feel it's going to be a great rental property, read carefully the section below on Vacation Rental Strategy.

§ Consider a partnership with family or friends. I have set up a lot of LLCs to own a shared vacation property where owners split expenses and use by 25 percent, 50 percent, thirds, or various combinations. **A quality LLC Operating Agreement can outline weeks for use, taking turns regarding management, and how costs will be shared.** It could make it much more affordable, and you won't feel so guilty when you aren't using the property.

RANDY LUEBKE

If you are going to partner with family or friends, **make sure you have clearly defined terms regarding use and costs, including repairs.** I've seen some nightmares regarding damages to the property or simply the costs to put on a new roof. If you don't have the procedures for a worst-case scenario in writing, they may not be your friends any longer or family reunions will be extremely uncomfortable.

Options for Those Already with a Vacation Home

Now that several years have gone by and the reality has set in, the extended family is still enjoying the property on your dime, while meanwhile you are setting up your own personal intervention session with your financial advisors, assuming you know you need a change, what do you do? You essentially have four options:

1. *Run the numbers and sell.* You might take a loss after all the improvements and selling costs, or more than likely, you at least feel like it's a loss after all the blood, sweat, and tears you put into the property. Perhaps those nights at the Ritz Carlton would not have been that expensive after all. *Bottom line*: **don't get emotional about the property and selling. If the numbers don't make sense—get out!**

2. *Keep it no matter what.* But you really do like your vacation home. You love the area and you enjoy yourselves after a couple days, once you've completed all the necessary work. Maybe the opportunity cost is worth it. **That's OK, just be real with yourself, enjoy it, and quit complaining.** Your guests at the home don't appreciate the ranting.

3. *Partner with family or friends.* I mentioned this above to those considering buying a vacation home. Maybe it's time to call up some of those that signed the guest book and make them an offer they can't refuse. They could come in for 50 percent, 25 percent, or any variation thereof. It's a great way to share costs and an LLC will shield you from the liability of others while the property and the Operating Agreement will define the rules of ownership, use, and shared costs. *Bottom line*: **it's their turn for an intervention. Tell them they can't keep using the cabin if they don't share in the costs and you're going to sell if they don't buy in.** It just might do the trick and be the perfect equation for your pocketbook.

4. *Time to create some rental income.* **Rather than sell, you decide to rent it. After all, it's vacant most of the time anyway.** Now, I know this can be uncomfortable for some of you to realize tenants are going to be sitting on your couch and using that Sleep Number bed you put in the master bedroom for those long weekends, but hey, why not cash in on that downtime, generate some income, and mitigate some of those expenses? This might be a viable option and help make the numbers work

just enough so you can keep the home for your use during those special holidays. But are you ready for what this entails? Please read further regarding the Vacation Rental Strategy below.

Vacation Rental Strategy

Buying a vacation home that's *also* creating rental income can be a fantastic idea if all the pieces come together. Please don't assume that just because you want to vacation in the area, and it appears there are lots of nightly rentals, it's going to be a success. I have had a lot of clients sorely disappointed with their vacation rental strategy. **I strongly encourage you to do extra research and due diligence on the property and area, even more than you would with a typical rental property.** There are a lot of unique aspects to a vacation rental property.

First, consider looking for a vacation rental that is already a part of a rental group. Maybe it's a condo in a community or building that has a built-in rental booking and cleaning service. There are several benefits of this in that it already has a track record with a "rent roll" (showing prior days and income of rent), it is clearly zoned and currently being used as a rental, and it will of course come furnished with rental-friendly furniture. **You might pay a little bit more for a property already creating cash flow, but at least you are buying a known commodity, or otherwise stated, you clearly will know what you are getting into.**

Next, if you have a property that you hope to use as a nightly rental, keep in mind you just got in into the hotel business. Not only do you have to consider the amount of hotel/motel space in town, you now have to market your home with the other rental units in town. I suggest you immediately play "renter" on several websites and see what your options are in quality and price. See where your property measures up, and see if you are OK with the rental rates your property would demand.

Don't forget repairs and the type of furniture and fixtures already in your property. You thought that a lot of things broke while you were gone and not using your home. Wait until you see what breaks when strangers use it. **If this is a new property you are purchasing, get some advice from other vacation rental owners on what type of furniture and fixtures to buy that can handle the wear and tear.** If you are starting to rent a property you've already furnished for your personal use, you will more than likely have to start transitioning your furniture into more durable-type pieces.

Now comes the booking, cleaning, check-ins, checkouts, linens, towels, and other supplies. **This is where you will start to work with a vacation property rental manager and create a system for the property.** I'm sure you know there is a growing number of entrepreneurial property owners renting out vacation homes to travelers. Evolve Rental Key Network shows that profits can be as high as $23k to $27k in annual net incomes across several vacation rental platforms for the typical rental. You'll want to find the right platform for your type of property and area, using services such as Homeaway, Airbnb, VRBO, AirBand, Bookings, Tripadvisor, etc. if you can provide a vacation rental to visitors who prefer to become (or try to become) a part of the community rather than a visitor or tourist.

A word of caution, however: Many communities HATE having vacation rentals in their neighborhood. After all, they purchased

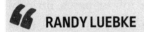

RANDY LUEBKE

Before buying your rental vacation property, make sure you confirm what the local rules are regarding nightly rentals in that specific neighborhood. Don't make any assumptions, and don't stop there! Call the city or local jurisdiction that manages this issue and see if there is legislation in the works and if they are holding hearings. You can even check the local paper in the area to see what the rumblings are. Several of my clients have bought properties that were zoned for rentals at the time, and then had the carpet pulled out from under them with legislation that came down shortly thereafter prohibiting nightly rentals in the neighborhood of their new property.

a home where they are living year-round. They like to come and go, and everyone enjoys a level of regularity in their home life and surroundings. The last thing they want is "party family," or worse "party friends," moving in for a few days who are coming and going, staying up late, and making plenty of noise. Also, some people don't want vacationers who have no respect for the people in the community and may leave garbage on your lawn, around the neighborhood, or anywhere they choose. The potential for crime is also a concern.

As a result, many people have purchased second homes with the anticipation of renting them only to find resentment and opposition from the locals. Moreover, if those locals can become organized and grab the attention of the local government, sometimes they can pass ordinances to ban short-term rentals altogether, blowing a great big hole in your business model. It's important to look at local laws, including HOA rules, as to what your options are for a vacation rental and the rules you need to follow.

Regrettably, I also have to mention taxes. Sorry. All of that incredible net income and profit comes with a cost. **Remember how I stated above that you are now in the hotel business? Well, that's exactly how the IRS sees it as well.** Thus, you have to report this rental activity on a Schedule C, and not Schedule E (as you would with a typical rental). It's not the end of the world, but you need to implement a little creative tax planning to handle the tax impact (a topic beyond the scope of this book). A simple meeting with your tax advisor should address this issue.

Also, don't forget the hospitality tax that many local jurisdictions are implementing. If a local city or township doesn't directly prohibit nightly rentals in your area, they can very well impose a hefty hospitality tax to discourage the rentals in that area or simply as an effort to cash in on the fun as well. Make sure you research this issue carefully before jumping in with both feet.

Bottom line: **the point of this section is that as an entrepreneur, you should understand that owning a vacation rental is clearly owning another business.** You may find that there is value in having a nice place in your favorite vacation spot and not having to worry about where you stay when you visit, but just make sure to do your homework and run the numbers.

Timeshares—Not a Bad Idea

Then, there are timeshares. **The concept behind a timeshare is brilliant. As most people understand their second home will be vacant 50 weeks a year, why not buy only a week or two instead?** That seems very practical in comparison to owning it all by yourself. Moreover, you will have an HOA and a professional management team to take care of the maintenance and repairs. You will have the comfort of knowing that you will return time after time to a place you liked and you won't have any of those bad surprises, checking into the hotel overlooking the air conditioner banks. **Plus, you can trade your weeks with others and stay virtually anywhere in the world.** You've got the flexibility to travel, and compared to whole ownership, the timeshare is a bargain.

All that being said, I have discovered three things that make the difference between happiness and a headache. One, buy your timeshare in the place you want to travel to most in the event that renting it out does not produce a net benefit to you (in which case, you'll be the one using it most). Second, don't count on being able to swap it out with others. Many think that the timeshare will open up all these other potential properties to use—guaranteed. That's not always a realistic perspective. Make sure you can live using that *specific* timeshare if you have to and be comfortable with the cost.

Third, and most importantly, buy it used, and not new— period. There is a used timeshare market out there that you may not be aware of. For instance, a new timeshare has to pay a large

---

TIP FOR FINANCIAL FREEDOM

Don't buy a timeshare from the retail market.

> ## ❝ RANDY LUEBKE
>
> For some of the larger developers like Marriott, for example, there is a team in place to sell timeshare units. It's literally almost like having a Multiple Listing Service (like buying and selling a standard home) to market your timeshare. The big difference is that the commission you pay to sell is much higher than you would pay for a traditional real estate transaction. I could go on, but I think you get the picture. **Don't buy while the circus is in town and everyone was there in attendance. Once the circus has moved on, you could have a very illiquid asset to sell.** HOWEVER, you can visit countless websites selling timeshares of owners with buyer's remorse willing to sell at a deep discount from what they originally paid. **I have personally purchased a timeshare at a 90 percent discount from its original price, and the owners were happy to sell it.** ❞

commission to the sales team. That's a reality. **However, many times people who did purchase a timeshare want out, and you can capitalize on this!** Perhaps they don't like owning even two weeks, or it's the expense of the HOA over which they have no control that gets to them. Whatever the situation, they want out and are now faced with some major hurdles. Top on the list is how do they find a buyer? After all, they are only at their condo two weeks a year. How would they show it to a prospective buyer? What almost always occurs is a market for resales.

The resale market is exactly where you want to buy your timeshare! Often, those discounts can be substantial. Why? Because the owner doesn't use it enough and wants to get out from under it. You can save thousands of dollars and see what the market *really* thinks that timeshare is worth. **Don't trust the high-pressure salesman at the resort when they give you a 90-minute pitch in a conference room overlooking the pool.** Been there, done that!

$ $ $

TAKEAWAY 1—If you already own a vacation home that is costing you, consider four alternatives: Keep it and know the true opportunity cost, sell and cash in—hopefully not at a loss, split up the ownership with other owners, or turn it into a vacation rental property.

TAKEAWAY 2—A vacation rental property can be a good investment, in fact a very profitable one, but it can be extremely tricky. It's important to do even more research and due diligence than you would with a standard rental.

TAKEAWAY 3—If you follow my two rules of buying timeshares, 1) buy where you love to travel, and 2) buy used on the resale market. You will likely be very happy with your purchase, and you will also get the use and the value you anticipated. Leave out either one, and you will likely regret it.

THE PROPER ROLE OF INSURANCE IN YOUR PLAN

As I stated earlier in Chapter 3, I am grateful and honored to have Randy Luebke, an independent voice, contribute to this book. As such, I have asked Randy to author this chapter as an expert and licensed professional to instruct on and sell insurance products. The BENEFIT of having Randy write this chapter is your and my opportunity to get straight answers about how entrepreneurs should view and utilize insurance in their investment portfolio.

$ $ $

Many people are just opposed to life insurance altogether. Even Woody Allen makes jokes about life insurance and life insurance salesmen. But life insurance is no joke, and for those of you who are opposed to life insurance altogether, I ask you to don the coat of possibility for a moment. **Please, at least for the next few paragraphs, be open to the idea that life insurance has a purpose and a place in most everyone's financial plans.**

Life insurance? It's almost an oxymoron, isn't it? First of all, you are not really insuring life. You are insuring against death. Unlike, say, fire insurance where the insured may or may not experience an actual fire, how can you "insure" something that will inevitably occur? Yet, that is exactly what life insurance does, and it has done this in an extremely efficient manner for a very long time.

According to Niall Ferguson Harvard University professor and author of *The Ascent of Money: A Financial History of the World* (Penguin Books, 2009), says the Church of Scotland Ministers deserve the credit for inventing the first true insurance fund more than 250 years ago, in 1744. Since then, the life insurance industry has grown and evolved so that today the variety of programs available is simply mind-boggling.

Yet, even though life insurance has been with us for so long, and even though the product has been marketed and promoted to great lengths, and even though life insurance is owned by millions of consumers, the fact is that most people do not understand what life insurance is or how it actually works. All that is going to change for you—right here, right now.

Insurance Is Not a Waste of Money, It's Leverage

As a financial planner, I'm often told by both consumers and other financial professionals that life insurance is a waste of money. It's just a scheme to enrich the life insurance companies off the backs of their unsuspecting clients. These claims could not be further from the truth, and every day, life insurance companies around the world pay death benefits to the beneficiaries of these policies, providing them with needed and certainly welcome funds. In essence, life insurance provides leverage. **You can pay a relatively small amount of money to the insurance company in the form of a "premium," and the**

insurance company will provide a guaranteed payout of a relatively large amount of money upon the death of the insured. It is that simple. Think of it as a bet you make with the insurance company. The insurance company is betting that you will live longer than you think you may live. Again, an oxymoron because if you win the bet, you lose your life. On the other hand, if the insurance company wins, and you're living longer, you win as well.

 MARK J. KOHLER

My greatest concern with any investment using insurance as the vehicle or tool is the commitment the owner of the policy is making to pay premiums. I have seen so many nightmare experiences of entrepreneurs purchasing cash-value insurance that are not in a secure financial position to make ongoing premiums. Within a few years of buying the policy, their business takes a small downturn; just enough to put a strain on cash flow, and the business owner quits paying the premium. What happens next is sickening. **The policy pays for itself for a short while, then it collapses, and the only winner is the agent and insurance company, with the business owner left holding the bag.** I ALWAYS want to ensure that any of my clients investing in insurance products have the financial depth and wherewithal to continue making payments in good and bad times.

The first element of life insurance is to understand how an insurance company can actually "insure" something that is inevitable, death. The answer is found in what is called the law of large numbers. The law states that if you have a large pool of similar participants that they will exhibit similar and predictable results.

Now, in English: If you toss a coin, there is a 50/50 chance it will land on heads or tails. That said, we also know that if we toss a coin, oftentimes it will end up being heads again and again and again. In our minds we think that since it has been heads so many times that the odds are great that the next time it will come up tails. **While it is** true that it will eventually land on tails, the fact is that it does not matter how many times you toss that coin, the odds of it landing on heads or tails is always 50/50.

Now, instead of having just one coin, what if you had a hundred of your friends, all with coins, and you all tossed those coins at one time. The result would be that some would land on heads and others would land on tails. If you added them all up, you would see the result would be much closer to 50/50. **In fact, if you had a million friends toss coins all at the same time the results would be even closer to 50/50.** That is how the law of large numbers works. Predictable results obtained by similar participants acting in a similar way. The larger the number, the more similar the participants and their action, and the more predictable the results.

Life insurance actuaries can predict that a 34-year-old male living in Florida with no health issues today, not participating in any risky professions or hobbies, with a family history of good health has a predictable life span. Put enough of these guys together into one pool of insureds and, guess what? Those predictions will be very accurate. With this understanding, a life insurance company can offer a life insurance product to all the consumers that fit into that pool for a small premium relative to the death benefit knowing that some of these insured will live longer than predicted while others will not. But, overall, the insurance company will make a profit from the process, and the insureds will have the peace of mind in knowing that if they don't win their bet, their families will receive payment in the form of a death benefit. **A relatively small premium payment in exchange for a relatively large death benefit—yes, life insurance is a leverage play, pure and simple.**

Two Types of Life Insurance

While there are thousands of different life insurance plans available, they all fall into two categories: term and permanent insurance. Term, as the name implies, provides a benefit for a fixed period of time; 10 years, 20 years, and so on. Permanent insurance is in place for life. It's really that simple. Choosing the right insurance plan for you? Well, that is not simple at all.

Term Insurance

This is the most efficient way to purchase life insurance. The premiums paid are calculated to accurately represent the risk of your dying based on your age, your health, and so on. For a very small amount of money, in general, you can purchase a very large amount of benefits so on the surface, it is a great deal. Term insurance has a purpose. Term insurance is not a commodity, even though it is often sold that way. There are many features, issues, and concerns that need to be addressed before purchasing a term policy, and just picking the one with the cheapest premiums is not the proper selection process.

The primary issue with term insurance is that it rarely delivers on its promise. That is, the large majority of term insurance policies, north of 90 percent, will never pay a death benefit. Now, before all you life insurance naysayers jump on the "I hate those crooked insurance companies" bandwagon, you need to understand why this is in fact true. **The fact of the matter is that most people will either outlive the term of the policies or just stop paying the premiums.** These facts contribute to the profitability of these products to the insurance companies, which enables them to keep the premium costs lower. From my perspective, however, I certainly don't want my clients to waste any money and sincerely hope that they outlive the term of the

> ❝ **MARK J. KOHLER**
>
> Keep in mind that this book is not designed to be a resource on life insurance—not even a primer. **We just want to point out that life insurance should not be summarily dismissed as worthless, nor should it be embraced as the ultimate solution to every problem.** It's just another tool in the toolbox, and you should learn about what it can do for you. ❞

policy, as most people will purchase a 20- or 30-year term policy in their 40s or 50s. Consider this: if you win because you live a long life, you lose the bet you made with the insurance company. If you win, you lose? I don't like that concept, so once again, we need to find a way to fix this situation.

Permanent Insurance

It's expensive, right? Well, it can be, but it does not have to be. Traditionally, when people think of permanent insurance, they think of "whole life." The benefit of whole life insurance is that everything is fixed and guaranteed. The premiums are fixed, the death benefits, the cash values—everything is written into the contract. **The problem is that those guarantees are expensive because the insured is shifting all the risks.** The investment risk, the risk of dying, inflation risks, every risk sits on the shoulders of the insurance company. While the insurance companies are used to this and they know how to live in that realm, they also know how to charge for it, and they do.

By the way, I'm going to take a timeout here to speak to those who feel that insurance companies make too much money. I would say, maybe they do; however, I want them to be profitable—very profitable. Why? I want them to be profitable and have lots of money stashed away because I'm paying a premium today hoping that the insurance company will be there in 30 or 40 years to pay the benefits I was promised. Rest assured, insurance companies are very profitable. They have stood the test of time. They were around before our country was founded. They have survived depressions, recessions, wars, and everything else thrown their way over the years. So, yes, I want them to make money so they will be there for me when I need them.

Universal Life Insurance

OK, there's a third type of insurance, a hybrid model—today, there are hybrids in everything. Universal Life, or UL, is a term insurance plan that lives inside the shell of a permanent insurance policy. Designed correctly, a UL will provide the most efficient cost of benefits, which can also be guaranteed for your entire life. **Designed improperly,** the UL can become an even bigger waste of money than a term policy.

Living Benefits

When most people think of life insurance, they think of dying and leaving a financial legacy for their loved ones. **Modern insurance policies, however, contain many benefits you can enjoy while you are still alive.** These "living benefits" range from tax-free accumulation of investment earnings to zero-interest loans. They can provide cash should you become seriously ill or if you need cash for a down payment on your home. There are scores of living benefits available in today's life insurance policies, making them much more useful and beneficial than ever.

Income, Savings Protection, and Tax Diversification—Bank on Yourself

With living benefits so prevalent, more and more ways to utilize them have become popular. Among these is a strategy called Bank on Yourself. **The essence of this strategy is to take advantage of the tax-deferred growth on the earnings within life insurance policies and using tax-free loans to access the cash when needed.** The idea is to borrow the money from yourself instead of the bank. Then pay yourself the interest instead of the bank and repay the loan you took from your policy.

Once again, on the surface, this appears to make sense. However, it takes discipline to ensure you actually do repay yourself, and what's the point of paying yourself interest? **After all, it is your money—all of it! It's just another way to trick yourself into saving more. I'm certainly not opposed to that.** I am opposed to the marketing hype seen on this topic, whereby they claim magical results from this "little known secret used by corporate executives and politicians for years, to paraphrase some of the advertisements I've seen over the years.

The truth of the matter is having your money grow tax-deferred and having the ability to access that tax-free is very powerful when you have a positive arbitrage—that is, when you can borrow money at a lower rate and invest it at a higher rate. Remember, this is what banks do all day long. They borrow the free money from your checking account and other very inexpensive sources like the Federal Reserve, and then they lend it out at a higher rate and make a fortune. **Let's go down this rabbit trail for a moment to ensure you clearly understand how arbitrage works.**

Let's say that you could borrow money at an interest rate of two percent and you were able to borrow $100,000. Over the year, the $100,000 loan would cost you $2,000 in interest expense. Now, let's say you invested that $100,000 in a home and you flipped that home, netting you $104,000 and, after all expenses, making you a $4,000 profit. One might be tempted to say that you made a 4 percent return on that investment, right? Well, that would be wrong because you did not invest $100,000. You borrowed it from someone else. You invested only $2,000; what you paid out of your money in this deal. So in reality, you earned $4,000 on a $2,000 investment, or a 100 percent profit. That is the power of arbitrage.

As usual, we need to consider the opposite situation as well. That is, what if the rate you earn on your investment is lower than the cost of borrowing? This is called "negative arbitrage." Using the same example, if you were to borrow $100,000 and net the same 4 percent, or $4,000 profit, but this time the cost to borrow the money was 5 percent or $5,000, now you have lost money on the deal.

You see, arbitrage is just another form of leverage. If you have a positive arbitrage, the more leverage you apply the better. In our example, we borrowed 100 percent of the money needed to acquire our flip, and because of the positive arbitrage, we made out like bandits with our profits. Conversely, with our negative arbitrage, borrowing more money just made our situation worse. After all, had we paid cash for the property, we would have made a nice 4 percent profit. Borrowing the money, we took a 1-percent hit instead ($100,000 + $4,000 − $5,000 = $99,000).

Why is this relevant? The reason is that to access the cash tax-free from inside a life insurance policy while you are alive, you borrow it. If

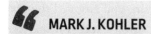

> **MARK J. KOHLER**
>
> Do these insurance strategies with tax-free loans to the policyholder work? Yes. Does insurance provide an amazing way to build wealth tax-free? Yes. In fact, all these amazing strategies with insurance work, are legal, and are legitimate . . . but with one condition. The owner can continue to make the premium payments! As I mentioned earlier, my greatest concern with the insurance strategy is making sure my business owners have a mature business and other buckets of wealth that they can turn to in order to make premiums if they have to. Make sure you don't bite off more than you can chew with insurance policies.

the rate you pay for your loan is less than the return you make on your investment, then you win. If it is not, you lose.

Most modern life insurance contracts offer very favorable terms on their loans starting at 2 percent. Borrowing money at 2 percent interest is a very good deal in 2017, but back in 1980, you could have taken the money out of your insurance policy, walked down to your local bank, deposited that money into a Certificate of Deposit, and earned 16 percent on it. Now, that is a VERY positive arbitrage and a risk-free investment as well. Some insurance policies will allow you to borrow the money at 0 percent interest after you hold the contract for 10 or 20 years. **Now you are like the bank, borrowing money for free.**

The 2 percent or zero percent loans are written into the contract and guaranteed for life. They are referred to as a "spread loan" and a "wash loan," respectively. You can go even one step further and get what is referred to as a "participating loan" as well. You see, with the spread or wash loans, you borrow your money out of the policy, and therefore, you cannot earn any interest on it.

In fact, think about this for a moment. With the spread loan, you paid the insurance company 2 percent interest just to have access to your money. Talk about making a profit. Again, you enjoyed the tax-deferred growth of your money and you are able to access it tax-free via these loans, but I don't even know how to calculate the return on investment for the insurance company when you are paying them to give you back your money!

That said, what if you could continue to earn interest on your money inside the insurance policy even after you borrowed it out? That is how a participating loan works. The money you borrow is loaned to you at one rate, say 5 percent. However, the insurance company will continue to invest your money as though it was never taken. Now, let's say you earn 7 percent on your investments during the year. **Remember, when you borrow money at a lower rate and then earn a higher rate, you have a positive arbitrage.** You could have put that money under your mattress, and you would still have more money at the end of the year.

The arbitrage door swings both ways. What if you only earned 1 percent on your investments with the insurance company that year? Once again, with the numbers reversed, you have a negative arbitrage and will lose money.

66 MARK J. KOHLER

These policies are very flexible and have many features and options that could be very beneficial. With flexibility comes complexity, however, and you really need to not get caught up in the hype and the marketing of these products. Can they provide the benefits they advertise? Of course. The question really is, will they work? Does the sun and moon have to align perfectly for them to deliver the numbers you are presented by the life insurance salesman, or are you looking at realistic assumptions? Get a second opinion whenever you hear something that sounds too good to be true and always do your due diligence on *any* advisor selling you insurance with incredible promises of returns and use of the money. 99

In my opinion, life insurance policies designed properly with the right guarantees and terms can become a very valuable and beneficial financial planning tool. They should be considered in almost all circumstances, but realize that they may not always be the best option. The tax-deferred growth, the tax-free access to your cash while living, and the tax-free death benefits at your passing all provide compelling reasons to look into this strategy. **However, as we wrote earlier in this book: "Hope for the best, plan for the worst, and expect that you will end up somewhere in between."** If you consider using life insurance as part of your financial planning strategy, like all other investment options, remember those words. If you have done your homework and you can live with those possible outcomes, then you can make the right decision for the situation.

Super-Charge Your 401(k): The Role of Life Insurance Inside and/or Alongside Traditional Retirement Plans

As a postscript, I want to offer up a 401(k) strategy that has a lot of merit. This is one of the strategies I deploy in our 401(k) Super-Charger Plan, and it is a good one. It works like this:

Most 401(k) plans and similar retirement plans have few options for great investments. They may offer a wide variety of stocks, bonds, and mutual funds, but all they offer are stocks, bonds, and mutual funds. They never offer the universe of possible investment opportunities available. Yet, as a W-2-only employee, these plans may be the only option available to you for tax-deductible savings and tax-deferred growth.

Most 401(k) plans do offer a "get out of jail free card" in the form of a loan. Keep in mind that all 401(k) plans offer access to your money for specific hardships and other reasons. These are not what I

TIP FOR FINANCIAL FREEDOM

When the time is right, insurance is an important part of your plan.

---

am addressing here. **I am talking about borrowing your money from yourself again.** This time, however, the interest rate you pay for your money, you pay to yourself. That alone is a good reason to consider this strategy as it effectively allows you to contribute additional money into your retirement plan in excess of the annual contribution limits.

In this strategy, I'm going to purchase a life insurance policy with the money I borrow. Why would I want to do that? For two reasons. One reason is because $1 inside my 401(k) will provide my family with $1 if I were to pass away. In other words, $1 of value provides $1 of benefits. Plus, there are all kinds of strings attached to those dollars in terms of taxes and/or restricted access to the money, etc. The second reason is that once that money is moved out of my 401(k) and into my life insurance policy, not only will I have tax-free access to my cash if I want it in the future, but also I have the benefit of leverage where my $1 would provide my family with $1,000 as a tax-free death benefit should I pass away.

I'm not talking about withdrawing the money from the retirement plan. That would trigger taxes and possibly penalties as well. I'm advocating a loan, which would be repaid over the course of one year. **If you were to repeat this process for five years, you could have fully funded a properly designed life insurance contract.** Your money is now inside the insurance policy to be accessed when you want it or need it to invest in anything you want, and you have multiplied the value of your 401(k) contributions many times over.

The only major risk to this strategy is if you leave your job, if you are let go from work, or you want to work somewhere else. When this occurs, the loan needs to be repaid. That said, if you use this strategy as I've described it, you did not borrow that much money. You borrowed just enough to be able to repay it within a year. It is a risk, but remember— "Hope for the best, plan for the worst, and know you will likely end up somewhere in between."

By the way, if you want to really double-down on this strategy, try this: After you fund your insurance policy for a couple of years, you may now have a sizable amount of cash accumulating there. Then, what if you borrowed some of the cash inside your policy and used it to purchase a rental property that provided a nice positive cash flow? Now, your tenant would be helping you repay your 401(k) loan, and your life insurance would be paid for as well. Or you could use the money as a down payment on a home for yourself. You lose the benefit of having a tenant foot the bill, but you gain the benefit of owning a home which you can be living in while enjoying all the tax benefits associated with that, and, once again, your life insurance comes along for the ride. Keep in mind that with every level of complexity I've added in this example comes added risk. That said, consider your situation and weigh out the risks. In many instances, the worst choice is to just leave your money inside your company's 401(k) and risk it to losses in the stock market.

$ $ $

TAKEAWAY 1—Despite the popular criticism, life insurance can serve as a valuable form of leverage and tax-deferred/tax-free wealth accumulation. The key is to buy the right kind of insurance, structured in the correct way to deliver the benefits you want. You don't buy a hammer to push in a thumbtack. You don't buy a tweezer to pick up an elephant. Buy the right tool for the job, and you will get the results you want and expect.

TAKEAWAY 2—Life insurance is not a panacea. It is not a one-size-fits-all solution to every financial challenge. Life insurance is expensive and a complete waste of money if you don't have it long enough to receive the benefit you want. Be careful to ensure that your financial advisor is licensed and quailed in a variety of strategies to ensure that you don't buy insurance for the advisor's financial benefit versus yours.

TAKEAWAY 3—Understand that the benefits of life insurance will likely not be received for a VERY long time—maybe decades into the future. Therefore, it is very important to only work with companies that are likely to be around for a VERY long time as well. While no one can guarantee that one company will survive so far into the future, working with a company that has already been operating for several decades or possibly even several centuries is a good indication that they know how to run their business in a sound manner.

WHAT YOU SHOULD BE BUYING FROM WALL STREET

As with the last chapter, I have asked Randy to author this section on what we should be buying from Wall Street. What's ironic is that although Randy is a licensed financial advisor with all the credentials to sell stocks, bonds, and mutual funds, he is vocal about his hatred and disdain for Wall Street. Frankly, it's refreshing to have a so-called "insider" with his level of knowledge to share these feelings. I hope you too can benefit from Randy's thoughts, advice, and commentary on the options you have to invest in Wall Street and the approach you should take with your investment strategy.

$ $ $

Of all the chapters contained in this book, this one has to be one of the most important. Volumes of books have been written on this topic by authors with much more knowledge and insight than I would likely ever hope to attain. **Why then should you take the time to read a short chapter on such a broad topic written by an author who professes to not be the most knowledgeable person on the subject anyway?** The answer is quite simple. One, Wall Street affects everyone on the planet, and that includes you. Two, although I may not be the utmost authority on the topic, I do have some incredibly valuable insights to share with you that will likely have a profound impact on the way you view Wall Street investments and, ultimately, what you should be buying from Wall Street.

If you only have a small amount of money to invest, then you must understand that your options will be very limited. **For simplicity and safety's sake, you could simply keep your money in cash or money market accounts until you grow your stockpile to a more substantial amount.** Frankly, there is nothing wrong with this strategy, as safety should be your number-one priority.

Think about it. If you only have $1,000 to invest and you invest it in a risky strategy that may return, say, 25 percent, but it has a potential loss of 25 percent as well, that is a fair bet with 50/50 odds of winning or losing. With $1,000 to invest, you would have an upside opportunity of $250. If you had $1 million to invest, then that same investment would return $250,000. Obviously, the upside is wonderful regardless of the amount of money invested. However, the downside loss of $250 is not nearly as significant as $250,000 in that you could likely re-earn and resave that small amount of money relatively easily. With a large loss, however, it would likely take considerable time and effort to recover.

If you are willing to accept the risk of loss, then investing in an ETF (Exchange Traded Fund) is a good option to consider. ETFs have very low costs, and they are easy to get into and out of, generally with the click of a mouse via an online trading portal. That said, what is absolutely critical to understand is that the decision as to what and how much to invest in any strategy is based on a number of factors: your age, your income, your marital status, the number and age of your children, and so on. For me as a financial advisor, or anyone else for that matter, to attempt to provide a generic recommendation without knowing the details of your situation would be ludicrous. It would be similar to a doctor writing a book about health suggesting that everyone should take an aspirin as soon as they begin to feel ill. That would be terrible advice at best and more like malpractice instead.

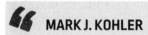

MARK J. KOHLER

My basic approach is that all of us will have something in the Wall Street or banking industry. The question is where we put it and how much of our available resources. In the beginning, I want my younger clients to start immediately saving, even if it is just $100 to $200 a month, and open an IRA or ROTH as a vehicle for those funds—THEN LEAVE IT ALONE! The longer you can leave it there, and *ignore* the ups and downs of the market, the more you will have later. Trust the system over time. This is what Dave Ramsey, Warren Buffet, and Tony Robbins have all taught and preached, including the esteemed author of this chapter, Randy Luebke. Save, put on your blinders, and be patient.

Again, my point is this: with little money, you have few options. With more money, you will have more. However, in all circumstances, you need to fully understand and evaluate the risk of the strategy that you are considering. That is why I am dedicating the remainder of this chapter to this topic. **I hope that you will take the time to read it and learn from it because it may be the most important concept you will ever tackle.** Please don't be like the majority of people and ignore risk. Understand it, embrace it, and make informed choices and decisions based on that knowledge. If you want to understand risk, then you need to continue reading because I'm going to describe and define risk in a manner that you will likely never have considered before.

Understanding the Risks of Wall Street Investing

The vast majority of wealth in the United States and likely the world is in real estate. That said, there is a HUGE amount of money in Wall Street as well, and some of it is yours. If you own an IRA, 401(k), or any other type of retirement plan, rest assured your money is in the hands of Wall Street. **Often, as individuals we have little or no control over the investments made with our money on Wall Street.** That said, when we do have the opportunity, wouldn't we like to make the best choices and decisions as to how it is invested?

Back in Chapter 9, we introduced the concept of "The Perfect Investment"—one that was 100 percent safe and liquid and that produced tremendous returns that were all tax-free. In fact, you would get a tax deduction for investing in it and access all your money tax-free as well. Oh, and of course you did not have to do a darn thing to make it work. If you just invested your money in that perfect investment, then all these wonderful magical things would automatically occur.

I also want to introduce the concept of "The Three States of Money," whereby money can only exist or be used in one of three ways and only one at a time. You can either:

1. Spend your money
2. Lend your money
3. Invest your money

Spending incurs more than the cost of what you buy. Once spent, that money can never again earn a return, which is referred to as "the opportunity cost." Lending is what most people end up doing, albeit unwittingly, with their money as they deposit their earnings in a bank checking account, thus lending the bank their money at 0 percent interest. Some people make formal loans, of course; however, most people are completely unaware that they have loaned their money to someone. The phrase "What's in Your Wallet?" takes on extra meaning when you consider those greenbacks in your pocketbook are essentially interest-free loans to the federal government. We buy bonds and make deposits into our checking and savings accounts, all forms of lending at terrible rates of return. Finally, we have investments.

Again, investments connote "ownership" and presume some rate of return and/or an increase in value. That's it! That's all you can do with your money, and there are no other choices or options. Your money will be in one of these states and only one at a time.

Understanding that there is no such thing as a perfect investment and understanding that you cannot avoid investing with Wall Street, I think you would agree that it is only prudent to learn about some fundamental strategies to improve the odds of winning. Let's consider three more concepts:

1. Risk
2. Drawdown
3. Decumulation

Understanding Risk within Specific Investments

We tend to ignore the true meaning and impact of words we use often. "Risk" is no exception. When we refer to risk as it relates to investments, to really understand the impact, we need to use the word in the context of a sentence rather than just the one word itself. In other words, ask yourself, "What is really at risk?" It's your money, of course. Then ask, "Risk of what?" Answer = Loss? Put it all together, and the meaning and impact of risk becomes very clear. What is at risk is the loss of your money, and that is what you need to focus on when evaluating the risk of any investment.

- § Risk is like oxygen: it's invisible, everywhere, and all around us.
- § We may be unaware of it, but we cannot ignore the influence and effects of risk.
- § Too little risk, and we won't survive.
- § Too much risk, and it can explode.
- § With the proper amount of risk, however, we thrive.

In my example of "The Perfect Investment," one of the characteristics is that it would be 100 percent risk-free. In the investment world, we tend to refer to risk-free when that investment is backed by guarantees or the solvency of the entity issuing the investment. For example, no one even considers the risk with the cash in their wallet. After all, it's backed by the United States Government. Yet, in reality, that money in your wallet is really just almost worthless paper.

MARK J. KOHLER

In general, low-cost index funds, or Exchange Traded Fund (EFTs), may be the best place to start for a novice investor just getting started in saving and investing. However, the more money you can build, the more you have to invest. Your age, your income, and your family situation all play into the equation. **The important thing in my opinion is to not get overwhelmed with the options and at least start saving now.** Ask, if not demand, from your financial advisor the simplest approach to your investment strategy so you understand what you are doing. If you can't explain what you are doing and understand it, don't do it.

My point is that any investment has some risk associated with it. Most investors do not understand the risk, and/or they ignore it altogether. Going forward, vow to never do this again. With any investment, take the time to learn about and understand the risk involved. **It's always present, regardless of what the salesman tells you.** Regardless of the guarantees provided, there is risk. Then, with a clear understanding of what the risk of the investment is, ask yourself, "If I experience the result of the risk, can I afford the loss?" If you can't, then don't invest! It's really that simple.

Lottery tickets are a great example of extreme risk and reward. The odds of losing 100 percent of your money are almost certain. The odds of winning anything is minimal, and winning big is near impossible. Yet, can most people afford to "invest" a dollar on a lottery ticket? The answer is obvious that most of us can because even if we experience the full magnitude of the risk exposure, we lose it all, that one-dollar investment will not severely impact one's life going forward. **If this is such a simple concept that everyone understands, they why is** it that we invest trillions of our hard-earned money with Wall Street every day without considering the risks of doing so? The answer, great marketing!

For decades, Wall Street has spent billions on making the general public feel "safe" when investing with Wall Street. Using little orange bunnies and green lines and colorful balloons, good-looking models and clever taglines have us feel like anyone can make money from Wall Street investments. Moreover, if you don't invest, you are foolish and missing out. Every day, money is taken directly from our paychecks and handed over to Wall Street with little thought about the real risk associated with those investments. The reality is that Wall Street almost always wins (makes money) even when you lose everything. In fact, like a casino, that is when Wall Street wins big—when the players lose and the house cashes in. **The point that I've now made in a variety of ways is that your money is going to be invested in something (one of the three states of money), and it's going to be exposed to risk.** Your job it to be aware of this reality, and instead of blindly going into an investment, you need to make informed choices and decisions about what to invest in with your money.

> **Drawdown**—The historical loss of an investment is calculated by subtracting that investment's lowest value from its highest value over a market cycle. (It is very important to note that the recovery from drawdown is not linear, which is why the average rate of return of an investment can be markedly different from the real rate of return.)

As I go around the country giving workshops or having one-on-one meetings with my clients, I always ask them if they understand the phrase "average rate of return." Inevitably, everyone says they do understand average. After all, you add up all the values in a set of numbers and divide that total by the number of values in that set. We learned this in grade school.

Here is a math test for you. Take an investment and increase its value by 50 percent. Then, lose 50 percent of that investment. What's left? To answer the question, let's start by determining the "average" return on that investment.

50 percent increase in value − 50 percent loss in value =
0 percent Average Rate of Return (ROR)

Therefore, if I invested $100,000 into this strategy, I made some money and lost some money, but at the end of the day, I would still have $100,000.

$100,000 x 50 percent = $50,000

Therefore,

$100,000 + $50,000 = $150,000

Right? Well, not so fast. I would actually only have $75,000 in my brokerage account had I experienced that sequence of returns ($150,000 x −50 percent loss = $75,000 balance). **While my average ROR would have been zero percent, my "real" ROR would have been a negative 25 percent instead.**

Now ask yourself this question, "When was the last time I saw an advertisement for an investment that stated the real ROR?" The answer is never. Why? Because the real ROR depends as much on when you invest as it does on what you invest into. The real ROR of an investment is also referred to as CAGR. Look for that value in your investment disclosures. Seeing it there is, if nothing else, an indication that the investment offering is attempting to be honest. More often what you will see, however, is the average ROR followed by the phrase *"Investments are risky, and actual investor returns may vary from those illustrated here."*

What this math problem (see Figure 17.1 on page 179) illustrates is the effect of "Drawdown." As the definition states, recovering from a loss is not linear. It is exponential. If I lose 50 percent and then earn 50 percent, I am not whole. I need to earn 2 x 50 percent, or 100 percent to make up for a 50 percent loss. Look at the drawdown and recovery chart noted below.

The next table (Figure 17.2 on page 179) is a great way to illustrate why it is more reasonable to accept more risk when you are younger

Beginning Balance	Loss Percentage	Loss Amount	Net Balance	% Needed to Recover
$100,000	-50%	($50,000)	$50,000	100.0%
	-45%	($45,000)	$55,000	81.8%
	-40%	($40,000)	$60,000	66.7%
	-35%	($35,000)	$65,000	53.8%
	-30%	($30,000)	$70,000	42.9%
	-25%	($25,000)	$75,000	33.3%
	-20%	($20,000)	$80,000	25.0%
	-15%	($15,000)	$85,000	17.6%
	-10%	($10,000)	$90,000	11.1%
	-5%	($5,000)	$95,000	5.3%

Figure 17.1—Recovering from Drawdown Losses

Percent Per Year to Recover					
Years	Years	Years	Years	Years	Years
5	10	15	20	25	30
20.0%	10.0%	6.7%	5.0%	4.0%	3.3%
16.4%	8.2%	5.5%	4.1%	3.3%	2.7%
13.3%	6.7%	4.4%	3.3%	2.7%	2.2%
10.8%	5.4%	3.6%	2.7%	2.2%	1.8%
8.6%	4.3%	2.9%	2.1%	1.7%	1.4%
6.7%	3.3%	2.2%	1.7%	1.3%	1.1%
5.0%	2.5%	1.7%	1.3%	1.0%	0.8%
3.5%	1.8%	1.2%	0.9%	0.7%	0.6%
2.2%	1.1%	0.7%	0.6%	0.4%	0.4%
1.1%	0.5%	0.4%	0.3%	0.2%	0.2%

Figure 17.2—Time to Recover from Losses

because with more time to recover, the returns can be much smaller. A 50 percent loss would only require a 3.3 percent ROR to fully recover. By the way, the effect of compounding over 30 years would also be much more profound, meaning it would take an even smaller ROR to fully recover over a longer period of time.

Let's say you were about to retire in 2008, and the market crashed. You could have lost 50 percent of your retirement nest egg right before you planned to access that money. Many people did find themselves in that exact situation and had to postpone their retirement as a result, hoping the market would recover and the value of their accounts would be restored. **That said, do you know how many times the stock market earned 20 percent for five years in a row? Never!**

What if you don't have time? What if you are going to retire and you do need to spend down your nest egg? Figure 17.3 shows what could happen.

Year	Age	Beginning Balance	Annual ROR	Cum. ROR	Change In Value	Net Account Balance	Inflation Rate 3.0%	Withdrawal Rate 4.0%	Ending Account Balance
0	65	$1,000,000				$1,000,000	$0	($40,000)	$960,000
1	66	$960,000	7%	7%	$67,200	$1,027,200	$1,200	($41,200)	$986,000
2	67	$986,000	7%	14%	$69,020	$1,055,020	$1,236	($42,436)	$1,012,584
3	68	$1,012,584	7%	21%	$70,881	$1,083,465	$1,273	($43,709)	$1,039,756
4	69	$1,039,756	7%	28%	$72,783	$1,112,539	$1,311	($45,020)	$1,067,518
5	70	$1,067,518	-15%	13%	($160,128)	$907,391	$1,351	($46,371)	$861,020
6	71	$861,020	7%	20%	$60,271	$921,291	$1,391	($47,762)	$873,529
7	72	$873,529	7%	27%	$61,147	$934,676	$1,433	($49,195)	$885,481
8	73	$885,481	7%	34%	$61,984	$947,465	$1,476	($50,671)	$896,794
9	74	$896,794	7%	41%	$62,776	$959,569	$1,520	($52,191)	$907,378
10	75	$907,378	-15%	26%	($136,107)	$771,272	$1,566	($53,757)	$717,515

(Correction Percent -15.0%; Average ROR 2.6%; Frequency (In Years) 5)

Figure 17.3—Steady Gains with Periodic Losses

There is a whole lot of data going on here, so let me break it down for you. First, you start out with a $1,000,000 nest egg. You're feeling pretty good because you believe that if you follow the 4 percent rule you can safely withdraw $40,000 from your nest egg when you retire, and with a 3 percent inflation rate, you can continue to withdraw more money each year. According to the 4 percent rule, you have a 95 percent chance of not running out of money over 25 years of retirement. Think about that statement for a moment. If you turn that statement around, then 5 percent of these retirees will also have a 100 percent chance of running out of money, and at 85 or 90 years old, there would be no chance of recovery—no "investing for the long term."

Figure 17.3 also illustrates the reality of the stock market. Wall Street uses the expression that "No tree grows to the sky," meaning the stock market does not go up and up forever. Eventually, it goes down, referred to as a "correction," and what that means is you lose money. In my example, I make a 15 percent market correction occur every five years. Even though my investments are earning a nice consistent 7 percent ROR, my retiree is completely broke at 89 years old. Drawdown has a profound impact in earnings. The problem is only exacerbated if you make withdrawals. This situation is referred to as "Decumulation."

> **Decumulation**—A condition whereby investment withdrawals occur while, simultaneously, the principal remains invested. Therefore, as withdrawals are made there is still potential for ongoing gains. There is also the risk of ongoing losses.

Decumulation is what every retiree faces with their retirement nest egg. After all, one has to take some risk. **Remember, risk is like oxygen. Without it, we die. With no risk, there are no market losses. There is also no earnings, no ROR.** The result is my retiree is now broke, at 81 years old. Risk, drawdown, decumulation—are you beginning to understand the problem? We need to invest with Wall Street. It's almost impossible to avoid it. Yet, even modest losses at the wrong time can blow up a retirement plan completely over a short period time.

Can I paint a bleaker picture? Of course I can. Let's introduce one last concept—a bonus to our list of investment risks. It's called the "Sequence of Withdrawal" risk.

> **Sequence of Withdrawal Risk**—If an investment is not protected from losses while withdrawals are made during a down market, that investment is subjected to profound negative effects, which are exacerbated by those withdrawals. If one takes withdrawals and simultaneously experiences serious losses, then there is very little chance of recovery and the investment will likely be depleted entirely over a relatively short period of time.

This is how it works. Figure 17.4 on page 182 is a random sequence of investment returns.

Year	Age	Beginning Balance	Growth Rate		Change In Value	Net Account Balance	Inflation Rate 3.0%	Withdrawal Rate 0.0%	Ending Account Balance
			Average ROR	7.0%					
0	65	$1,000,000	Annual ROR	Cum. ROR		$1,000,000	$0	$0	$1,000,000
1	66	$1,000,000	5%	5%	$50,000	$1,050,000	$0	$0	$1,050,000
2	67	$1,050,000	10%	15%	$105,000	$1,155,000	$0	$0	$1,155,000
3	68	$1,155,000	15%	30%	$173,250	$1,328,250	$0	$0	$1,328,250
4	69	$1,328,250	20%	50%	$265,650	$1,593,900	$0	$0	$1,593,900
5	70	$1,593,900	25%	75%	$398,475	$1,992,375	$0	$0	$1,992,375
6	71	$1,992,375	30%	105%	$597,713	$2,590,088	$0	$0	$2,590,088
7	72	$2,590,088	10%	115%	$259,009	$2,849,096	$0	$0	$2,849,096
8	73	$2,849,096	-10%	105%	($284,910)	$2,564,187	$0	$0	$2,564,187
9	74	$2,564,187	-15%	90%	($384,628)	$2,179,559	$0	$0	$2,179,559
10	75	$2,179,559	-20%	70%	($435,912)	$1,743,647	$0	$0	$1,743,647

Figure 17.4—Sequence of Withdrawal Risk—Positive Years First

As you can see, if you were to total up these returns, you would have earned 70 percent on your investment over ten years. On average (there is some rounding involved), you would have earned 7 percent per year.

Now, what would happen to our retiree had she encountered negative returns before receiving the positive returns during retirement? Figure 17.5 illustrates that change.

Year	Age	Beginning Balance	Growth Rate		Change In Value	Net Account Balance	Inflation Rate 3.0%	Withdrawal Rate 0.0%	Ending Account Balance
			Average ROR	7.0%					
0	65	$1,000,000	Annual ROR	Cum. ROR		$1,000,000	$0	$0	$1,000,000
1	66	$1,000,000	-20%	-20%	($200,000)	$800,000	$0	$0	$800,000
2	67	$800,000	-15%	-35%	($120,000)	$680,000	$0	$0	$680,000
3	68	$680,000	-10%	-45%	($68,000)	$612,000	$0	$0	$612,000
4	69	$612,000	10%	-35%	$61,200	$673,200	$0	$0	$673,200
5	70	$673,200	30%	-5%	$201,960	$875,160	$0	$0	$875,160
6	71	$875,160	25%	20%	$218,790	$1,093,950	$0	$0	$1,093,950
7	72	$1,093,950	20%	40%	$218,790	$1,312,740	$0	$0	$1,312,740
8	73	$1,312,740	15%	55%	$196,911	$1,509,651	$0	$0	$1,509,651
9	74	$1,509,651	10%	65%	$150,965	$1,660,616	$0	$0	$1,660,616
10	75	$1,660,616	5%	70%	$83,031	$1,743,647	$0	$0	$1,743,647

Figure 17.5—Sequence of Withdrawal Risk—Negative Years First

As you can see, even with the negative years coming first, the investment still earned 70 percent overall and averaged a 7 percent ROR as well. **You see the sequence of returns does not matter during the accumulation phase, that period of time when you are saving for retirement.** You can have good years followed by bad ones, and in any sequence over time, you get the same results. After ten years, both accounts would have grown to $1,743,647 in value. The math during the decumulation phase, however, is profoundly different, and the sequence of returns very much matters. Figure 17.6 shows the value of one of my retiree's accounts. He wisely chose to retire, and within the first seven years of his retirement, he benefited from a generally positive stock market and corresponding investment returns. **Our retiree was able to consistently withdraw an ever-increasing amount of money from his nest egg, and he never ran out of money.** In fact, after 35 years of retirement, he still has over $2.6 million to pass on to his estate.

Year	Age	Beginning Balance	Growth Rate Average ROR / 7.0%		Change In Value	Net Account Balance	Inflation Rate 3.0%	Withdrawal Rate 4.0%	Ending Account Balance
			Annual ROR	Cum. ROR					
0	65	$1,000,000				$1,000,000	$0	($40,000)	$960,000
1	66	$960,000	5%	5%	$48,000	$1,008,000	$1,200	($41,200)	$966,800
2	67	$966,800	10%	15%	$96,680	$1,063,480	$1,236	($42,436)	$1,021,044
3	68	$1,021,044	15%	30%	$153,157	$1,174,201	$1,273	($43,709)	$1,130,492
4	69	$1,130,492	20%	50%	$226,098	$1,356,590	$1,311	($45,020)	$1,311,569
5	70	$1,311,569	25%	75%	$327,892	$1,639,462	$1,351	($46,371)	$1,593,091
6	71	$1,593,091	30%	105%	$477,927	$2,071,018	$1,391	($47,762)	$2,023,256
7	72	$2,023,256	10%	115%	$202,326	$2,225,582	$1,433	($49,195)	$2,176,387
8	73	$2,176,387	-10%	105%	($217,639)	$1,958,748	$1,476	($50,671)	$1,908,077
9	74	$1,908,077	-15%	90%	($286,212)	$1,621,866	$1,520	($52,191)	$1,569,675
10	75	$1,569,675	-20%	70%	($313,935)	$1,255,740	$1,566	($53,757)	$1,201,983

Figure 17.6—**Retiring in An Up Market**

But what if our retiree was not so fortunate? What if he were to have retired into a negative market instead, reversing the order of returns? Let's look at Figure 17.7 to see what happens to his nest egg.

Year	Age	Beginning Balance	Growth Rate Average ROR / 7.0%		Change In Value	Net Account Balance	Inflation Rate 3.0%	Withdrawal Rate 4.0%	Ending Account Balance
			Annual ROR	Cum. ROR					
0	65	$1,000,000				$1,000,000	$0	($40,000)	$960,000
1	66	$960,000	-20%	-20%	($192,000)	$768,000	$1,200	($41,200)	$726,800
2	67	$726,800	-15%	-35%	($109,020)	$617,780	$1,236	($42,436)	$575,344
3	68	$575,344	-10%	-45%	($57,534)	$517,810	$1,273	($43,709)	$474,101
4	69	$474,101	10%	-35%	$47,410	$521,511	$1,311	($45,020)	$476,490
5	70	$476,490	30%	-5%	$142,947	$619,437	$1,351	($46,371)	$573,066
6	71	$573,066	25%	20%	$143,267	$716,333	$1,391	($47,762)	$668,571
7	72	$668,571	20%	40%	$133,714	$802,285	$1,433	($49,195)	$753,090
8	73	$753,090	15%	55%	$112,964	$866,054	$1,476	($50,671)	$815,383
9	74	$815,383	10%	65%	$81,538	$896,921	$1,520	($52,191)	$844,730
10	75	$844,730	5%	70%	$42,237	$886,967	$1,566	($53,757)	$833,210

Figure 17.7—**Retiring in a Down Market**

With just three negative years of returns during the initial years of retirement, this poor fellow is dead broke at just 88 years old. **Clearly, "Sequence of Returns" has a profound effect on retirement.**

The solution to this problem is simple. **Simply, never choose to retire immediately prior to a market downturn.** As long as you can predict the future accurately, then you can avoid the sequence of withdrawal risk altogether. Figure 17.8 is a chart of the history of the stock market going back many years.

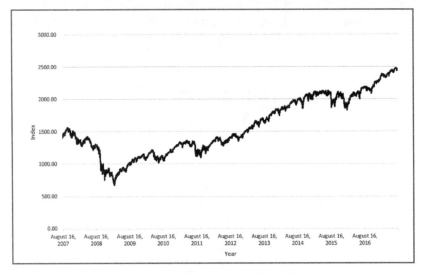

*Figure 17.8—*The History of the S&P

You should observe a couple significant points from this chart. **One, overall the market has increased over time. Two, it NEVER increases in a straight line.** The market goes up, then down, then up, and so on. Bull markets are always followed by Bear markets, and until we experience a cataclysmic collapse like the fall of the Roman Empire, I think it is fair to assume that this cycle will continue.

We now know that it really does not matter when you start investing in the stock market because given time, and if you don't have to make any withdrawals, you will make money in the stock market. That said, just looking at this chart, can you tell me what is going to happen next? Will the market continue to go up? Or, will we experience a correction next and move down? The answer will surprise you. If you chose up, you were right. If you chose down, you were also right. **Both answers will be right given enough time.**

I'm going to layer on one more level of risk into the equation. (I promise, this is it!) This risk may be the biggest risk of all, however. **It's called "Investor Behavior," or sometimes referred to as the psychology of investing.**

Investor Behavior works in cycles as well. One example is the "Greed/Fear" cycle, whereby most people will be willing to jump into the stock market after they have seen evidence that people are making money. They see it on the nightly news. They hear about it at cocktail parties. The market is up. Everyone is making money, so the typical investor jumps on board to join the party and not miss out on the fun. **This is the "Greed" stage of the investor market cycle.** In reality, of course, most of the profits in the market have already been made. After all, that is what the news has been reporting on, right?

Then, a market correction sets in. At first, the loss may not be significant. Markets also do not decline in a straight line. A brief upturn in the market helps to recover some of those losses, so the average investor hangs on, hoping to regain all their losses. As soon as they become whole, they will get out of the market. This, of course, does not happen, and the market takes another big hit. This is followed by a nice rally. Once again, our typical investor is not necessarily looking forward to a full recovery, but wants to get back some of the money he lost, so he hangs on and stays invested. **This of course is followed by more losses, and eventually, after our investor simply cannot endure any more pain suffered from these repeated losses, gets out of the market.** At this juncture, he is scared, tired, and content to earn nothing with his money sitting in cash as at least he will no longer lose sleep over another loss in the market.

Unfortunately, and with almost absolutely certainty, this is when he should be getting into the market, not getting out. The market rallies. The news is still reporting the recent losses, and after riding a zigzag road downward, surely those rallies will be followed by even more losses. So our typical investor once again will sit on the sidelines, fearful to get back into the market until when? At the top of the next market cycle, right?

You see, market averages represent absolute values whereby someone had the discipline and fortitude to ride out the bad markets and wait for the good one to develop. Over time, you've seen the math. You make money. **The problem is that most people are far too emotional. They follow the crowd during both the Greed and the Fear stages of the market cycle.** The result is that most investors will NEVER see the returns on their investments that are possible. Instead, they will see the augmented and generally much worse returns created by their emotions. Truly, investor behavior may be the biggest risk of all.

As I conclude this chapter, you may be asking yourself, "what the heck should I do?" You know that you are going to invest with Wall Street one way or another. In fact, you know that you should because Wall Street, while it may appear to be a big casino, has an unbelievably important purpose. It provides business with the capital it needs to grow. Even from the most cynical perspective, anyone should want everyone to prosper as it makes the world a better place to live.

What Should You Do About Investing with Wall Street?

1. Be smart, and do your homework. Understand the true risks involved with your investment options.
2. Be realistic, and understand that there is no such thing as the perfect investment.
3. Plan ahead, creating a long-term financial plan to better understand your financial needs and the time horizon you face.
4. Do something as doing nothing will guarantee failure. Get involved learn, and be willing to take an appropriate amount of risk.

The bottom line is that Wall Street is not going to tell you as much as it wants to sell you. Let the buyer beware.

§ § §

TAKEAWAY 1—Everyone invests with or lends to Wall Street. It's unavoidable. Therefore, you need to educate yourself about the various investment and lending options that are available. If you don't, then you need to accept the fact that you are going to go along for the ride.

TAKEAWAY 2—Know the risk of the investment you are considering. If you truly understand the risk and are willing to accept the worst-case outcome, then you are making an informed decision and not relying on luck.

TAKEAWAY 3—Do not invest with a focus on winning. Invest with a focus on not losing, and in the long run, you will be better off. Hitting a number of singles and doubles over and over again will put you much further ahead than attempting to hit a home run and striking out.

PART

IV

EXIT STRATEGIES FOR YOUR BUSINESS

"Blue Sky is in the Eyes of the Beholder."

We've all heard the old adage that "a business is worth whatever someone is willing to pay for it." Sounds simple, right? However, it's much more complicated than that. The problem is that not all businesses are the same, nor are the owners, the products and services, or the type of customers, not to mention the region or area where the business is located. The list goes on and on.

In this section of the book, I want to discuss things you can do to prepare for the process of selling your business, the valuation methods that will be used to evaluate your business, and, most importantly, what you can be doing now to *increase* the value of your business.

In fact, one of the greatest factors driving the value of a business, and thus the asking price, is the type of buyer and the legal transaction involved. For example, if a family member is involved, it could be a much longer process with a gradual buy-in and flexible pricing. If it's a third party, the price could be hotly contested, but the transaction could be completed much more quickly, or at least the anticipated handover.

Because of the complexities of these issues, I have dedicated five chapters to this topic, including various valuation methods and three types of buyers for your business.

CHAPTER

18

PREPARING TO SELL YOUR BUSINESS

I suspect many of you reading this book have gone through the exciting, yet stressful, process of selling your home. When you recall this presumably stressful process, you didn't just wake up one morning and decide to stick a sign on your lawn or tell a Realtor™ to list it on the MLS (Multiple Listing Service) that very day. In fact, you took weeks and months to prepare for the sale. You may have even invested over a year's time and thousands of dollars to maximize the value of your home.

The same process couldn't be truer for the sale of your business, and it's in fact probably far *more* involved. But before we get into the complexities of valuation and the types of buyers you may entertain in the sale of your business, there are steps you will need to take to prepare your business for sale.

The more organized you are, the less stressful the process will be, and will also inevitably increase the value of your business.

Later, I will go into detail regarding valuation methods and how to increase the intrinsic or hard core *value* of your business. In fact, these are things you can not only start to do immediately, but also may take a few years in order to prepare for the sale and maximize the value of your business (see Chapter 18). For now, let's get into the process of finding an appraiser, determining what you will disclose to potential buyers, how you can protect yourself in the process, and finally, preparing your "books" or "financials" for buyers and appraisers to review.

The Appraiser

A business appraiser will be almost a must when you are serious about selling your business. The two biggest reasons why an appraiser is going to be in the mix is to utilize the different valuation methods to arrive at a value for your business. They also provide an arm's-length valuation that the two parties may be able to agree upon. **Believe it or not, your business may not be worth as much as you may think (please read Chapter 2 if you haven't already).**

Now with that said, keep in mind that each valuation method could be an entire book or training manual unto itself. In fact, you may be surprised to know there are several associations in the business appraisal industry providing training, testing, and accreditation for licensed business appraisers. **You will want to make sure the appraiser you choose has credentials issued from an organization such as the National Association of Certified Valuators and Analysts, or International Society of Business Appraisers, just to name a couple.**

Additionally, www.bvresources.com and www.hadleycapital.com are a couple of prominent business appraisal service companies in the industry that may be a good starting point for you when the time is right. I suggest you interview several appraisers in the process of selecting the right professional for you.

In the end, a business appraiser will use a combination of several valuation methods to arrive at an "average" or "fair market value" for the asking price. Moreover, it's important as a business owner that you at least understand the basics of these methods because it will help you learn how to increase the value of your business now *and* give you a range of what your business may be worth before you officially engage a broker or appraiser.

The Disclosure

When the appraisal begins, it is based on the financial disclosures of the seller. This will most certainly be uncomfortable for you as the business owner, but it is expected and a common practice. To protect you in this process, all the parties involved (especially ANY potential buyers) will be obligated to sign a nondisclosure agreement, or NDA, as they are called in the industry.

Just as the seller is nervous to disclose information, the buyer is generally also concerned about signing an NDA. The buyer doesn't want to be held back from still moving into the industry (even if they don't buy the seller's business). For example, a buyer could learn something insightful in the process (even unintentionally), and they won't want the seller to later claim that they, the buyer, "stole" a secret that threatens the seller's business if the buyer doesn't follow through

❝ RANDY LUEBKE

The disclosure covered by the NDA will typically be the seller's current and prior year's financials, with up to two to three prior years of tax returns, an asset list, and even a list of debts that may be assumed by the buyer in the deal. These financials are critical for both parties and should be as accurate and honest as possible. I'm not suggesting that you offer a full-blown set of "audited financials." Doing so is a very time-consuming and expensive process. In fact, most business sales aren't based on audited financials; although in larger transactions, they may be more common before the deal is done. **❞**

with the sale. **As such, the NDA is carefully drafted to protect both parties and, again, it is highly recommended for both buyer and seller to sign and abide by its terms.**

It's also typical that a new term will start to get thrown around during the discussions and valuation: the concept of the normalized financials. These are financial statements that are adjusted from a business owner's tax returns or financials he or she may give to a bank. **Essentially, the owner needs to create a normal set of financials or books for a buyer to review and get a sense for the value and health of the business.** Why do the financials need to be adjusted, you may ask? Well, a good business owner should be writing off a variety of expenses particular to their family needs or tax strategies.

For example, the seller may have justified four-wheelers in the warehouse for moving supplies around or travel expenses to attend a semi-annual convention and taking the board of directors (typically the spouse and older family members) along for the trip. These are costs that a buyer would probably cut out. The seller wants to show "normalized financials" with these types of costs removed so it drives up the profit and thereby a potential valuation and asking price.

Finally, the financials disclosure will need to indicate the owner's compensation. It will need to be set forth clearly as to whether the owner was taking a salary, a draw, or a combination of the two. A buyer wants to know how turnkey this operation will be. In other words, they want to know how the buyer will replace the seller's personal service in running the business. Will the buyer need to hire anyone, one person or maybe several, to replace the seller? This is a scenario buyers need to be prepared for at this point.

Understanding EBITDA

The goal in the disclosure process is for the buyer to get as clear a picture as possible of the profitability of the business. Then the buyer and seller can engage the business appraiser to tear apart the financials and list of assets and liabilities to come up with a valuation. This is where EBITDA comes into play. But what *is* EBITDA?

EBITDA is an equation and stands for:

Earnings Before Interest, Taxes, Depreciation, and
Amortization

It's certainly a mouthful, but the equation itself is really quite simple: **subtract expenses from revenue (excluding interests and taxes) without depreciation and amortization.** The remaining number gets to the heart of the cash flow the business might produce and provides clarity for the valuation.

As I stated earlier, one of the first priorities in the appraisal process, is to get to a set of agreed-upon normalized financials or normalized EBITDA. As such, there are positive and negative "add-backs" you can make to EBITDA depending on the party's perspective, goals, and needs. The term of procedure of "add-backs" means you will add back to income or expenses certain dollar amounts that are personal or particular to the current business owner that won't apply to a buyer if they were to take over the business. Let's look at some examples.

To determine sustainable cash flow, some positive add-backs that increase EBITDA may include:

§ Owner's excess compensation
§ Rental expense above market rates
§ Owner's benefits that are not required to run the business, such as automobiles, vacations, etc.
§ Tax strategies particular to the owner's family or personal/business lifestyle
§ Unnecessary employees that are part of the owner's family or friends

Add-backs that may decrease EBITDA may include:

§ Rental expense below market value
§ Increased expenses due to special rates or deals exclusive to the owner's contacts
§ Recent or significant annual capital expenditures
§ Additional salaries required when the owner departs

Once "normalized EBITDA" is determined, the owner, buyer, and appraiser can start to implement various valuation methods more clearly and start to arrive at a fair asking price for the business.

Bottom line: **starting to fine-tune your financials and engaging an appraiser early on can help you understand what your true income is.** Please allow me to caution you and suggest you brace yourself. It's very common for business owners to be living off their business and be implementing creative tax strategies that give a seller the impression the business is worth more than it really is. **Remember, a buyer may not value the same benefits or strategies you do.** Get your financials dialed in, and start to look at valuation methods and learn what steps can truly increase the value of your business—our next topic and chapter!

§ § §

TAKEAWAY 1—Choosing the right appraiser for the sale of your business is critical to having a smooth sale and maximizing the value of your business. Make sure to interview several professionals before deciding on a specific appraiser or appraisal company.

TAKEAWAY 2—Be prepared to disclose everything from assets and liabilities, client and asset lists, and the systems and procedures of your company. Your buyer should be equally prepared to sign a Nondisclosure Agreement, and it's important to have an ironclad legal document for this purpose.

TAKEAWAY 3—You need to know your EBITDA (Earnings Before Interest, Taxes, Depreciation, and Amortization). During the process of calculating EBITDA, you will also prepare normalized financial statements to reflect the true profitability of your company.

PRICING YOUR BUSINESS AND INCREASING ITS VALUE

No matter who you are going to sell to, or over whatever timeline, your process has to start with an asking price. Now, whether the price is proposed by the seller or the buyer, the asking price isn't pulled out of "thin air." **It's always based on a valuation; in fact, it's generally based on a blend of valuations or an "average."** As I discussed in the last chapter, the appraiser you engage will go through a variety of valuation methods to try to come up with the highest and most fair price for your business.

The top six methods of valuation when it comes to pricing a business are:

1. Multiple of cash flow method
2. Balance sheet method

3. Cost to create method
4. Capitalized earnings approach method
5. Discounted cash flow
6. Comparable sales

Before I explain the basics of these valuation methods, it's important to recognize that a significant benefit of going through this whole process of "appraising," and why I want to take you through the most common methods of valuing your business, is that **this process can give you a roadmap for what might actually increase** *the value of your business*. Because of this side benefit, below I break down the most important steps to take years before you want to sell in order to maximize the value of your business. But for now, let's dive into the six valuation methods listed above.

1. Multiple of Cash Flow Method

This is probably the most common method and a great starting place for a buyer and seller to begin negotiation. Appraisers will typically apply a multiple to the annual normalized EBITDA to estimate the business's value.

Most companies (not a dotcom with wild expectations) typically trade for between three to five times their normalized EBITDA. Thus, a company with $400,000 in annual profit (EBITDA) and a "multiple" of five would sell for approximately $2 million. It's hard to explain where these multiples really started to become commonplace and industry averages for lack of a better word. Some have suggested it's a realistic estimate as to the number of years it would take to pay off the purchase price if profits remained the same as in the year of purchase. Nonetheless, these multiples vary based on several factors. The difference in the multiple is generally the result of a variety of characteristics specific to your business, including:

§ Sales growth rate
§ Gross profit margin
§ Location and expansion possibilities

§ Working capital requirements

An appraisal will take all these factors into consideration and then continue with various other valuation methods to arrive at an average.

2. Balance Sheet Method

Rather than focusing on the profit, an appraiser will also consider the assets and liabilities of the business. Sometimes, a business is worth more because of its assets, not necessarily the cash flow. For example, the land, buildings, intellectual property, or even expensive machinery that could be tooled or modified in a way that could be extremely valuable to a buyer would all contribute to the overall value.

When a seller has volatile cash flow or a difficult business to market, it will be in their best interest to focus on the assets and not the income/loss. In turn, a savvy buyer may see underlying value in the assets and may be able to offer a price to an unsuspecting seller who doesn't realize the assets they are sitting on hold great value because the profit and loss has been less than impressive.

These assets could also be intangible (not physical), such as a customer list, patent, trademark, intellectual property of some sort, or even a brand recognition or logo. In the hands of the buyer, such intangibles could be worth even more if utilized in their distribution system or market reach to expand the brand or to exploit the customer list.

3. Cost to Create Method

There are times when a buyer will purchase a business simply to avoid the difficulties of starting a new business from scratch. I've met with many clients using this approach because they don't want to "reinvent the wheel." Welcome to the Cost to Create Method.

Moreover, a buyer needs to consider the time and effort to create trust with customers and the value of the seller's name and recognition. It can be very unpredictable for a buyer to create a new

> ## 66 RANDY LUEBKE
>
> Sometimes, the cost to create this method is referred to as the "leapfrog startup method," and the buyer calculates the startup costs in terms of dollars and time. When I reference "time," I'm not talking about the hourly cost of the buyer's time, but the opportunity cost of lost time. For example, the buyer might determine it would take three years to develop a new business to the point where the buyer is already operating. That could be three years of lost profit that needs to be factored into a competitive offering price for the business. 99

product, service, and brand. Although the buyer may think it is easy to reproduce, simply acquiring the seller's business could minimize a lot of risk.

A buyer can use this valuation approach as leverage or a threat to the seller, explaining that the buyer is coming into the market no matter what. I once used this argument on behalf of a buyer in a carpet business transaction and told the seller that my client would be taking at least some market share of the seller's customers and further tried to motivate the seller with a generous price, rather than see their profits go down when there is another player in the market.

4. Capitalized Earnings Approach Method

Under this valuation method, a buyer has an expectation of a rate of return based on their investment in the purchase. This return can have a lot of different labels, such as Return on Investment (ROI), Cash on Cash Return, CAP Rate, or Internal Rate of Return (IRR). In fact, there are many other terms that could be used, but essentially, it means that the value is going to be based on an expected return in relationship to the investment.

The rate of return is based on the investment of the buyer divided by the annual net income after taxes. For example, if the buyer pays $2 million for a business with a $500,000 down payment and loan for $1.5 million, the investment is really $500,000. Let's assume that after debt service (payments for the $1.5 million loan), the cash flow is $50,000 after taxes; then, the ROI is 10 percent. This equation may sound simple, but it's important to compare apples to apples when negotiating. Lawyers and appraisers are notorious for using the definition that supports their value and can easily change numbers and terms creatively to fit their argument.

One of the prominent theories of this ROI approach is that the buyer should be able to sell the business at any time and get their initial investment back. Because of this, risk becomes a critical factor to consider. **A buyer will compare their investment in a seller's business to other options, such as an annuity, mutual funds, or some sort of moderate risk.** This puts the investment in perspective for the buyer and involves a lot of comparisons to help the buyer make an informed decision.

The type of buyer interested in this valuation method is typically leaning on the "turnkey" concept often referenced in real estate deals: that the buyer can purchase the business, replace the buyer with a manager/executive (a cost inserted into the normalized financials), and then, the buyer can sit back and see the profit roll out without having to personally oversee the day-to-day operations or put significant time or labor into the business.

5. Discounted Cash Flow Method

This is a type of calculation based on the future cash flow of the company and what a buyer is willing to pay now for those future cash flows. It starts with a seller and buyer first agreeing as to the current cash flow being generated by the company and then projecting that cash flow into the future based on any trends taking place in the business.

Once the parties agree as to the future cash flow, the appraiser will take into account the time value of money and calculate the present value of the future cash flow. That is essentially what the word discounting means and really entails. Buyers can then use this method to determine what the asking price *should* be and if the seller is asking too much or too little for the business. In reality, there are several variations of this valuation method to consider, and each is based on multiple variables. Such variables include: the estimated cash flows, timing, cost of capital, and the trend or growth rate. A change in any one of these variables can have a big impact on the estimated value of the company. Thus, this is again another method used to come up with an average price during the appraisal.

6. Comparable Sales Method

Comparable sales are obviously a pretty straightforward method here, but worth mentioning because of its importance and common use. If and when possible, an appraiser will try to pull comparable sales of a similar type and nature of business. **The difficulty is finding a business that sold within a reasonable amount of time, in a similar market, and that has common characteristics.** Nonetheless, with certain types of businesses, it's easier to find these types of comparables. For example, a restaurant of a similar size, type of food, and city demographics could be easy to find and help a seller and buyer in appraising a business.

Increasing the Value of Your Business

I have had many meetings with clients interested in selling their business, and as we start to go through the different valuation methods, together we quickly discover that they are a few years out before selling. It's not that they aren't interested in selling; it's just that they have come to the realization that they have to take some action to create more value for a potential buyer.

The importance of trends and growth rates cannot be overstated. When a seller can take several years to build a compelling growth rate and trends of sale demands or production output, buyers will take notice.

What happens is that sellers begin to understand how buyers perceive and view the value of their business and are grateful to learn that there are steps they can take to truly increase the value of the business and then legitimately be able to prove it under various valuation methods.

Business owners know deep down where the problems are within their business, and when they are forced to deal with them in preparation for a sale, the value of the business will certainly benefit. It's actually really exciting. Probably the most important step to take in preparing your business to sell is simply "systemization," and I mean systemization of everything.

I learned this critical principle when working with a professor of entrepreneurship, Mark Morris. I learned from Morris during our consultations that as he worked with family-owned businesses trying to pass on the company to the next generation, if "processes are implemented to replace key personnel, the business had a much higher value and probability of success." **A buyer wants to buy a system— not a handful of key people who could leave and/or essentially destroy the business for any reason.** Ironically, by creating systems and processes in your business that are probably far past due for implementation, you start to find a little financial freedom and even increased profitability (a side benefit I'll discuss further below).

Nevertheless, regardless of the specific issues you know that need to be cleaned up in your business, here is a list of other important items to get in order as you prepare to value and look for a third party.

- $ *Assessing company employees for readiness.* Are the proper personnel in place to run the business for a third party? What are the strengths and weaknesses of the management team? Do you need to do more training or make some hard decisions and let some people go?
- $ *Reviewing company systems and procedures.* Just as I stated above, review *every* aspect of your business for processes and systems that could be improved or implemented. This includes production, admin, sales, delivery, and customer service. Is there anything you could do to systemize and increase productivity without adding more staff? Consider engaging a business consultant to review your company operations from an outside point of view.

§ *Tightening up the books.* Is the bookkeeping in good order? Are tax returns accurate and be reasonably tied to the operational books? It may take a couple years to bring the financials in line with true operations, but start now. A buyer will want to see at least a couple years of solid books that tie to bank accounts, credit card statements, and tax returns. This also includes improving your accounting systems and immediately starting to prepare annual financial statements.

§ *Reviewing your software systems.* Is your technology outdated? What is now commonplace in your industry, and what are your competitors using by way of software and automation in the technology sector? It may be time to upgrade your hardware, software, wiring, and even move items to the cloud. The investment could pay off tenfold as a buyer sees that you aren't running on outdated technology that would have to be upgraded after a purchase.

§ *Wrapping up any litigation or potential claims.* You will ultimately need to sign documentation verifying that all outstanding claims are either settled or nonexistent. Don't let a potential plaintiff screw up the sale of your business. Start reviewing your relationships with prior customers, vendors, and employees, and settle. Get rid of these "problem children" so they will not taint the sale before *or* after closing.

§ *Determining what regulations the buyer will have to satisfy.* If you are in an industry that requires city, state, or federal approval, find out about the process. Who can qualify to buy your business, and what hoops are they going to need to jump through? Get the list now, and create a path for ownership so the process can be streamlined.

§ *Update your marketing plan.* Implement an organized, long-term marketing plan that integrates current technology and social media. Does your website need a facelift, and are all of your social media platforms up-to-date with a regular posting schedule?

§ *Intellectual property.* File any necessary documentation to lock down your brand, logo, catch phrases, images, and any intellectual property unique to your business. Do you need to file any patents or trademarks? These can create significant value in the eyes of a buyer.

Finally, it may simply be in your best interest to engage an appraiser as I discussed in the previous chapter. **By hiring an appraiser, there is a good chance you will discover many of the problems or holes in a higher valuation.** Even a semi-successful appraiser should give you a list of areas to improve that would significantly increase the value of your business.

The Unexpected Side Benefit

What is interesting is that in every instance that I have helped a client go through these steps of preparing to sell their business, they discover an ancillary benefit: they remember the passion they had for their business! In fact, I have even had clients get a renewed interest and excitement for their business that puts the sale on hold.

 RANDY LUEBKE

As business owners, we can get stuck in the trees for months, if not years at a time, but by stepping back and looking at the forest like a buyer might, it can truly be exhilarating for a business owner burned out and wanting to sell. As they organize and systemize the business for a valuation and buyer, they *finally* take the time to step back and look at the big picture.

Essentially by going through this valuation process, it always involves long-term analysis and planning regarding sales, structure, costs, employees, vendors, systems, and the unique characteristics of their business, which literally takes their business to a whole new level. Profits increase almost immediately. No matter what, the business improves because of this new perspective—this new way of looking at the business.

§ § §

TAKEAWAY 1—Understanding the most common valuation methods used by business appraisers will help you obtain a realistic view as to the value of your business and help you better negotiate with a buyer and direct your appraiser through the process.

TAKEAWAY 2—By going through the valuation process, you will quickly learn where the weaknesses are in your business. Moreover, there is a long list of things you can do now to increase the value of your business for a future sale.

TAKEAWAY 3—Don't be surprised when going through this process if you discover a renewed excitement and passion to take your business to the next level. You will inevitably increase the value and profit of your business that could very well change the timeline as to when you will sell.

TAKEAWAY 4—Make a plan now for the sale of your business two to three years from now, and you'll be amazed at what you can accomplish and the difference it will make in your business.

HELPING YOUR PARTNERS OR EMPLOYEES BUY THE BUSINESS

Selling to your partners or employees can oftentimes be the best option on the table for a business owner, perhaps even more than a family member. There are a lot of options to structure the deal in a win-win relationship, and a business owner can take the time, even over years, to groom the right buyer or buyers from within the business. Let's dig into how both these options might work.

Partners

Selling your business to a partner is probably the most common ownership transfer among small businesses. **The reason for this is that your partners have a clear picture as to the value of** the business, its potential, and what they need to do in order to replace you in the operations.

Selling to a partner is often one of the easier transfers to handle legally—**not that partners don't have their battles and disagreements—but most buying partners want to make the transition smooth and get the selling partner out quickly and painlessly.** Many times, I feel that partners are amenable and anxious to define the transaction and process so that they themselves can utilize the same method with a good conscience in the future.

The document that typically lays the groundwork for a partnership sale like this is called the "Buy-Sell Agreement." These types of agreements are drafted daily by law firms around the country and are actually implemented for more reasons than a partner wanting to sell. In fact, we include standard provisions for a buy-sell situation in our LLC Operating Agreements so there is at least something to fall back on if there isn't a more formal Buy-Sell Agreement signed separately.

In a more elaborate Buy-Sell Agreement for a more mature or established partnership, the document will cover issues of divorce, death, disability, and a requested departure or exit (the subject of this chapter). I call these the "Four Ds," and each is important to address with predefined terms.

The primary purpose of the Buy-Sell Agreement is to define the procedure for the transfer of ownership, price, terms, and transition well in advance of any event causing a transfer. This is a powerful tool because it prevents a partner from holding another partner hostage at a price or process in the heat of emotions when the transfer is needed.

For example, if all partners (or more) understand the process to determine the value well in advance, then they can work more clearly towards increasing the value of the business. Each party also knows that they are all held to the same equation and process if they were on the other side. This way, it will be fair when the time comes for each partner to leave the partnership (at least, that's the goal of the document and can certainly minimize the chance of a lawsuit). Here are some details you need to know about the Buy-Sell Agreement:

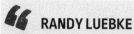

RANDY LUEBKE

Having a Buy-Sell Agreement is very important. It provides everyone with a roadmap and set of instructions when things, well, go wrong. It's interesting to note that no one would ever start a business with the idea that it won't work out. After all, every pro-forma spreadsheet model I've ever seen, the business owner will create a set of books that makes the business look incredible even if it's failing. Right? Things do go wrong, of course. Businesses are always subject to the four D's—Death, Disability, Departure, and Divorce. All these situations are bad. However, of the four, death of a partner is the easiest one to deal with. Typically, when a partner or key employee passes away, the business will want to buy out that person's share of the business. It will likely want to replace that valuable person, and that new person may want a seat at the table (ownership) as well. Or, the surviving partner(s) may not want to go into business with the deceased spouse as that person is not likely to have the same skillset as the departed partner or they may have a conflict in personalities, etc. Whatever the reason, the business wants to buy out the partner's estate, and they will need money to do this. The Buy-Sell Agreement generally makes it very easy to determine the appropriate value. The biggest problem is where the heck does the business get the cash to pay for the buyout?

Most entrepreneurships run a pretty lean balance sheet, and as we've mentioned repeatedly, they often reinvest all their money right back into their business. Even if the business did have the cash to buy out the deceased estate, that would likely not be the best use of that money. The solution is to have life insurance purchased by the company for this purpose. Life insurance provides a tax-deductible method to fund a buy out, and, because life insurance is a huge leverage opportunity, just a small amount of cash outlay can provide a huge tax-free death benefit. Having a larger amount of tax-free liquid cash at the time of a partner's death can be a huge relief to the business and, of course, the deceased estate.

§ *Determining the value.* Most Buy-Sell Agreements require the partners to agree to the value of the company on an annual basis and record it in the annual partnership meeting. This may seem arbitrary, but if everybody agrees (typically requiring a unanimous vote) and everyone knows that the value applies to everyone, then who cares what anyone from the outside thinks? If the partners can't agree, then a third party appraiser is brought in to do a formal valuation if a buyout is triggered during the upcoming year.

§ *Terms.* Oftentimes, the terms are based on a note, with interest, paid out over five to ten years. This can obviously create the retirement income a partner is looking for, and over the period of payments, it will spread out the tax bill as well. Some Buy-Sell Agreements require the remaining partners to obtain a loan for a good portion of the purchase price and then finish off the rest with a Note. This allows the departing partner to invest the initial money received wisely to create additional cash flow and prepare for when the payments under the Note end.

§ *First right of refusal.* Typically, there is a first right of refusal that must be given to the remaining partner(s) when a partner wants to leave or sell. This means that before a partner can run out into the open market and look for another buyer, they first have to offer their ownership interest to the other partners. This obviously can create some hurdles for the partner wanting to sell because they first have to find a third party willing to buy into a partnership where they may not be welcomed with open arms, probably be in a minority position, and then have to wait around for the other partners to exercise their first right of refusal. But again, it's a protection mechanism that "cuts both ways" and protects all the partners.

§ *Security.* To protect both parties, there can be a provision requiring the departing partner to sign a noncompete, and also the remaining partner or partners to "pledge" the partnership interest they purchased as security or collateral for the Note they are paying off. Thus, if the buying partner(s) defaults, the selling partner can come back into the company as an equity partner to try to recover the remaining sales price or value sold in the original agreement.

If a partnership doesn't have a Buy-Sell Agreement, it's okay, but it can increase the tension in the case of a partner selling when the remaining partners didn't foresee the situation and don't have the wherewithal to buyout their partner. In these situations, I tell the partners to turn immediately to their partnership agreement (typically an LLC Operating Agreement) to understand what the governing document allows for when it comes to a partner that wants to get out or sell.

Bottom line: if you are in a partnership and you ever, and I mean if you have the slightest thought that you might, want to sell in the next ten years, and your partner might, just maybe, be the buyer, then implement a Buy-Sell Agreement immediately. Don't mess around with the disaster that can be created in a partnership when it becomes volatile or a partner up and decides they want out.

Employees

It is actually not that common of a situation for a business owner to sell to an employee or employees, for three major reasons. First, employees typically don't have the capital to complete the purchase, even if they know the inner workings of the company and could do a good job running the business.

Second, an employee may also not think the business is worth as much as you do because they are privy to the inner workings and dysfunctional aspects of the business.

Third, it's generally not a good idea to start approaching your employees and telling them you are interested in selling. Employees tend to get a little concerned and skittish because they see a situation where they may not have a job if you can't find a buyer or find an objectionable buyer, and they tend to start looking for other employment.

However, in those unique, and I mean very unique, situations where you can approach one or more of your employees who want to buy your business, or have expressed an interest in doing so, you can often be in the driver's seat regarding price and terms. **In fact, an employee may have an insight into the future value of the**

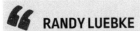 **RANDY LUEBKE**

Another benefit or strategy when selling your business to employees, or anyone else for that matter, is to create an installment sale. The installment sale will potentially defer all the taxes that would otherwise be due upon a cash sale as with an installment; you do not pay taxes until you receive the money. This strategy does have downsides of course. While this may be a great solution from an income tax perspective, still that money (your money, your golden goose) is still tied up inside that business. Worse yet, once you sell the business, you give up control of it. What if the new buyers blow it and can't repay you? The solution can be in the form of a Deferred Sales Trust (DST). With the DST in place, the seller can effectively cash out their ownership position, taking the risk of the new buyer's inability to repay the seller out of the equation. To mitigate the tax issue, the proceeds from the sale do not go into the hands of the seller directly. Instead, those proceeds go into a trust. Then, with money in hand, the trust can slowly distribute the proceeds, yielding similar tax benefits to what would have been received under the direct deferred sale. Keep in mind that this is a relatively complicated strategy, and it is definitely not a DIY project. If you want to consider this strategy, you must seek competent legal and tax advice before you proceed or you will likely regret it. By the way, the DST strategy can also be used to rescue a 1031 exchange. If a seller in the 1031 cannot find a suitable exchange property within the time limits imposed by the exchange, a DST can become a bailout strategy. The DST can be a great strategy to delay taxes on the sale of any highly appreciated asset. Again, if you do venture down this path, proceed with caution and find a well-trained guide to walk along your side.

business and passion to carry it on. Thus, you may be able to get the price you want, set up a promissory note, and have the security and collateral to come back in and take over the business if you have to for lack of payments by the employee/buyer.

For example, in a situation where the employees are buying, there will typically be a Note, paid by the profits of the company and the stock of the company securing it. The owner will have regular reports regarding the financials, and if sales or profits start to go south, the owner can take back control over the company to rein things back in. This is a typical provision and fair to the owner in order to protect the company, which is essentially the asset paying off the Note.

Take Your Time with Employees

A suggestion we make to business owners in this situation where the owner has already established a strong relationship with one or more employees is to take their time in the process with the transition of ownership and leadership.

First, start with training and leadership. Make sure the employees who think they can buy the business can handle it once they have the reins. Consider signing an agreement that starts the process and then give them more important roles, not necessarily with extra compensation, but with the written promise that ownership will be transferred as they prove themselves. This proving period could be showing things like maintaining profit levels and production quotas, maintaining morale with key employees, or simply showing leadership skills with good decisions when the owner steps back a little from operations.

Next, consider appointing the potential employee/buyer an officer of the company or adding them to the board of directors

---

TIP FOR FINANCIAL FREEDOM

If you are carrying the "paper" you need to monitor the business.

---

or management team. You still control the process and the positions as the owner/shareholder/member, but they need to be given a little rope to either win your approval or that of the other employees—or hang themselves in the process.

As the process evolves and the employee or employees show they have what it takes, you will then be duty-bound to start transferring ownership of the company; however, there can still be strings attached. This is called a vesting phase under what is known as a "vesting schedule," where real equity ownership and voting rights will transfer to the employee only under certain conditions and over a certain period of time. In turn, the purchase and sale is executed as stock transfers and the employees start to pay off the Note with the profits they are receiving and getting taxed on during the transition.

Finally, some owners choose to begin transferring a majority of the equity ownership through nonvoting stock or similar types of ownership interest, which allows the owner to maintain control through owning a majority of the voting interest while selling the equity or profit interest that is funding the buyout. **Don't be afraid to be creative and demand protection for yourself during the transition.**

Let me tell you now, because someone else may not be in the position or have the guts to tell you, letting your company go to a partner or employee—due to the close relationship or friendship—isn't easy. You're going to want to step in and be the hero at times and will want to stay emotionally attached to the company, customers, and employees. Don't do it!! Be strong, and let the transition take place. I guarantee you won't like certain ways they are running the company.

However, it doesn't matter what their style or approach to the company is **as long as they are making a profit and are financially successful!** Keep your eye on the ball. You sold the business so you could have more financial freedom, flexibility, and/or retirement—you didn't sell the business to leave a legacy in the community or neighborhood. **Let the business evolve and the new owners move onward and upward.** As you get quarterly reports and IF you notice that the new owners are starting to drive the business into the ground, you can jump in—but only then. Otherwise, you'll undermine the buyers and potentially blow up the whole deal. Stay out! Watch from the sidelines. Cash your checks and go on a cruise or something.

$ $ $

TAKEAWAY 1—The Buy-Sell Agreement is your secret weapon, your most powerful tool, that can define the procedure for the transfer of ownership, price, terms, and transition all in advance of the event causing the transfer. It prevents a partner from holding up the sale due to pricing or other considerations.

TAKEAWAY 2—Get on the same page as your partner when it comes to how the business will be run and later sold to them. You and your partner need to take ownership of the agreement and share a thorough understanding of how it will govern your business.

TAKEAWAY 3—Selling to employees is a tricky business. Make sure you have all of the information you need to proceed before making your plans public knowledge. Create a long-term procedure for the transition with a Promissory Note that gives you control to protect both the business and the "deal."

HOW TO FIND AND SELL TO A THIRD-PARTY BUYER

Although selling to a partner or employee, a third party, or a family member have the same basic elements, the process or steps of selling to a third party are the most distinct and straightforward. The waters tend to get a little muddier with a family deal or an "in-house" partner/employee deal. People will cut corners, which I certainly don't recommend, but because of the close relationships, there tends to be more of a DIY (do it yourself) approach.

However, sellers don't cut those same corners in a third-party transaction. Business owners are more wary of getting ripped off and hence more willing to follow proper or traditional steps, including hiring a broker, appraiser, attorney, CPA, and a variety of other professionals to help them through the process.

Now, although on the surface it may seem that you are less likely to screw up the deal because of the support you are receiving or paying for, with more "cooks in the kitchen," it's actually easier to have a deal hijacked or cost you more in excessive fees.

Thus, in this chapter, I want to focus on the most common issues faced by a seller in a typical third-party transaction and help you avoid some of the pitfalls I've seen clients fall into over the years. First, allow me to put this process of selling a business to a third party in perspective by describing the typical steps you will go through to ultimately sell your business successfully. Figure 21.1 is a diagram to put a visual to it:

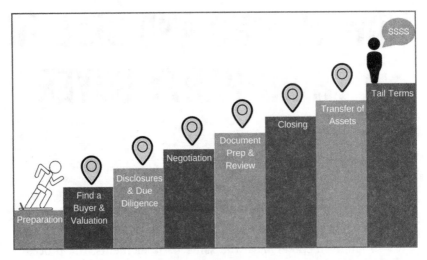

Figure 21.1—General Steps in a Business Sale to a Third Party

I understand that different businesses, buyers, and situations will drive the process. In fact, every business transfer tends to be different. **There is always some hiccup or hurdle, and it's important to expect those to pop up and not be dismayed when they do.** However, the steps are generally the same in the end. Let's talk about each of these steps in more detail.

Preparation

As I discussed in detail in Chapter 18, it's critical to start years in advance of when you may want to sell, especially, if you are going to shop your business to third parties. You'll want to be able to put your best foot forward when the time comes. Don't shortchange yourself. A mistake that many business owners make is that when they want to sell their business, they want to sell it NOW. This results in them selling far below the value of their business. In fact, circumstances in life can arise where the owner waited too long, and it's now an issue of "must" instead of "want." **Please review the steps in Chapter 18 that you can take now to increase the value of your business for a potential sale so you don't end up in a "must" situation.** Doing the work now and envisioning a day in the future when you will sell can make the process much easier for you down the road.

Finding a Buyer and Valuation

I discussed the valuation techniques and options in detail in Chapter 19, but that doesn't solve the problem of finding a buyer. This can be one of the biggest challenges with this type of transaction. A seller may not have a partner, employee, or family member with the will or interest to step up and buy the business. Thus, you have to take on a sales role you have never experienced before. You can put a great price tag on your business, and it could even be a great deal, **but how do you find that perfect buyer who can pay the price and still not run your business into the ground?**

To frame that question, let's first consider the real issue here: many business owners don't want to start advertising that they want to sell. Doing so can cause serious problems with employees or key management personnel who don't want to deal with a buyer and will jump ship out of fear before you could even present an acceptable buyer to your internal team. Yes, you are going to have to "sell" the buyer to your employees and management as well. This is something the third party is also going to require (and it's typically in the purchase and sale contract)—that you help make it a smooth transition and minimize the loss of any staff.

You also may have the problem of vendors and customers getting nervous and jumping ship if they hear you might be selling. You want to present the narrative of who the new buyer is at the *right* time and

RANDY LUEBKE

Keep in mind that when you sell anything, both parties need to benefit. Often, it's tempting to see things from our own perspective and become unrealistic. It's not easy to become unattached, unemotional, and objective when selling your business. That said, just ask yourself this question, if I were shopping for a business today, would I be likely to purchase my business with the terms I am offering? How do you judge fairness? I have a story that explains it very well. I don't recall where I first heard this story, but I've told it many times. It goes like this: Two boys want to share a candy bar. Each of them wants an equal share, of course. The wise parent overhears their conversation and tells the boys, "One of you gets to cut the candy bar in two. The other gets to pick which half he wants first." Problem solved, right? If it's a fair deal for both of you, then that is the best deal. That said, often-times that is not the situation and one person has an advantage over the other. Perhaps the seller needs the cash. Perhaps the buyer has to complete a 1031 exchange or face a huge tax bill. In both situations, the motivations are unequal, and the candy bar will not likely be split equally. In fact, it does not have to be split equally. That said, when it comes to a situation like this, here is my rule, "Whoever wants it most, loses." Another way to look at this is, "Whoever has the most leverage, wins."

not get blindsided with a rush of social media or rumors that you are selling for some terrible reason.

Bottom line: **it is safer to try to keep your plans to sell as confidential as possible with your employees, customers, and vendors.** I've seen a number of clients hijack the deal themselves by having a "big mouth" and talking about selling. You may be excited about it, but that doesn't mean everyone else will be. Take your time, be very "tight-lipped" about the topic, and you'll know when the time is right to tell key people. Don't brag or complain that you are anxious to sell. It's not professional, and again, it can screw up your deal in ways that could surprise you *and* the potential buyer you are courting.

So, once you have committed yourself to silence and put on a poker face around the office, how do you find a buyer? First and foremost, don't be dismayed. I think you have several great options that could surprise you as a qualified buyer. Let's walk through some of the options you have for finding potential buyers:

- § *A business broker.* Yes, just like realtors help you buy and sell a home, there is a robust business broker community out there you may not have even been aware of. These are very skilled and qualified agents, for lack of a better word, who can help you find a buyer and act as a huge resource to you throughout the process. **Yes, you will pay a fee for the service just like with a Realtor™, but it can be totally worth it.** There really isn't a Zillow© site for business sales; so start researching companies on the web that could help you in your particular industry, interview several before choosing, and make sure you meet offsite and never at your place of business. Again, be incognito.

- § *A vendor or supplier.* You may be shocked to discover that a vendor or supplier could be interested in expansion and getting into your line of business. **Again, you have to be careful on how you approach them, but you probably have a contact at most of these organizations that you could "swear to secrecy."** Such a contact would be appropriate to float the idea by to see if it's worth having more in-depth discussions. If you do start having discussions, make sure you sign an NDA early on (discussed in Chapter 18). Privacy is again critical, but your company data and security are even more important.

- § *A competitor.* It could be tricky to approach them, and it might show weakness or give them a competitive advantage with the knowledge you might be selling, but everyone's business is different. **It could be a great strategy for you to approach a competitor if the political climate is appropriate to do so.**

Disclosure and Due Diligence

In Chapter 18, I discussed the disclosure process in detail and the NDA (nondisclosure agreement). These elements are vital to your process, but I think it's important to also address something called *due diligence*. In this case, that means you understand your potential buyer will be doing their due diligence by asking to see all documents and records associated with your company. **Don't be shocked when this happens and a buyer wants to see everything about your business, and I mean everything.** You are probably asking a pretty penny for your business, so it should be expected that the buyer will want to double-check all your data and assertions.

In actuality, you prepared for the due diligence step and process back in the preparation phase we discussed in Chapter 18. You should be excited to show them how cool and amazing your business is! Show them the details of your normalized EBITDA, your systems, procedures, and intellectual property. With a proper NDA, this is your time to let your business shine and show why you are asking so much for your business. Don't be intimidated by the due diligence phase—embrace it!

Negotiation

Now, it's time to negotiate. I bring up this topic as an important step and process because of the competing issues facing a buyer and seller. Because there are many moving parts to a sale, negotiations can hinge on any of hundreds of complex topics. For example, let's say you want to do a stock sale for a better tax result. Your buyer may want to simply buy your assets so depreciation is a possibility. Then, if you do settle on an asset sale (which is most common in small business), then how are you going to allocate the purchase price to different assets? The buyer and seller will generally not be on the same page in such a scenario. That's just one example of how the structure of a deal could affect the negotiations and outcome. Everything—and I do mean *everything*—is negotiable.

Now, you may have an asking price *or* you and the buyer have agreed to have an appraisal, the structure of the deal can be just as much a negotiation as the purchase price. **Unless you negotiate on a regular basis in your business already, I suggest you read a number of good articles and/or books on negotiation before going into this process—it certainly won't hurt.** You are negotiating your financial freedom!

This can also be the phase of the deal where your advisors, and especially your lawyer, can be worth their weight in gold. A good lawyer can close the deal and find a way to make it a win-win for everyone. A bad lawyer can screw up the deal so fast it will make your head spin. Style and personality will play a big role in this process. Make sure you are extremely comfortable with your attorney and the role they are going to play.

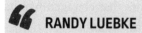 **RANDY LUEBKE**

One of my favorite stories is one that Jon Huntsman, Sr., recounts in his book *Winners Never Cheat: Even in Difficult Times* (Pearson FTP Press, 2008). In 1986, after lengthy negotiations with Emerson Kampen, chairman and CEO of Great Lakes Chemical Co., there was an agreement to buy 40 percent of a division of Huntsman Chemical for $54 million. A handshake between Mr. Huntsman and Mr. Kampen sealed the deal. After seven months of lawyers haggling the details and drafting documents, they were finally ready to sign. In the interim, the price of raw materials had decreased substantially. Mr. Kampen called Mr. Huntsman, saying the price of Huntsman Chemical had increased greatly during that time and that he would pay half the increase in value. Huntsman's answer was no. Kampen said it wasn't fair to the Huntsman Co., but Huntsman stuck to his handshake agreement. We need to understand how important it is to keep our word and negotiate with fairness and integrity. Don't let your representatives in a deal sacrifice your character to gain advantage or get a few more dollars. It's never worth it in the end. Huntsman summarized, "We will be remembered for truthful disclosures and promises kept."

Document Prep and Review

Ah, the part lawyers love. I joke about this for a reason. I have truly been shocked at the price lawyers have charged for helping to conduct the sale of a business. It is sometimes highway robbery (I guess that doesn't surprise some of you when I bring up the lawyer topic), but seriously, shop around to find the right lawyer to write up the docs.

Watch out for attorneys who charge large flat fees or a percentage of the deal because *this is their expertise and what they do.* You can certainly find excellent business attorneys that will charge hourly and be accountable for all the time they spend. **Just this past year, I was shocked to see a lawyer charge nearly a six-digit fee for a generally simple business transaction where an owner only sold 10 percent of his company.** Yes, there were a lot of dollars that changed hands, but that was no reason for the excessive fee in my opinion.

So, who is the right lawyer? **Regrettably, your family attorney may not be the best to handle the transaction.** Although you trust them and they won't rip you off, they may not handle purchase and sale agreements on a regular basis. There are a lot of tax issues and legal exposure topics that just aren't common in other areas of the law. Try to get a business attorney to handle the transaction, and make sure they have a strong tax background, or ensure that your tax advisor is at the table at all points of the discussion.

I also want to summarize the two primary options small-business owners use in the documentation to transfer and sell their businesses.

Asset Purchase Agreement

This is probably the most common method used to sell a small business because it allows for a seller to classify some of the sale as "goodwill" and recognize capital gains for tax purposes. Conversely, the buyer is able to get "stepped up basis" on a lot of the assets and start depreciation and amortization to also benefit from some tax planning. In other words, the buyer can begin to "write-off" a lot of the purchase, even over time, and thus create expenses from the purchase to save taxes in future years. The foundation of the transaction is the Asset Purchase Agreement, but there can be a host of ancillary documents like the Promissory Note, Noncompete, Nondisclosure, Security Agreement, Lease Agreement, and Consulting Agreement, just to name a few.

Stock Purchase Agreement

This type of transaction is more rare in the small-business world and far more common on Wall Street and with large companies. Yes, for the seller, a stock purchase is fantastic for tax planning but it is typically a disaster for the buyer—at least to a small-business owner. As such, this isn't a typical transaction for me or my clients. Nonetheless, it's important to be aware of this strategy because during negotiation, it can impact the purchase price if thrown on the table. Of course, all the other ancillary documents are similar to the ones I listed above that are oftentimes included with an asset purchase agreement.

As I indicate above, there can be competing interests between the buyer and seller regarding which method to use for the purchase. This can certainly make for a more robust negotiation regarding the price to be paid for the business. Figure 21.2 is a diagram to illustrate the pros and cons of each method.

Finally, and most importantly, make sure you understand every line of the contracts and agreements. The primary purpose of the lawyer

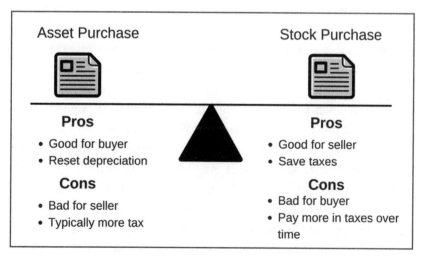

*Figure 21.2—*Asset Purchase versus Stock Purchase

is to draft the agreement *and* explain it. **If you don't understand something, stay at the table until you do. Remember—you are paying them, so get your money's worth.**

Closing and Asset Transfer

Believe it or not, closing and transfer of assets don't always happen on the same day. In your situation, it may be as easy as tossing the new owner the keys to the front door, but that's not always the case. Inventory, equipment, and client relationships may need to be carefully handled in the transfer. This is what I alluded to earlier when it came to employees, vendors, and customers and letting them know when and how the purchase will take place at the right time.

You will want to work closely with a buyer to make sure the transition is handled in the most appropriate way to create a win-win. I suggest you work really hard at being a politician and diplomat after closing, even if you aren't paid a consultation fee. Don't run out the door and jump on a plane to Bermuda. The buyer's ability to pay is oftentimes directly related to the ongoing success of the company. **Help them to succeed without giving away too much of your time, but ensure they are off and running smoothly.** Also, this is your legacy, after all. Help cultivate it for success with the new owners. Your knowledge of your business is limitless in value—share it with the new owners so they can continue your tradition of excellence.

Typically, the closing will be at an escrow office or title company, but they can also be handled between law firms, the procedure and goal being that the "keys" to the business are handed over at the same time the money/down payment is delivered and documents signed. Does this next point even need to be made? Yes, it does because I see a case like this every year. **Do not, and I mean do not, take money or give control of your business until everything is reviewed, approved, and signed.** It shocks me how many people start the transfer of a business on a handshake. I wish everyone would keep his or her word, but it also is a situation of memory loss. Many of these situations turn into selective memory issues and a "he said/she said" argument resulting in a lawsuit. Regrettably, you can't trust anyone. I'm sorry, but we live in a different day and age. Protect yourself, your assets, your business, and your legacy.

Tail Terms

You may think after closing and after the assets, customer lists, equipment, and keys have been handed over to the buyer that the deal is complete. However, typically that is not the case, and it results in 'tail' terms, or agreements and obligations after closing. **Oftentimes, in a small-business purchase and sale, the owner is asked to stay on board for a few months or even years.** This is typically in the form of a consulting contract, and I think this can be a really good fit for both parties.

As a prior owner, you can typically set up a new S corporation for the earnings you will earn as a subcontractor and can keep deducting a lot of the personal business expenses you have become accustomed to. It is also a good emotional transition. **Leaving the business, believe it or not, can be a difficult transition. The business was your baby, and you want to make sure it's in good hands.** Starting a new consulting company (even if the only business you will consult with is the one you just sold) helps you move on and focus forward while continuing to influence the original company you worked so hard to build.

Also, the buyer can really benefit from a consulting contract with you since you are the prior owner. It can help in the transition with employees, management, vendors, and certainly customers

> ## ❝ RANDY LUEBKE
>
> If you sell your business, you owe it to yourself, your clients, and the buyer to do everything you can to ensure its continued success. It may be difficult to be inside your business and watch someone else make all the choices and operational decisions you once made. Do your best to stand aside and let it happen. Be helpful, be supportive, but most importantly, be quiet if at all possible. ❞

because you will be a familiar face upon whom they can call. **Of course, boundaries and duties need to be clearly defined.** It's not uncommon to have miscommunication regarding the expectations for this role on both parties. **Prior owners sometimes try to do too much and step on toes; then, in other instances, they do too little and think the consulting contract is simply another payment for the sale of the business.** Work with the new owner to create a set of expectations and role responsibilities (and boundaries) that satisfy both of your needs.

Other "tail terms" include the seller signing a noncompete agreement to protect the buyer from the seller turning around and starting a competing business. Also, if there is a Promissory Note to be paid by the buyer (which is typical), the seller should have the stock of the company as collateral and regular reports from the buyer as to the condition of the company's finances. It's very common that documentation will allow the seller to step in and take over control of the business if the buyer defaults on the Note or starts to run the business into the ground.

We've covered the basic steps of preparing your business for sale to a third party, and it all looks good in theory, right? It does. **That said, we all know that when humans are involved, so remember that anything can happen.** Even buyers and sellers with the best of intentions can fall victim to sloppy preparation, loose contract language, and general misunderstanding.

In summary, books, classes, entire careers, and businesses are built on this important transaction of the purchase and sale of a business. I realize this book, and even this chapter, is a 10,000-foot look at the process, and I humbly hope that these thoughts and points on the sale of your business to a third party are helpful.

§ § §

TAKEAWAY 1—Have backup or contingency plans in case any deal to sell fails.

TAKEAWAY 2—Vigilantly guard your company information and always use a nondisclosure agreement (NDA).

TAKEAWAY 3—The culture of the company may be diluted, changed, or erased once you're gone. Be prepared for a new sheriff in town once you're gone. If you want some control after the sale, negotiate a consulting agreement so you can shepherd the business through the "new owner" phase.

TAKEAWAY 4—If you don't receive the majority of the cash upfront, make sure you have protections in place to retake control of the company if the buyer can't stay current with the note.

SELLING TO YOUR FAMILY

In my experience, it is quite common to have a family member purchase the business from the owner. This could be as small as a real estate office, insurance agency, or landscaping business or as big as a chain of restaurants or larger retail locations. I truly believe, and maybe I say this because I'm a business owner myself as well as a family man, that **most business owners hope deep down that someone in their family will see the value of what they are doing and want to take over the family business**. I suppose it could also be just visions of grandeur, but whatever the reason, this probably contributes to so many multigenerational businesses.

With that said, it doesn't always happen that way. Many businesses, in fact, simply shut down because the family doesn't want to carry on the torch. If the owner is lucky, the business is sold successfully to a third party as a contingency plan. **Then in some of the most regrettable situations, the business transfer is handled within the family inappropriately, and it's a disaster**. However, luckily many businesses pass to the next generation without a lot of hiccups.

I have actually helped many business owners over the years prepare for and successfully follow through with, a family member purchasing the business. Here are some important considerations and ways the transaction between family members can and should be handled.

Assess Yourself and the Company

Ask yourself, "If I left tomorrow, would my company crumble under the direction of my family members? What about in six months?" How independent is your company? Is your family even physically and mentally up for the challenge? **Be realistic with yourself and about your family members**. Even Don Corleone in the *The Godfather* knew the ultimate heir to his business needed to be Michael as much as he didn't want him to be involved. Sonny and Fredo just didn't have the temperament and skills. That's what you're looking for when selling your business—a Michael.

As you read in Chapter 18, whether you are selling to a third party or a family member, the preparation stage is absolutely critical. You certainly want to set them up for success and not failure. The more you can systemize the business and prep it for transfer, the better. Please read the sections on the preparation stage in Chapters 18 and 19 if you felt you could skip them because you were determined to sell to a family member and jumped directly to this chapter.

Pros and Cons of a Family Member Buyer

OK, it's time to get real. It's time to be honest with yourself. Do you have a "Michael" in mind? Or is your family a who's who of Sonny's and Fredos? Honestly, there is never one perfect person, one shining example of the ultimate business owner who can nurture your legacy, in any family. Why? We're all human—complete with faults and shortcomings. **That said, you can probably identify at least one family member, whether it's a child, grandchild, niece, or nephew, who just has that thing—the thing that lets you know they will be good stewards of the business you've worked hard to build.**

If you're lucky, you have more than one person in the family that could take over the reins, but you also don't want a heated competition between family members fighting for the position. That inevitably creates a whole other set of challenges. However, take some time to make yourself a good, old-fashioned list of potential family members who might buy your business, and consider the advantages and disadvantages of each. Here's what to keep in mind about selling to family:

Advantages

- $ Your successor grew up around the business. They are familiar with your ethos, your client base, and your product or service.
- $ They know the language and day-to-day flow of the business. They understand the terminology associated with your product or service and have experience communicating with clients, customers, and vendors.
- $ Most likely, they will preserve the culture of the business. In other words, they will not change the heart and soul of what you've built. Branding stays in place, as do business practices.
- $ It can be a reward for working in the business and working for reduced pay over the years. In other words, is selling your business to a family member a nice way to reward them for their loyalty? For many family members who have worked up through the ranks of the family business, taking ownership is a point of pride.
- $ There are tax advantages for selling to a family member. Because it's family and there is a higher degree of trust, there can be a lot more creativity in the structure and transaction, leading to more tax benefits to help paving the way for financial success of your entire family.

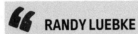 **RANDY LUEBKE**

Selling to a family member is great if you have a qualified buyer. Building a business into a legacy for your children has to be one of the greatest rewards one can have in life. I don't know, personally, as my kids have zero interest in what I do for a living. They have their own careers, and I'm happy for them. My point is simply if your children have the attitude and aptitude and the willingness to do what needs to be done to run your business, congratulations! Not only have you raised a great kid, but you've also got an awesome buyer who will benefit from all the hard work you put into your business and, hopefully, allow his family to enjoy the spoils of that work for the rest of their lives as well.

Disadvantages

- § Both parties know the weaknesses of the other and can cause aggression from the successor—and hesitation from the owner.
- § Passing on a business to a family member will not happen all at once. There are lots of details to work out. It's a long process that can be arduous for both parties.
- § Owner will most likely not get money from the sale all at once. Payment is often dealt out over a much longer period of time than a traditional sale to a third party.
- § Some businesses are not easily taken over, which may require additional education on the part of the successor.
- § One of the greatest disadvantages is that the owner may not get what they want for the sale of the business or at least what they need to retire on comfortably. This can be a balancing act as Figure 22.1 on page 235 illustrates.

Thus, if we are going to try and exploit the advantages, avoid the disadvantages, and do our best to get mom and dad (presumably the owners selling the business) the money they need to retire, we need to follow a process. **It certainly isn't something you can craft together**

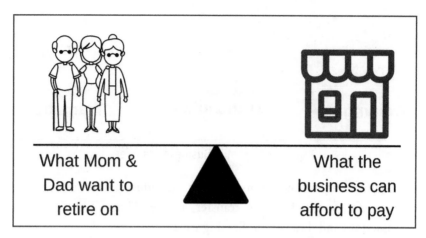

Figure 22.1—Balancing Retirement and Affordability

on a college-ruled notebook at the kitchen table, and you know what I'm talking about. Let's focus on what you need to do in order to make this transition a success.

The Process

Selling to family is similar to selling to a third party, but typically, it's a more simplified process that happens over time. I actually don't recommend a long, drawn-out process. Please understand that your family member(s) buying the business have lives and dreams, too. **If you are going to sell the business, make a plan and a timeline, and stick to it.** I have seen children leave the business because mom and dad made promise after promise to sell the business and step away from management, but it never came to fruition. Situations such as that can really put a lot of stress on the family, and I felt it was truly destructive to the child.

So get serious! If you're going to do it, then get to it. Have a plan and a timeline agreed upon in writing. Maybe it's 5 years, 10, or 15, but be clear about what you want and all your expectations. Have the respect for your family member to treat them like a third-party buyer. That means you should provide them with the preparation you would afford any other buyer. Good documentation in a family business transaction keeps the family together and the family reunions civil.

Figure 22.2–Family Business Transfer

Many family business consultants in the industry have summarized a successful family business transfer as the Three T's: Training, Transaction, and Transition. See Figure 22.2.

Training Your Successor

As I mentioned above, hopefully it's obvious who the buyer is going to be and who has the skills, personality, and temperament to step up and run the business. However, this doesn't mean they are automatically ready for the job or could handle it in the near future. **This business is something you have built from the ground up, and you need to make sure you have chosen the right person**. Make sure the person you're passing it down to is not only ready and interested but also competent. This is where training comes into the equation and could take years.

Remember that you don't need to be in a rush to exit either, but you certainly want to have a plan—and a written one at that. **Early on, "anoint" the family member that will be taking over the business, edify them, and build them up.** If it's a family member already working in the business, your employees, vendors, and customers should be expecting the transition. Of course, this includes getting them the proper training as well. **Don't be afraid to invest in this process either.** It shows the family member and the other employees of the company, that you want to "do it right" and not cut corners.

Document the training plan, and set benchmarks for achievement and a date for when official ownership transfer documentation will be signed and put into motion. The family member needs to certainly earn the right to buy the business, but they also don't want to feel

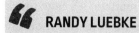

RANDY LUEBKE

I have seen business owners require the child that was going to take over the business get an MBA before the parent would sign the transition paperwork. I've also seen families require them to work at another company in the same industry, not only to pay their dues, but also to bring other product and systems knowledge back to the family business. I've even seen owners require the family member to work at a lower level position within the family business to better understand company culture, and to show other employees that the family member wasn't going to have the business handed to them on a silver platter without them learning the inner workings of the business.

the carpet may be pulled out from under them or the training process continues to be an endless process of jumping through hoops and no official paperwork is ever signed.

The Transaction

Family transactions tend to be a little more relaxed on the topics of the NDA, valuation, and negotiation. This is understandable, but it can also lead to other corners being cut in the documentation process as well. **A family should do their best to keep the transaction process professional.** Involve a lawyer in the process and maybe even a legitimate business appraiser to provide an outside voice as to the true value of the business. Again, in almost every situation it's typical that the owner thinks the business is worth far more than it really is, and they believe the family member should simply be grateful they are getting the business—even though they expect them to pay for every red cent. This can require the family to have an intervention or reality check with the owner as to the real value of the business. Thus, an appraiser can be a good idea even in a family transfer.

However, the reason why the valuation tends to not be as critical is that it's something we typically "back in to" in a family sale. For example, it's not the value of the business that matters; it's how much mom and dad need to retire on. Thus, once we find the monthly income needed to support the seller, we can work backwards to arrive at a price. Sometimes, the price ends up being under market value; other times, it's a price that a third party would never pay in exchange for the business. *Bottom line*: **the goal is that the buying family member can carry on the business, and in turn, mom and dad get a payment every month for life**. Again, this can sometimes be unrealistic, but other times, it's a good fit. It really comes down to the numbers and lots of conversations around the kitchen table.

Although the steps may be simplified or truncated compared to a partner/employee or third-party purchase, the actual structure and documentation tends to be more creative. As I stated earlier, because it's family, more trust and flexibility is offered by all parties and typically with the universal goal to stick it to the IRS as much as possible. Over the years, our office has handled many of these family business transfers, and each one can vary dramatically depending on the type of business and players involved. Here are a few examples:

- § If kids sell the business to a third party, the Note is paid off in a balloon to the parents.
- § When mom and dad die, the Note is forgiven as part of the estate and use of the unified credit.
- § Loan payment is considered an installment sale made up of four parts: interest, ordinary income, LT Cap Gain, and return of basis.
- § If there is a building or land, a lease agreement is executed to help support mom and dad. Passive income is not subject to SE Tax.
- § When mom and dad pass away, the building is bequeathed tax-free with a stepped-up basis to the family member who bought the business and made the lease payments over the years.

Transition Phase

If you as the seller want to stay involved in the business, that's great. But if it's not handled very carefully and the relationship isn't clearly defined, it can end up in a case of the seller stepping on the toes of the buying family member at the least. **Typically, I encourage the seller to just do their new job, keep their head down, and don't stick their nose into everything.** You are getting paid under a purchase contract and may have a consulting or employment contract—but only for a specific job. Now, I know this is very difficult to do, but stick to your assignment and stay out of the way.

 RANDY LUEBKE

Again, I've never had the opportunity to sell a business I've created to one of my family members. However, if I did, then after agreeing to the terms of the sale, I would:

1. Agree what my role will be in/for/with the business going forward, if any

2. Get out of the way, and let my buyer do their job!

Your family member taking over the business may have a new vision or direction, and as long as it doesn't risk profits or your Note, then give them the latitude they deserve and paid for. Something I recommend strongly is having the prior owner (oftentimes mom and dad) serve on the board of directors (if a corporation) the board of advisors (if an LLC). This is not just a figurehead position, either. **During the training phase, there should have been a focus on regular meetings and trainings to help the upcoming family member take over the reins properly.** Oftentimes, when the baton is handed over, a whole new set of problems occurs and usually with unexpected challenges. More than ever, those regular board meetings need to take place to help in the transition.

It is certainly common to also have the prior owner work with specific customers that could leave if the owner completely disappears. I really believe looking at the current client list and setting up meetings and experiences for the new owner to meet key customers is critical.

For example, golf outings are a classic example where the "old boys club" brings the new owner into their fold through relationship building—an important part of the transition. This also goes for vendor relationships. Sometimes, the business has been given great pricing by vendors, deals on delivery, or accounts payable terms, and the new owner needs to strengthen these bonds through the help of the seller. Plan for this, and expect these types of meetings and activities.

Potential Pitfalls

Now that we've nailed down the advantages and disadvantages of selling to family, let's talk caution. I've worked in these types of transactions and business transfers for more than 17 years, and I have seen lots of scenarios between family sellers and buyers. **In fact, every year, I'm surprised with new twists and turns that families can throw at me**. With that said, here's a few pitfalls I suggest you consider that could very well keep everyone friendly at the dinner table and family reunions pleasant for years to come.

§ DO NOT make one family member "lord" over the other family members or create a situation where there are competing interests. For example, this can happen if one member is given the real estate that the store is on, and the other member owns the actual store; they can argue for years about what a fair rent payment should be. If one member owns the land the store is on, and the other owns the store, they can argue over who needs to pay for what.

§ DO NOT split the business between two members where one is active and the other is not. There are other options, such as selling other holdings separate from the business, or passing down life insurance benefits to the inactive member while giving the business to the active one.

§ DO NOT make continued promises to sell the business but never sign anything or take active steps to complete the transaction. It could cost you your retirement and relationship with the younger family member.

§ DO NOT sell to a family member just for the sake of keeping the business in the family. It's OK if you sell to a third party. Your retirement *must* be a major consideration, and your family members can still be guaranteed employment or roles in the business with proper documentation between you and the third party.

$ $ $

TAKEAWAY 1—Before you commit to selling your business to a family member, consider all the pros and cons. Be guarded in what you say to everyone, including the member who could "be the one" to purchase the business.

TAKEAWAY 2—Once you decide to sell to family, ensure you choose the right person, and begin a rigorous training schedule and timeline for the transition. Put it in writing, and outline the process so everyone has disclosed their expectations and everyone is on the same page.

TAKEAWAY 3—Take advantage of creative structuring for tax-planning purposes, but follow a well-documented transition so that it's as smooth a transition as possible. Be aware of pitfalls, and get good advice and professional support in the process.

V

PROTECTING YOUR HARD-EARNED ASSETS

Sometimes, the words "asset protection" can sound cliché, and I too feel they are overused—or at least used in vain to oversell unnecessary plans to unsuspecting business owners. In my opinion, protecting our assets is FAR MORE than registering just a couple LLCs or corporations in another state or even adding some type of creative trust structure.

I wanted to add this section to the book to address some of the less frequently discussed topics that truly destroy a family's assets faster than they can spell asset protection. Think about health-care costs, identity theft, or a lawsuit from a texting and driving accident.

You may ask, "Is there really anything you can do if you have a catastrophic situation like cancer, a teenage driver accident, a cybertheft, or scam?" **Frankly, the answer is yes! You can actually do quite a bit to prepare for the unexpected**, and it's more than just buying insurance to protect yourself from "mayhem" in a dark suit in a clever commercial.

Humor me, and carefully read the next three chapters. **You'll quickly see that a major aspect of building financial freedom is to make sure it's protected**. I also recognize that in some ways, I just scratch the surface of quality asset protection strategies and techniques. For a more in-depth discussion and more chapters on the subject, please see my last book, *The Tax & Legal Playbook: Game-Changing Solutions for Your Small-Business Questions*.

ASSET PROTECTION: INSIDE AND OUTSIDE

I'm convinced that the term "asset protection" and the goals of asset protection are misunderstood by millions of Americans and even by the bulk of attorneys. Far too much legal planning is implemented and paid for in the name of asset protection but doesn't come close to accomplishing what was envisioned.

Simply stated, asset protection is the concept of protecting your assets from the claims of a potential creditor. However, many think that by setting up an LLC, corporation, or estate plan or trust, they are finished planning and are good to go. That is the furthest from the truth.

What I want to do in this chapter is cut to the true core of asset protection and what many attorneys or self-professed

gurus don't talk about. Essentially, I'm going to pull back the curtain and explain what real asset protection means when it comes to potential lawsuits.

Now with that said, I have written two books on asset protection, and this one chapter certainly doesn't do the topic justice with all the nuances and variations on asset protection. Nonetheless, this summary will give you the basic concepts to measure against your current plan, and at the very least, it will help you understand where to get started. Frankly, when it comes to financial freedom, how can we consider ourselves truly "free," at least to some degree, if we don't consider the risk of a lawsuit that could take everything away?

Let me break this down into four core concepts that will provide clarity and by so doing save you thousands of dollars and get you started on the *real* asset protection you desire.

1. Where's the Beef?
2. Two Types of Risks
3. Automatic Protection
4. Targeted Strategies

Where's the Beef?

For those that grew up in the '80s or remember that iconic era, there was a famous commercial I'm sure you haven't forgotten. It involved a typical fast-food commercial like you would see today with a B-roll of patrons eating their value meals and featured a little old lady (actress Clara Peller) looking at the skimpy amount of beef on the burger and asking the question, "Where's the beef?" Classic '80s fodder.

I use this TV commercial as an important example because we have thousands of clients come to our office seeking asset protection out of fear. **They want to check the next box off their list in building wealth, and they have a false sense of urgency.** As soon as I discover their feverish concern for "asset protection" imposed on them by some company firing them up unjustifiably, I ask them, "Where's the assets? Where's the beef? What are you stressed about protecting?"

TIP FOR FINANCIAL FREEDOM

If asset protection is such a concern for you, tell me what these assets are that you are trying to protect.

This poignant and direct question accomplishes two important goals:

1. *We decide if asset protection is even necessary.* If there really aren't any assets to protect, or they are already afforded protection, with automatic provisions (as discussed below), then we can move on to more important topics like actually building wealth. **This is often a break-through moment or realization for the client when they understand that they have been overly fixated on asset protection, rather than spending time on** *building* **those assets to protect in the future.** I love to turn the conversation to goal setting and practical legal planning to take their ideas to the next level and produce some real income and assets.

2. *We determine what assets need protecting and then can hyperfocus on the assets themselves, taking an asset-by-asset approach to targeted protection.* For example, we can create a holding company for a specific asset that is just what the doctor ordered for *real* asset protection.

To better advise and focus your attention on what matters most when considering asset protection, Figure 23.1 on page 248 is a list of assets that will drive the rest of the discussion.

Two Types of Risks

Once we determine there are actually real assets that need protection, we can then start talking about the risks. I have classified risks into two simple categories; I refer to them as "inside" or "outside" risks or liabilities. This principle is at the heart of real asset protection and thus the title of this chapter.

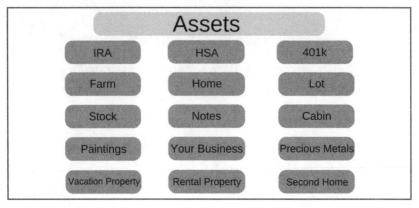

*Figure 23.1—*Potential Assets

Inside Risk Is the Exposure Created By Doing Business

These risks are created inside your business. For example, if you are going to start a landscaping business, you just created a bunch of risks that if something goes wrong inside your venture (such as an employee or bystander getting hurt), you have just threatened your personal assets or even your home. By doing this specific analysis, we can isolate the issue to a direct correlation we can begin to focus on. See Figure 23.2.

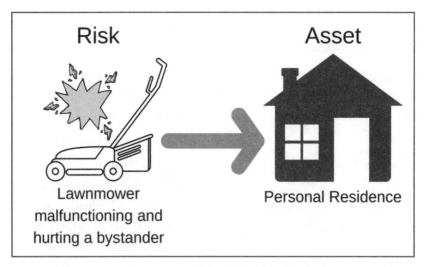

*Figure 23.2—*Risk to Your Assets

Outside Risk Is the Liability You Create in Your Personal Life

This has nothing to do with your business. It's outside of your business activity but is still a critical risk assessment we often forget to consider. For example, if you are texting and driving down a road and seriously injure a pedestrian, you have just created a significant risk to your assets, and it had nothing to do with your business. This is when the discussion of real asset protection begins to take form and shape into a constructive conversation.

I realize this can seem complicated, but this is truly the core of asset protection planning. Some see it as a fresh look compared

---

CASE STUDY

A few years back, I had a client with a teenage driver in the house. (Yes, you know what is coming.) There was an accident one weekend, and two third-party individuals were terribly injured. It was a devastating situation for everyone involved. Of course, a lawsuit followed, and my clients scheduled a meeting with me to assess the potential damages and risk to their assets. Early in the meeting, the parents said something I'll never forget and initiated my quest to teach this inside/outside concept. They stated confidently, "Well, at least we set up LLCs for our rental property that is paid off, so at least that is protected." I regrettably had to tell them that the LLC didn't protect them from this type of lawsuit. They were shocked and confused. **I said that the LLC protected them from the rental, but it didn't protect the rental from them getting into a lawsuit.** I went on to explain further that the LLC protected their home and a number of assets from a lawsuit inside the LLC or from the rental (like a tenant gone bad), but the LLC didn't protect the property and them from a personal lawsuit—something that happened outside the LLC (like a teenage driver). **This reality is a shock to many people when they realize that the typical LLC protects them but doesn't protect the asset.** It sounds odd, right? Please read on further.

---

to the advice of traditional advisors. Let me give an example that
will make sense of this unique approach to analyzing your risks and
assets.

**The good news is that there are structures—and yes,
LLCs—that will protect the asset and not just protect you and
your personal assets from the business.** This type of LLC is called
a COPE entity or Charging Order Protection Entity, and I discuss
more fully below as one of my targeted strategies. This could be a
perfect fit for your family if you have equity or assets other than your
personal home worth protecting.

Automatic Protection

Sometimes, you get lucky, and you have asset protection already built
into a plan or product that you are using. This means you are already
covered—to some degree—in case creditors come after you.

Once you have made a list of your assets that need protection and
identified your inside or outside risks, it's important to understand
which assets may *already* have automatic protection. Our federal and
state government has felt it's critical to our economy and the American
way that certain assets are protected from most lawsuits. **We, as a
society, have generally decided that we don't want to throw
people to the curb with no assets at all when they go through a
debilitating lawsuit.** Thus, we have created certain classes of assets
that are excluded from a creditor's reach in a lawsuit.

This topic of automatic exclusions is a big one and difficult to do
justice to in one section, of one chapter in this book; however, I want
to summarize the "Big Five" exclusions, as I have come to call them,
and how they may impact a client's asset protection analysis.

§ Homestead Exemption
§ Retirement Plans
§ Life Insurance
§ Tenancy by the Entirety
§ Garnishment Limits

Homestead Exemption

This concept is one of the bedrock principles of debtor protection outside of bankruptcy, the concept being that a creditor can't take every last penny of value from your home if you lose in a lawsuit. If there is equity in your home, you get to walk away with a few bucks to start your financial life over again after settling the claim. Interestingly enough, state governments dramatically vary on how much that exemption should be for your home after a lawsuit.

Retirement Plans

Many Americans don't realize how protected their retirement plan really is against any type of lawsuit. This includes every type of retirement plan, from an IRA, to a Roth, SEP, 401(k), and even an HSA. There are only two people that can get into your retirement account without some sort of creditor exclusion, and it's the IRS (federal government) and your ex-spouse in a divorce.

Now, you may not think this is a big deal, but **everyone I explain this to seems to be able to relate to this concept with an aha moment when I explain how through all the ups and down of O.J. Simpson's legal problems, he has kept his NFL 401(k) from creditors.**

States can sometimes have the ultimate say about the exemption amount and how certain retirement accounts are protected. Regrettably, IRAs aren't as protected as 401(k)s, but it's still pretty amazing the protection you can get. In this asset protection context, there are really two types of retirement plans: those that are covered by ERISA (aka the Employee Retirement Income Security Act of 1974, which set minimum standards for protection for most voluntarily established pension and health plans in private industry) and those that are not. For example, a 401(k) is covered, but non-ERISA plans (such as IRAs, SIMPLEs, SEPs, and KEOGHs) vary from state to state when it comes to having automatic protection. **The bottom line is if you are relying on your retirement plan as an asset protection vehicle, make sure you understand the rules in your state.**

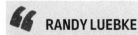

RANDY LUEBKE

In general, I feel that most people make too big of a deal over asset protection. So many people are afraid of the bogeyman or the proverbial "slip and fall" guest at your rental. The odds of something happening to you or your business that would be catastrophic are very small. That, by the way, is why insurance is such a bargain. For a small fee, you can protect yourself from catastrophe. That said, I also feel that most people do not truly understand risk or the risk of their particular situation. Remember, risk is like oxygen. It's everywhere and all around us. You cannot see it, smell it, or taste it, but it's there. You cannot survive without it, but too much risk, and you can explode.

Aside from business risk and market risk, the biggest risk that most of us ignore is our ability to earn an income. Financial plans look great when one spreadsheet lays out 20 to 30 years into the future the future earnings, savings, and compound growth. But what if you don't get 20 to 30 years? What if you can't work due to health-related issues or you are laid off and unable to find a replacement job? Oh, yes, then there is that one absolute certain risk, as we will not be around forever. Once again, often the best "asset protection" can be as simple as having an adequate long-term financial plan that involves your business and every possible option.

Life Insurance

Life insurance can be used for asset protection as well as for investing and estate planning. Essentially, life insurance is afforded some protection under federal bankruptcy exemptions, but protection across the states varies drastically. Some states give blanket protection of all the accrued cash value inside an insurance policy. Others may give just a limited dollar amount of protection. There are even limitations on the ability of the IRS to collect against the cash value, or the proceeds, of life insurance. Of course, if you have term life insurance, which does not build up liquidity inside the policy but simply pays out a death benefit upon your passing, there is no cash value to worry about protecting.

I still don't think the primary reason to purchase life insurance should be for asset protection. It can be expensive, and you should have other important goals you want to accomplish if you are going to make such an investment. Therefore, I don't recommend that anyone rush out and buy life insurance just to protect their cash in the bank. **Rather, I encourage my clients to make the wisest possible decision for the investment of their liquid assets and real property.** In sum, be cautious about being oversold on insurance for the purposes of asset protection.

Tenancy by the Entirety

If your state allows it, you can title your personal residence as "tenancy by the entirety," which offers unique a protection: if one spouse is sued, the property cannot be attached or bifurcated by the lawsuit. **Essentially, tenancy by the entirety holds that if a husband gets into a terrible lawsuit, it's not fair that the wife loses the house when the lawsuit had nothing to do with her (or vice versa).** There are approximately 15 to 20 states that have this law on the books, including Hawaii (as if you needed another reason to move to the Aloha State).

Garnishment Limits

Garnishment limits are imposed by state law to limit how much a creditor can withhold from a paycheck so people can still make enough money to live.

Targeted Strategies

After analyzing your asset list for any automatic protection, you will likely determine that you still have risks and assets that are exposed to these risks. We can then implement targeted strategies that are effective *and* affordable. Moreover, we can use strategies that make sense so as not to overdo our asset protection.

Many times, nonlawyers, coaches, gurus, and document prep companies will oversell one-size-fits-all strategies that don't actually protect anything. To add insult to injury, they will accuse your lawyer of being a liar and then charge excessive fees for their silver bullet protection that costs far more than what a skilled asset protection attorney may charge. (This issue alone was the impetus for my first book *Lawyers are Liars: The Truth About Protecting Our Assets* (Life's Plan Publishing, 2007) and later chapters in my book *The Tax & Legal Playbook: Game Changing Solutions for Your Small-Business Questions*). In both of these books, I have appendices that list how the various states treat your retirement accounts, life insurance, or primary residence in regards to asset protection.

I want to propose three targeted strategies that a competent asset protection attorney can at least present and discuss, then tailor them to a client if it's a good fit for their situation and will work in the state in which their client resides. Again, state domicile and where the asset is can play a big part in the planning.

Charging Order Protection LLCs

In a nutshell, a Charging Order Protection Entity (COPE) protects your assets from personal liabilities that arise outside your entity holding the asset. Now, the Limited Partnership (LP) in most states and a limited number of states give this COPE protection to the Limited Liability Company (LLC).

I'll talk about LPs in the next targeted strategy because LLCs and LPs have one major difference when doing COPE planning. The IRS treats the LLC much more favorably when it comes to rental property—no matter what type of rental property. **Essentially, you are going to get far better tax treatment with an LLC when it comes to rentals and flow-through depreciation, something you don't get with an LP.** Discuss with your attorney *and* tax advisor the types of assets that are best for an LP.

Now, the COPE is exactly the protection I was talking about at the beginning of the chapter that will protect you from an outside liability. Many times, we structure a COPE to own all the other sub-LLCs or assets when we have a client with significant assets. Again, be careful of getting oversold this strategy when you are just starting to invest.

The legal principle of the COPE was developed in courts and then codified under some state laws, and allows you, the owner of an asset, to protect its equity inside an entity such as an LLC or limited partnership (LP). **Thus, by putting an asset like a real estate property or an investment account in the right type of COPE, you have protected the asset from an outside liability.**

The effect of this law is that a judge will give an order charging a debtor to pay creditors from the revenue of an entity but not allow the creditor to foreclose on or dissolve the entity to get at the asset. **However, this protection isn't provided in every state.** Approximately 13 states have COPEs for LLCs, while 40 or more provide the same protection through an LP. Again, your tax and legal advisor should collaborate to determine if and when you should utilize this strategy.

Domestic Asset Protection Trusts

This is one of the hottest structures in asset protection today. It's great for protecting your primary residence, and you should consider this to be the best use for a Domestic Asset Protection Trust (DAPT).

Essentially, a DAPT is an irrevocable, self-settled trust created and protected under state statute. Once you place your assets in the trust, after a certain amount of time (which will vary by state), the assets are protected indefinitely from future creditors. What makes DAPTs so popular is that they don't require you to file a separate tax return, nor do they have gift tax consequences. They are relatively affordable and easy to set up and maintain. **A DAPT can hold your personal residence, stock brokerage accounts, or LLCs that own your**

TIP FOR FINANCIAL FREEDOM

The more assets and wealth you have, the more asset protection you need.

---

rentals. Moreover, it is ultimately coordinated with your revocable living trust and enhances your estate plan (but doesn't replace it).

While a DAPT can own rental property LLCs, I typically have concerns when they are used for this structure because of the third-party trustee requirement and steps that need to be taken for distributions. For example, if you want money or assets out of the DAPT, you need to request the distribution from your trustee. This will typically be a friendly trustee who looks out for potential creditors against you before making a distribution, but it's an extra step that can be cumbersome.

Rather, I recommend a DAPT for assets that you will have for a very long time or make few changes to—such as a personal residence, farm, cabin, etc. In those cases, managing a DAPT and its assets can be simple, affordable, and straightforward. Moreover, you can be designated as the investment trustee, allowing you to make decisions regarding the sale and acquisition of assets within the DAPT.

Yes, in the end, the DAPT could ultimately fail when challenged in your home state by a creditor. At that point, it would be unlikely you could keep a creditor from reaching the assets held in your DAPT. But one of the key strategies of a DAPT is that the amount of time, money, and resources needed to reach the assets could potentially dissuade creditors from pursuing them.

$ $ $

TAKEAWAY 1—Before going to great lengths and spending a lot of money protecting assets, make sure you have assets that are worth protecting.

TAKEAWAY 2—Make sure you understand which of your assets may already be protected under an automatic exemption. Review how such protection works (or whether it counts) in your state.

TAKEAWAY 3—Consider a Charging Order Protection Entity (COPE) or a Domestic Asset Protection Trust (DAPT) as a targeted asset protection structure if you have an asset mix that warrants it.

24

CYBER SECURITY RISKS

As an entrepreneur, or simply as an individual, you may be asking yourself, "What does cyber security have to do with me, and even more so, what does it have to do with financial freedom?" **The answer is that the odds of you becoming personally affected by a cyber threat are growing every day.** At a minimum, a cyber issue could be an inconvenience. At its extreme, however, a security breach could cost you millions and irrevocable harm to you, your family, and your wealth.

The fact is that millions of people rely on the internet for so many assets of their business and their life. Frankly, most people have no idea how "connected" they have actually become. We're connected by everything, from cell phones with a GPS (Global Positioning System) tracking our location 24/7 to cell tower connections continually tracking changes to cell tower locations, to the built-in camera (or two) and microphone in our phone, computer, and other connected devices that can watch and listen to everything we do and say.

Yes, even the basic cell phone has connected everyone who carries it. Then, of course, there are the computers, the tablets, and those continually monitoring devices that are waiting for you to ask a question or request their help or advice. **From baby monitors to refrigerators to thermostats to light bulbs, we are all connected in ways most never dreamed of.** More importantly, we are connected in ways that most people are completely unaware.

The benefits of these connections are obvious, from making phone calls to knowing who is at your front door while you are perhaps thousands of miles away. However, unawareness of the indirect consequences of these connections is equally, if not more, important as the benefits we receive. We obtain tremendous power through these devices, and we give away tremendous power to those monitoring them. **However, as in any situation, with power comes responsibility and, rest assured, it is our individual responsibility to both monitor and control these connections to protect ourselves** as well as everyone else we are connected to, which essentially, is the world.

You Are Responsible

On Christmas Day 2015, a cyber attack was launched against Sony. No, there were no armies or planes or any of the conventional players one might envision being involved with an "attack." This was more "The Attack of the Baby Monitors," and they were not from outer space. They were from your kids' bedrooms. I'm being a little facetious; however, the concept is accurate. The attack launched on Sony was referred to as a DDOS, or a Distributed Denial of Service Attack. Without getting into all the technical aspects of a DDOS, the essence of it is this: thousands of connected devices all try to connect to one source at one time, and as a result, that source is overwhelmed and effectively shut down. As a result, the service, or access to others, is "denied." Think of it like thousands of people trying to get into a door at one time. Very quickly, the doorway is jammed with people, and all the others who are waiting to get in must continue to wait.

How does this happen? Again, without getting into the technical details, the attackers had been planning this assault well in advance and had been conscripting an army of computers to assist them. By using automated programs called "Bots" to search the web 24/7, they found and took control over thousands of computers. **The owners of these computers were unaware that their devices had been taken over. In fact, the owners of these computers were unaware that they were involved in the attack.** Regardless, when the time came, these computers were summoned up by their new masters and all called Sony at the same time, the overflow shut them down to all the actual users who just wanted to activate their new PlayStations that they received as Christmas gifts or do anything else. Sony has the resources to

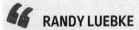

RANDY LUEBKE

Before we were connected to the internet, we were all protected and insulated from outside threats imposed by computer technology. Today, everything is connected, and I mean everything. Did you know that even those little automated vacuum cleaners that rove around your house are often connected to the internet as well? Did you also know that they know the size and dimensions of your room and that this data can be reported to the manufacturer via the internet? As of this writing, the Amazon Echo is the rage. Amazon is constantly listening for key words and then switches on to listen to every word you say and reports them to the mothership. Afraid of that dreadful eavesdropping Echo? You don't want to surrender your privacy to a device like that? Well, then you had better power-down your cell phone, too, because it has a built-in microphone and usually two cameras! Come on. Get real. Maintaining your privacy may be a "right," but it is absolutely a "fight."

overcome such an attack—it is, however, likely that as a small business, you would not withstand a cyber attack of such magnitude.

Why do I mention baby monitors? Well, it's because many of those devices today are connected to the internet as their method of monitoring. Many of these connected devices are full of holes that allow these Bots to enter their operating systems, and as a result, they are vulnerable to being controlled. Do you own a phone, a tablet, a computer, or any other "connected device"? If you do, then YOU are responsible to maintain its security. While this is not exactly simple, it is not altogether that difficult if you follow a few good "cyber-hygiene" techniques and strategies.

Continually Under Attack

The first step in protecting yourself is to understand that you are continually under attack. The number and variety of Bots roving the internet is mind-boggling. If you are connected, you are subject to their poking and probing. Therefore, your first job is to access what devices you own that are connected and understand how they work.

The modem (modulator/emulator) allows your devices to talk to the internet. Essentially, it pokes a hole into the internet and exposes you, and everything you are connected with, to all the internet has to offer—both good and bad.

Just a few years ago, modems worked primarily over your phone lines. You had to dial a phone number, and then you would listen to some squeaks and squawks as your modem connected to another device. When you were done, you "hung up" the phone, breaking your connection to the internet, closing the hole, and eliminating your exposure. Today, most internet connections are made via cable. **These connections run 24/7 and never shut down, leaving the hole open every minute of every day.** The modem is still with us; however, you no longer hear the squeaks and squawks, and once established, the connection is made and remains continually.

The modem is, essentially, a very small and very basic computer. It is also not very smart. It generally has just one job, which is to monitor and maintain communications between your home and the internet.

Essentially, it is an open door, and anything in your home can go out that door. **Conversely, anything outside the door can come into your home—anything! The result is that everyone has a hole into their home or office, and it needs to be guarded.** Because it is connected 24/7, the only thing you can do with this device is to maintain the software updates, which, for most of these devices, are NEVER provided by their manufacturers. (More on software updates later in this chapter.)

If the modem pokes a hole into the internet and exposes you to the world, it would make sense to install something to plug that hole to protect you, something that guards that gateway to the internet. That gateway to your home or office is generally your router. The router serves a number of functions; however, it is your primary firewall with the job of not allowing anything in or out of the hole made by your modem unless you give it permission. How do you give it permission? Most often, we use a browser, a software program designed to allow you to interact with other computers on the internet. Your browser tells your router that you want to travel to somewhere on the internet, another computer's web page for example. The router then gives your computer permission to travel to that other computer's location on the internet so they can talk with each other. **The communications between your computer and that other computer are "trusted" and thereby generally unregulated and unmonitored by your router.** In other words, you are once again exposed and on your own.

In this relatively simple example of how you, your computer, and the internet work together via your modem and your router, you can see that, well, it's not simple. In fact, it's very complex. Now, let's multiply the complexity by the number of connected devices you own and further complicate this by the number of family members and employees operating them, and now, you can begin to understand how unmanageable the problem of protecting yourself from cyber threats has become.

Take Action, or You Could Lose Everything

It's critical to not underestimate the seriousness of maintaining your cyber security. With virtually everything we own, everyone we know, and everything we do accessible via a cell phone you carry around in your pocket, protecting that information is extremely important. In a business situation, this would include your company records, perhaps your methods of operation, accounting, etc. In addition, you are likely to have important private information about your clients all maintained on your computers. **All this data is subject to exposure and/or loss and needs to be protected.** We've all seen news stories about hackers getting into listings of personal records stored at banks—this is no longer the unusual story but something that happens too often.

A few years ago, the biggest risk one had to their data security was hardware failure. You know, your computer stopped working, froze up, and the data became corrupted and inaccessible. A good backup program could fix your problem, restoring your data, and you were back on the road to productivity. This problem was more of an internal threat, and by maintaining and upgrading your equipment, it could be generally avoided. You should still be working to mitigate these internal problems.

Today, however, things are magnified because of the external threats as noted above with the mention of hackers. With our 24/7 exposure to the outside world, we face 24/7 attacks on our data in the form of malware or a more recent and what is becoming a much more frequent attack using ransomware. As the name implies, ransomware is software that forces you to pay money to someone to regain access

 RANDY LUEBKE

Your computer is going to crash or get hacked. It's inevitable. Back it up, regularly and automatically. Or, when something bad happens and you lose all your music, your photos, and all the digital information stored on your devices that you depend on and enjoy in our modern cyber world, then all you can do is blame yourself for being lazy and unprepared. Sorry to be so blunt, but you know what, sometimes that is what a good advisor needs to do.

to your data. Typically, when you obtain ransomware, a message will appear on your screen announcing that your computer has been infected and you no longer have access to your data. Then, it states that if you would like the infection removed and access restored, you must submit a sum of money via some untraceable method like Bitcoin or by money orders. **Ransomware has become a very lucrative, multibillion dollar industry affecting individuals and businesses alike.** The ransom can be relatively small, like several hundreds of dollars, or it can be very large, like tens or even hundreds of thousands of dollars. People will pay if they have no better alternatives, and the business thrives as a result. This is essentially a means of cyber extortion.

Basic Cyber Security Countermeasures

The first thing you want to do is one by one, shut down the holes that lead everything into and out of your home or office. These are your modem and your router. **People no longer bother to "hang up the phone," so to speak, or in this case, shut off the connections.**

Now, we've just begun to address the many problems associated with cyber security. Frankly, as we publish this book, I'm 100 percent certain that new and even bigger problems are on the horizon. The question is, "what can you do about it?" The answer is that there are a few simple countermeasures you can take to protect yourself that we have listed below. Again, this book is not written to be your guide to cyber security. It's your guide to financial independence. Therefore, the list below is meant to be a general reference, and it is incumbent upon you to take this information to the next level and implement these strategies.

Things to DO to Increase Your Security

▮ *Keep all your software up-to-date.* All computerized devices run on software. These are the programs that tell the devices what to do, when, and how. The bad guys are continually looking for ways to take control over these devices. To do this, they look for exploits, which are essentially flaws in the software's programming code that will provide a point of entry for the bad guy's software. For robust software platforms like Windows or Apple, there is a never-ending battle between the bad guys trying to find these exploits and the software developers to plug those holes. When the developers discover the exploits, generally, they will write a correction to their code, which is referred to as a "patch." These patches are then redistributed to all the users in the form of updates. **Therefore, to provide ongoing protection from the bad guys, you must keep your devices up-to-date and install the updates as soon as they become available.** If you don't keep your devices up-to-date by installing these patches, you are simply leaving the door open for all the bad guys to walk right on in and take over your devices.

§ *Back up everything, all the time; having one copy is not enough.* To be safe, you need three copies of everything: the original, a backup for yourself, and an off-site copy, which could be stored in the proverbial cloud. There are a number of affordable off-site backup systems that will continually monitor your data for changes and make copies of these changes as they occur, automatically and in the background. **To maintain a local copy, you will need a separate storage device, perhaps an external hard drive or on a separate computer. Flash drives are also inexpensive ways to store material.** Generally, saving information often, like hourly or daily, is recommended. With your original data on your computer, your changes saved offsite continuously, and regular incremental copies of your data stored locally, you have an adequate backup system that is relatively simple to implement and maintain, affordable, and automated. Don't get complacent.

§ *Become a limited user.* By default, most computers consider you an "administrator." As the name implies, the administrator can do virtually anything to the computer, including installing and removing software. Most cyber attacks rely on this vulnerability. In fact, most cyber attacks rely on YOU doing something to allow the bad guys in. That "something" may be as innocent as visiting a website that has become infected with malware so the second you land on that site, the malware goes to work infecting your computer. It's like someone with a cold sneezing on you in public. That person could be a friend or a stranger. Either way, they are sick, and even if they are unaware that they are ill, their sneeze will spread the disease. **However, if you are not an administrator of your computer, the bad guy cannot get it.** Why? Because only the administrator has the authority to make changes to your system's software. Therefore, if you operate your computer as a limited user, the bad guys will have limited access to your computer and limited ability to make changes, making you safe.

▮ *Use two-factor authentication.* Typically, we use passwords to provide some level of protection. The problem with passwords is they are difficult to remember, so often, people use the same password everywhere, and they make that password easy to remember. **From the bad guy's perspective, this provides a tremendous opportunity because if they can guess your password once, then they can gain access to everywhere you have used it.** Guessing your password is not that difficult. By using social engineering to survey Facebook or other public sites, the bad guy can often learn your birth date, place of birth, your high school and college, your religion, your work, affiliated social groups, and the names of your friends and family and pets. **Regrettably, there is a LOT of information out there in the public domain available to anyone and everyone to collect.** This makes any passwords associated with this information vulnerable. A password provides only one form of protection. Today, the perfect protection would require three forms of protection: something you know (a password), something you have (a device like a key fob), and something that is "you" (a fingerprint). **More and more devices are providing the "you factor" form of protection, which is wonderful. Use it!** While many devices do not provide this feature, a growing number offer something called two-factor identification. As mentioned, two-factor authentication requires that you have something in your possession that provides you with a random code that changes periodically, possibly every few seconds. **The bad guy may have learned your password, but they won't likely have this device in their possession, and without it, your password is ineffective.** Using two-factor authentication is a bit of a hassle, it is an extra step, but the additional level of security it provides is generally well worth the effort.

§ *Use strong, long, and hard-to-remember passwords.* Obviously, simple, short, and easy-to-remember passwords are convenient for you. However, as pointed out over and over again, they are also convenient for the bad guy, too. **You should use passwords that are long, at least 12 to 15 characters, and that make use of capital and lowercase letters, numbers, and symbols if allowed.** You could literally let your fingers randomly dance all over your keyboard with your eyes closed and create a GREAT password. You need to do this for every place you want protection, meaning you need to create a different strong, long, and hard-to-remember password over and over again. Now, the problem is obvious. How do you remember all these passwords, and when entering them, how do you do this without making a mistake? The solution is to use a password vault. **A password vault will safely and securely store all your passwords.** Many of these vaults will automatically enter your passwords when needed so you don't have to retype them. With the vault, you only need to remember one password—the one that accesses your vault. That password still needs to be long and strong, however, it can be easily remembered by you using a number of tricks like citing a quote or lyrics to a song. For example, the song title "TheL0ng&WindingR0ad," can be combined lwith lowercase letters, numbers, and symbols for 19 characters altogether. It's easy to remember, and no, it's not my password. There are many commercially available vaults, some better than other, of course. **Do your research. Understand their security. Remember, if any site maintains your password, it may**

not be secure. Frankly, you could store your passwords on a document file you maintain on your computer and cut/paste the passwords from there. Granted, that document is only as secure as your computer. That said, you could add a master password to access the document, thereby securing it from any bad guy who may gain access to it.

RANDY LUEBKE

Let me say this just one more time: use BIG, long ,complicated, and unique passwords every time you can. Two-factor identification is exponentially greater than just a password. Back up your stuff!

Things NOT TO DO That Will Expose Your Information

§ *Don't trust anyone. Always think before you act.* The bad guys will use your familiarity with friends, family, or businesses to hopefully put you at ease and let your guard down. You may receive an email from a "friend" with a link in it or a document attached to it. **Before you click on any link or attachment, pause for a second and ask yourself, "Am I expecting this email?"** This form of phishing is rampant, and people fall victim to it every day. With the barrage of emails we often receive daily, many from known/friendly sources, we are tempted to react to them and click on the link. You know what happens next, bad stuff. Often these emails can be detected by their use of bad grammar, misspellings, or weird comments. That said, sometimes the bad guys will go to great lengths to disguise themselves, recreating corporate logos to make it look like it came from a real trusted source. The variations on this theme are endless. If you assume that all unsolicited communication may be bogus and just take a second to think before you react, you would save yourself potentially hours of frustration. This also includes emails allegedly from your bank, the FBI, the IRS, and other official entities that are designed to look real and designed to scare you into opening them. Places like banks, will never send you an email telling you there is something wrong with your password that they need your account number or any such thing—these are bad guys clearly trying to get you to give them your information. Never respond to these emails.

§ *Don't become complacent about cyber security.* Instead, always assume that you are continually under attack from outside threats and internal problems with equipment and software. Never let your guard down.

§ *Don't solely rely on antivirus programs to protect you.* They cannot keep up with the threats and may, in fact, create vulnerabilities in your system that expose you to cyber security risks. They can also provide you with a false sense of security. You should, however, still have them in place because they can provide warnings and block certain types of malware or attacks. You should update them regularly, as directed.

Follow the "Dos" previously mentioned and avoid the don'ts, and you will be well protected beyond that which can be provided by any antivirus program.

Advanced Cyber Security Strategies

Good cyber security practices are like good hygiene: you must do something every day, consistently, and in many areas. Again, this book is not your guide to cyber security; it is your guide to financial freedom. That said, if you fall victim to a cyber threat in some way, large or small, it is going to threaten your financial freedom. At minimum, we recommend that all our readers complete the "Cyber security Audit," which can be found on our website for the book at www. ebooktofinancialfreedom.com. This simple assessment will help you to determine your level of understanding of cyber security as well as the level of risk you currently maintain. Then, depending on the results, you can determine what measures beyond those discussed in this book you should consider. Advanced cyber security methods can be both expensive and complex, and your decision to undertake them should not be taken lightly. However, should you find the exposure you have to cyber security risks to be great enough, obviously implementing these advanced strategies should not be ignored.

$ $ $

TAKEAWAY 1—Recognize that cyber security affects anyone using any type of communication device from computers to cell phones to baby monitors. Don't think a cyber attack cannot happen to you. It can and will if you don't practice good cyber hygiene.

TAKEAWAY 2—Back up your data often. Use external means (away from your computer), such as an external hard drive, thumb drives, cloud, etc. Hard copies may sound obsolete, but they are not—use them as well as external backup.

TAKEAWAY 3—Think from the point of view of someone who wants to get at your information. What logical steps could you implement to block yourself? From clever passwords, backups, and anti-virus software to updating software and not being the administrator, you need a multifaceted approach.

WHERE ESTATE PLANNING FITS INTO THE EQUATION

Building financial freedom isn't all about you. It's also about your loved ones, significant other, or even a charity that you might want to benefit when you're gone. Trust me—if you don't have a plan, your hard-earned money could end up going to lawyers, the government, or bickering family members. Leave a legacy. Leave a plan to make the world just a little better place by strategically planning where your wealth will end up after your death.

I included this chapter about estate planning in the book for an important reason. A Revocable Living Trust (RLT) and Will doesn't protect your assets from a creditor in a lawsuit, but it does protect your assets from the government or your family wasting your hard-earned assets. **Millions of**

Americans die each year without any type of estate plan in place, and this forces their families into the court system, where they experience the high cost and time delay characteristic of probate proceedings.

In fact, more than 50 percent of Americans don't even have a will or any type of estate plan. With that said, does everybody need to be scared into a RLT? Certainly not. Here's the truth: not everybody needs an RLT, and a simple Will may be all some of us need to plan for our estate upon our demise.

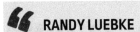

RANDY LUEBKE

While you are alive, having an advance health-care directive takes the burden and pressure off those who love you and want to do what is best for you. If you are unable to make and verbalize your choices and decisions due to your physical condition at present, wouldn't it truly be better for everyone if you had created a set of instructions for everyone to follow in the past? This is true when you pass away. Plan your estate and direct your assets, and you will help to mitigate the quarrels and frustration that may otherwise evolve among the survivors. Hey, they may still fight over your stuff, but you won't be around to hear it. At least you will have the opportunity to get your way just one last time.

There are three main reasons to implement an RLT:

1. You have provisions you may want to implement for minor children or special-needs adult children for managing their finances.
2. You wish for your family to avoid probate because you own a personal residence, a business, or rental properties.
3. You wish to minimize estate tax with a marital bypass trust.

A quality estate plan typically includes an RLT, as well as a number of ancillary documents, such as a will, powers of attorney for finances and health care, an advance medical directive or living will, burial instructions, a directive for organ donation, final instructions, etc.

Avoiding Probate with an RLT

One of the key reasons for using an RLT is to avoid probate, which means avoiding attorneys, judges, courts, and the state sticking their noses into the family affairs. Probate is essentially the court's process of determining if the will is valid and then executing its provisions. If there isn't a will, then the court distributes the assets according to state law.

In addition to helping your family avoid probate, the RLT becomes the instruction manual for how the estate is to be distributed among the beneficiaries. **The process is administered by the trustee you appoint and avoids a tremendous amount of wasted time and money spent going through court.**

In order to make sure the trust does its job, it needs to be funded by a holding title to four main assets:

1. Real estate (typically your personal residence)
2. Entities (such as corporations and LLCs for rentals)
3. Investment accounts (including retirement accounts with see-through provisions)
4. Life insurance (so that minor children receive it constructively)

Figure 25.1 on page 274 shows an example of a typical family trust structure.

Estate Tax and the A-B Trust Strategy

In the late hours of December 31, 2012, lawmakers in Washington, DC, passed the American Taxpayer Relief Act of 2012. Under the "fiscal cliff legislation," as it came to be known, the estate and gift tax exemption was set at $5 million. This means that the first $5 million of an individual's estate may be inherited (at death) or gifted (during life) before any estate or gift tax is due. This exemption amount is, has been, and continues to be adjusted each year for inflation.

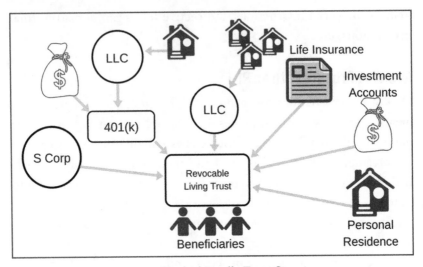

Figure 25.1—Typical Family Trust Structure

With a marital bypass trust, often referred to as an A-B Trust, a married couple can take advantage of both personal exemptions and thus double how much they can leave to their family without estate tax. This is a special trust that creates two subsequent trusts upon the death of the first spouse and thereby doubles the estate tax exemption of approximately $5.5 million. Obviously, this is a very complex aspect of estate planning and is typically only undertaken when a family's net worth is more than $5 million to $6 million.

Don't Give Property to Children—Let Them Inherit It

When you gift property during your lifetime, the tax basis in the asset transfers to the person who receives the gift. In other words, if you have a property you bought for $100,000 that is now worth $300,000, the person receiving the gift would get your $100,000 tax basis, so that when they sell the property, they pay capital gains taxes on anything above $100,000.

However, when someone inherits property upon death, they receive tax basis in the property at the fair market value at the date of death. So if the basis to the owner was $100,000, but the fair market value was $300,000 at their death, the heir would get the property at a $300,000 tax basis. When they later sell the property, they will only pay taxes on any gain above $300,000—as opposed to $100,000 if the gift had been made during the lifetime of the donor. Make sure these types of properties are transferred to the trust and inherited by the family—not gifted to them during life.

Creative Provisions for Children

Many parents and even grandparents don't realize how creative they can be in distributing their assets upon their passing. I realize that some folks believe it's immoral to control their children or family with money after their passing, but others feel they have a duty to leave their hard-earned assets in a constructive manner for their descendants' posterity. Whatever your position may be on the degree of control you want to exercise from the grave, here are a few options to consider:

- $ Require your trustee to hold children's inheritance in a trust until they reach the age of 25, 30, or 35. Give it to them in stages, e.g., a third at age 25, a third at age 30, and the final third at age 35.

- $ Use a joint trust for minor children until the oldest reaches age 18. Then split up the trust into individual trusts for each child. This makes it easier for the trustee to manage the trust while the children are minors. Then when different children pursue business, education, marriage, or even world travel, their trust is accounted for separately from the others.

- $ Consider having the trustee give the guardian of your children a specific amount each month to take care of the living costs of your minor children (room, board, clothing, school supplies, etc.). It could be something like $1,000 a month, adjusted for inflation as of the date of your trust.

- $ Place restrictions on inheritance if there is drug or alcohol abuse. An attorney can insert a provision that prevents a distribution to any child with an abuse problem and allow for the

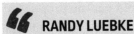

RANDY LUEBKE

Ideally, life should be like a banana split. You know, the banana split comes with all those great toppings and the ice cream, all that good stuff. The goal is, on that very last bite, to get just the right amount of everything on the spoon, and then it's gone. It's a terrible thing, to have a nut or two or a large pool of fudge left over with no ice cream to swallow along with them. It's just not right!

Life should be like that, too. You work, earn money, save some, stop working, spend some, and then on your last day on the planet, you spend the last dollar you have or give it away to anyone besides the IRS. Right? Wouldn't that be ideal?

Well, life is not as predictable and manageable as a banana split, so as this relates to your estate planning, follow my rule once again: "Plan for the worst, hope for the best, and know that you are going to likely end up somewhere in between." The operative word being "plan"—make one.

trustee to hold their funds in the trust until they have their life under control.

§ Give the inheritance in matching funds, distributing $1 for every $1 the child earns.

§ Give them a bonus for graduating from certain levels of college or do not allow full distribution until they obtain a certain level of higher education. However, still distribute funds for school or any secondary education program, skills training course, etc.

§ Distribute funds for education, or use their GPA as a "carrot": distribute funds only if children maintain a minimum GPA that you set. You could also tie funds for tuition or books to GPA to help keep the children focused on finishing school rather than becoming career students.

§ Distribute a certain amount of funds for a wedding.

§ Distribute funds for a church service, volunteering for the Peace Corps, or joining the military for a certain number of years.

§ Distribute funds to start a business upon the presentation of an acceptable business plan to the trustee. Name a board of advisors to approve any small business or investments by the children.

Disinheriting a Child

Perhaps you have a child whom you'd like to disinherit from your estate. If so, don't just leave their name out of the will and think this will accomplish your goals, as the laws in most states will presume you intended to have them inherit unless you specifically state otherwise.

After your spouse, your children are the presumed heirs to your estate by law in the absence of an estate plan. As a result, it is important to include a complete list of your children in the estate plan and to specifically mention any child who will not be an heir by stating something like, "It is the intention of the settlor [you] to disinherit the following child from the estate." It's that simple; just clearly indicate in writing that you specifically intend them not to inherit your estate, and they're out.

The Living Will/Health-Care Directive

A Living Will (or Health-Care Directive, as they are referred to in some states) is a legal document that can be used to make decisions as to whether you want to be on life-sustaining support or whether you want someone to pull the plug if you are brain dead or in a persistent vegetative state.

Dealing with the death of a spouse or other close family member is one of the most difficult situations a person will face. However, that experience is made even more difficult when family members must make life-ending decisions for their loved ones. A well-drafted estate plan includes a Living Will, aka health-care directive, whereby a person makes a legal decision for themselves about whether they want to be placed on life-sustaining support or whether they want to be removed from life support.

The Living Will can be relied on by family members and medical professionals. It also allows a person to declare if they wish to be an organ donor and/or want their body to be used for medical research. Hospitals are authorized and protected by law when they rely on a Living Will, and it makes family decisions at a hospital so much easier.

Top Three Mistakes with "Do It Yourself" Estate Plans

Families can easily and affordably prepare basic estate planning documents online these days. However, this increase in affordability and convenience found on the web has created a false sense of security and inadequate planning that has caused disasters for many families. **Many do-it-yourself estate plans fail to provide the benefits and protections that are included in a well-drafted and carefully planned estate.**

Below are the top three mistakes I've seen made by individuals who have completed their estate plan on their own. Two of the mistakes listed below are based on actual clients who hired our firm to represent them in a lawsuit with other heirs in probate court, due to the fact that their parents made the drastic error of completing their estate plan on their own.

1. *Improper signatures and witnesses for wills.* Most states require the signature of the person creating the will as well as two witnesses to the will. The only exception to the two-witness requirement in most states is a holographic will, which is a handwritten will with the signature of the person creating the will. No matter how good it looks or how many terms are included, failure to adhere to the signature and witness requirements invalidates the entire will.

2. *Failure to fund the trust.* Most individuals who create an RLT on their own fail to actually fund it with their assets. Funding a trust means that you put the assets you want to be controlled by the trust in the name of the trust. For example, if you want your

home to be subject to the terms in your trust, then you need to deed the home out of your personal name and into the name of the trust. If the property is not deeded into the trust, it falls outside the trust terms, and your heirs will need to go to probate court to get a judge to approve any transfers of title following your death.

3. *General do-it-yourself forms may not address your unique situation.* Most families have at least one situation unique to their estate that is typically not covered by standardized documents found on the web. For example, you might have a child who is financially irresponsible, but the rest of your children are not. **Do you know how to use prepackaged forms to create an adequate plan that takes into account the financially troubled child while not adversely affecting the inheritance of your other children?** Or maybe you have an estate that has more debt than assets. Do you know how to plan the estate to leave the most to your family and the least to your creditors? The list could go on and on. My point is that the unique situations that arise are rarely handled properly when you're doing your estate plan on your own.

The real benefit of a revocable living trust is that the structure allows a grantor or grantors to control, affect, and influence future generations. Think of your own family. How many of us can say we know the detailed life history of a grandparent or great-grandparent? I suspect very few. However, if that same relative had created a trust for our education and tried to positively influence our lives through an inheritance, I would argue that many of us would be very interested in the life history, personality, and character of such a grandparent.

TIP FOR FINANCIAL FREEDOM

Your trust isn't worth anything if you don't fund it.

❝ RANDY LUEBKE

From a financial planner's perspective, one of the biggest areas of concern is my clients not having proper beneficiary designations in place for those accounts that allow for them. The purpose of the beneficiary designation is to provide legal authority to take specific actions with an asset when it is inherited. Most people give very little thought as to who should be named as a beneficiary. In addition, over time, changes may need to occur so that the beneficiaries represent what you would want to do today versus 20 years ago when your brother was still alive. Now that he has passed, his ex-wife who you detest is going to inherit your money. Do you understand the potential problem? *The solution is to review your beneficiary statements regularly.* Like a trust, they should be revisited every five to ten years. You need to get copies of the actual beneficiary statements on file with the financial institutions to ensure their accuracy. You may have filled out the paperwork to establish the beneficiaries in the correct manner. However, the financial institution may not have recorded your requests correctly, or they may even have lost your documentation.

The other area to consider with beneficiary designation is when dealing with retirement accounts. Unless your attorney has the skill and knowledge to draft a trust that will allow your retirement account to pass through the trust to designated beneficiaries, then they do not belong in your trust. Many trusts do not have the appropriate language to facilitate that transfer. The result is that your retirement assets will lose their ability to retain their tax-deferred status, and a distribution of those assets is forced over a very short period of time, creating unnecessary and often unwanted income tax issues. **❞**

Leaving your family with an organized estate plan for your affairs is something they will truly appreciate. After your passing, that plan will allow them to focus on mourning and emotional wellness, rather than financial or court issues.

If you've already completed your estate plan on your own, consider having a lawyer review your documents and goals to ensure you have the right plan for your family. Or, if you know you're in need of a new plan, you can revoke the old do-it-yourself plan and replace it with one that has been carefully considered by an attorney experienced in estate planning. At the very least, complete a handwritten will. Then, create a binder, and organize a list of your financial affairs for your family. Also, consider a comprehensive estate plan to organize your affairs and make sure it's been reviewed in the past five years. Finally, make sure your trust is funded.

$ $ $

TAKEAWAY 1—You need a carefully thought out estate plan so that the assets you have planned to go to your family end up in their hands and not in legal battles in the courts. Estate planning is imperative.

TAKEAWAY 2—Work with a professional when doing estate planning as there are too many frequent mistakes that occur when you use do-it-yourself plans.

TAKEAWAY 3—Ensure that you have all the pieces and parts to a well-drafted estate plan, for example, a will included with your trust, powers of attorney for health care and finances, health-care directive, funeral and burial instructions, etc.

OUR FINANCIAL FREEDOM CHALLENGE TO YOU!

I truly feel that this book can save you thousands and thousands of dollars, help you build your wealth significantly, and most importantly, save you countless hours of heartache and pain because you don't have a proper financial plan.

As I have stated repeatedly, I am not a licensed "financial planner" as defined by Wall Street and the financial industry, but I am a tax attorney who meets one on one with clients daily around the country and assists them with their tax, legal, and business planning. Inevitably, many of these conversations evolve into a difficult "wake-up call" regarding their lack of a coordinated financial plan for their business and retirement.

Because of these thousands of meetings, I have seen and learned what "works" and what "doesn't work" when it comes to an *entrepreneur* building wealth and hopefully retiring on their business. I AM an ENTREPRENEUR, and I often feel I have benefited from these meetings more than my clients have. I wrote this book to share what I've learned and I am confident we share extremely similar goals in regards to the freedom we desire from financial burdens.

So I partnered with a licensed, independent financial advisor to "complete the circle of life" on this crazy topic of financial freedom. Randy Luebke's advice and contribution to this book, and my personal life, has been invaluable.

To HELP YOU find the right path for yourself, or at least start on the road to financial freedom, we created the **Business Owner's Financial Freedom Challenge™—** questions that will help you find your place on the Business Owner's Financial Landscape. PLEASE TAKE the time to answer these questions and see what your financial future may hold for you!!

Visit www.ebooktofinancialfreedom.com
to take the challenge TODAY!

ABOUT THE AUTHORS

MARK J. KOHLER, JD, CPA, MPrA, is a lawyer, Certified Public Accountant, best-selling author on asset protection and tax planning, national speaker, radio show host, blogger for Entrepreneur.com, and real estate investor. Mark is also a senior partner at the law firm Kyler, Kohler, Ostermiller & Sorensen (www.kkoslawyers.com) and the CPA firm of Kohler & Eyre (www.ke-cpas.com). Mark is a personal and small-business tax and legal expert, who helps clients build and protect wealth through wealth-management strategies, as well as business and tax remedies often overlooked in this challenging, ever-changing economic climate. His seminars have helped tens of thousands of individuals and small-business owners navigate the maze of legal, regulatory, and financial laws to greater success and wealth.

Mark has written three books previously; *The Tax & Legal Playbook—Game-Changing Solutions for Your Small-Business Questions* (Entrepreneur Press, 2015). *What Your CPA Isn't Telling You: Life Changing Tax Strategies"* (Entrepreneur Press, 2011), and *Lawyers Are Liars: The Truth About Protecting Our Assets* (Life's Plan Publishing, 2008). Mark has a loyal following of fans through his weekly radio show, which can be accessed at www.refreshyourwealth.com and is a top-100 podcast in iTunes under Investing. Mark is a proud father of four beautiful children and husband to his lovely wife, Jen. They reside in beautiful Southern Idaho, where Mark practices his fly fishing skills when he's not traveling and trying to squeeze in surfing on his trips. He has offices in Southern California, Phoenix, Southern Utah, and Idaho.

RANDALL A. LUEBKE, Investment Advisor Representative, RMA, CWPP, CMP, is an independent financial advisor and the principal and founder of Lifetime Paradigm Inc., an intellectual property company specializing in providing Real Estate Integrated and Self-Directed Retirement Planning, Asset Protection, and Estate and Tax Planning for Businesses, Home Owners, and Real Estate Investors. Going well beyond traditional financial planning and wealth management, Randy specializes in providing Cash-Balance Pensions, 401(k) Profit Sharing, and 401(h) Tax-Free Health Benefits Savings Plans. Randy's focus is on providing his clients with one thing, *"certainty,"* by helping his clients to achieve all their financial goals in a ***better, smarter, safer way***. With over 30 years of experience, Randy trains financial planners, attorneys, Realtors, CPAs, stockbrokers, and insurance agents from all over the country, teaching them how to become better stewards of their clients' money. His experience, knowledge, and proprietary systems have helped scores of clients live less stressful and more fulfilling lives. Randy is married to his beautiful wife Sandi, and they have two wonderful children, Jana and Kurtis. They reside in Southern California, where he and his wife enjoy art, great food, and mountain biking, as well as regular trips to Park City, Utah, for snow skiing and outdoor living.

INDEX